Television News
and the Supreme Court
All the News That's Fit to Air?

Beginning with the recognition that the Supreme Court is the most invisible branch of American government and the one that most Americans know the least about, this book examines the way in which television news, the primary source of the public's limited knowledge, covers the Supreme Court. The book relies on rich interviews with network news reporters who have covered the Court, coupled with actual videotapes of network newscast coverage, to develop a unique portrait of the constraints faced by reporters covering the institution as well as a thorough picture of the facets of the Court's work that are factually covered by television news. The analysis demonstrates convincingly that there are characteristics of the television news industry (such as its heavy reliance on dramatic stories and visuals) that, combined with the rules and habits of the Supreme Court (such as its refusal to allow cameras in the Court as well as its propensity to announce several critical rulings on the same day), make network news coverage of the Court infrequent, brief, and in too many instances, simply plain wrong. The book explores the implications of this situation for the public.

Elliot E. Slotnick is Associate Dean of the Graduate School and Associate Professor of Political Science at The Ohio State University. He is the editor of *Judicial Politics* and has published widely in such journals as the *American Journal of Political Science, Journal of Politics,* the *Yale Law and Policy Review,* and *Judicature.*

Jennifer A. Segal is Assistant Professor of Political Science at the University of Kentucky. Her research interests include the influence of U.S. Supreme Court decisions on public attitudes about the Court, the media's influence on public knowledge about the Court, and gender and racial representation from the federal bench. Her work has been published in *Judicature.*

Television News
and the Supreme Court

All the News That's Fit to Air?

ELLIOT E. SLOTNICK   JENNIFER A. SEGAL

CAMBRIDGE
UNIVERSITY PRESS

PUBLISHED BY THE PRESS SYNDICATE OF THE UNIVERSITY OF CAMBRIDGE
The Pitt Building, Trumpington Street, Cambridge CB2 1RP, United Kingdom

CAMBRIDGE UNIVERSITY PRESS
The Edinburgh Building, Cambridge CB2 2RU, UK http://www.cup.cam.ac.uk
40 West 20th Street, New York, NY 10011-4211, USA http://www.cup.org
10 Stamford Road, Oakleigh, Melbourne 3166, Australia

© Elliot E. Slotnick and Jennifer A. Segal 1998

First published 1998

Printed in the United States of America

Typeset in Ehrhardt 10/13 pt, in Quark Xpress™ [AG]

*A catalog record for this book is available from
the British Library.*

Library of Congress Cataloging-in-Publication Data
Slotnick, Elliot E.
Television news and the Supreme Court : all the news that's fit to
air? / Elliot E. Slotnick, Jennifer A. Segal.
p. cm.
Includes bibliographical references and index.
ISBN 0-521-57264-9 hardback – 0-521-57616-4 paperback
1. United States. Supreme Court. 2. Television broadcasting of
news – Law and legislation – United States. 3. Press and politics –
United States. I. Segal, Jennifer A., 1967– . II. Title.
KF8742.S56   1998
347.73'26 – dc21   97-47069
                                                      CIP

ISBN 0-521-57264-9 hardback
ISBN 0-521-57616-4 paperback

For Marcia
and
the memory of my parents, Herbert and Lillian Slotnick
Elliot E. Slotnick

For Dad, Jeffrey, and Julie
and
Mom, Ryan, Cassandra, and the memory of Paul
Jennifer A. Segal

Contents

Tables

Acknowledgments

Like a good many subjects worthy of scholarly inquiry, the project from which this book is derived had its genesis in our students' queries and comments about the Supreme Court, many of which appeared to us to be reflections of what they had learned from the mass media. Writing this book has been a remarkable learning experience for both of us, and we hope that readers will find it as valuable as our long-term collaboration has been rewarding. We have accumulated many debts over the course of our writing, some of which we would like to acknowledge here.

The research presented in the following pages was generously supported through grants from the Office of Research and Graduate Studies and the College of Social and Behavioral Sciences at The Ohio State University and the College of Arts and Sciences at the University of Kentucky. Several research assistants have helped us with numerous tasks throughout several facets of the research process. At Ohio State, our thanks go to Lisa Campoli, Lori Hausegger, Sara Schiavoni, and Rorie Spill. At Kentucky, we appreciate the assistance provided by Mike Gunter and Scott Peters. In addition, several colleagues have been invaluable critics of our work. We have benefited greatly from the thinking and comments of Larry Baum, Paul Beck, Greg Caldiera, Brad Canon, Steve Nichols, and Steve Wasby. We are profoundly grateful to our editor at Cambridge University Press, Alex Holzman, who has been unwavering in his support for and guidance of this project from the first day we proposed it to him. We also extend our thanks to Professor Susan Herbst at Northwestern University, who reviewed the entire manuscript and provided thoughtful and constructive comments and criticism. Additionally, we would have never seen the publication of this book without the remarkable skills, dedication, and patience of our production coordinator, Mary Byers, and of our copy editor, Louisa Castner. In the final stages of the production process we benefited greatly from the work of Marielle Poss, Wendy Watson, and Anita O'Brien.

This book would have been very different had many critical people been less generous with their time and expertise when responding to our inquiries and requests for interviews. Among them are several professional journalists who have reported on the Court for the television networks, including Fred Graham, Tim O'Brien, Carl Stern, Jim Stewart, and Pete Williams. We appreciate the insights of Linda Greenhouse and Lyle Denniston, who joined Fred Graham and Carl Stern in a panel discussion on reporting on the Supreme Court moderated by Slotnick at the annual meeting of the American Political Science Association in 1993. And we owe special thanks to Toni House, both for sharing her thoughts and unique perspective with us and for her aid (and that of the Supreme Court's Public Information Office) in responding to several of our inquiries. We are also grateful for the care, efficiency, and skill of the staff at the Vanderbilt University Television News Archive, which compiled and prepared the videotapes on which much of our analysis is based.

As is often the case in research projects of long duration, the final product owes much to the support of those people closest to the authors. Our experience has proven to be no exception and, indeed, in a setting where our writing took place both over a period of extended time and across long distances, our need for such support proved both great and continuous. Here we are indebted more than they can know to our families and, most especially, to Marcia Slotnick, whose patience and generosity went far beyond the call of duty, and to David Segal, whose astute insights and unfailing encouragement were, as always, invaluable.

While we have relied on the aid of many in the writing of this book, some of whom are acknowledged here, our analysis reflects our own judgments, interpretations, and conclusions about what we have learned. Thus, we, alone, are responsible for whatever may be lacking in the final product.

1

Television News: A Critical Link between the Supreme Court and the American Public

"If it didn't happen on network television, then it didn't happen."
Ron Nessen, former network news correspondent and
presidential press secretary (Quoted in Michael J. Robinson
and Margaret A. Sheehan, *Over the Wire and on TV: CBS and
UPI in Campaign '80*)

In democratic political systems, the interaction and communication between political elites and institutions and the mass public are considered of primary importance. Because democratic governments are established to serve their citizens, the flow of information between elites and masses is critical to the functioning of these governments and to their perceived legitimacy. Ideally, effective democratic citizenship requires that the people know about the activities of their officials and institutions so that they may protect their interests by evaluating and holding them accountable for their actions. Political information is significant for the optimal functioning of this process (Berkman and Kitch, 1986; Lippmann, 1922). As Michael Delli Carpini and Scott Keeter have argued, "[our] system can be very responsive to the interests of civically engaged citizens. But to take even modest advantage of these opportunities, citizens need a number of political resources. Central among these resources is political information" (1996: 59).

Knowledge and understanding about things political are sometimes attained through firsthand experiences. Our lives (or those of our family and friends) are influenced by the laws of the country, we may go to candidates' speeches, write letters to legislators and executives, and receive political pamphlets from them, and we may talk to our family members, friends, and colleagues. From these experiences, we may learn and form opinions about our government and the people who work there.

1

In addition to, and often in the absence of, this form of information gathering, citizens utilize the mass media as a method of learning about and participating in the activities of their government: "For the vast majority of Americans . . . use of the mass media, coupled with brief visits to the voting booth on election day, represents their total participation in politics" (McCombs, 1994: 1). This is certainly the case in the United States, where the news media have been recognized as the primary conduit of information between elites and masses. Ideally, as journalist and media critic James Fallows has noted, "What we read in the papers and see and hear on TV and radio should provide context that gives meaning to information" (1996:130). The significance of the media increases as issues, institutions, candidates, and officials are more removed from the daily personal activities of the mass public. Indeed, in some instances of particular "distance," the public is at the mercy of those who present the news. The choices made about the subjects to report, how they should be presented and by whom, and the depth of coverage all potentially influence what we know and understand about the operation of our government; moreover, and as important, our behavior as citizens in a democratic political system may be grounded in this information. As Delli Carpini and Keeter note, "a citizen who participates in, or who simply follows, the development of national policy and who understands the logic of that policy is better able, and when appropriate, more willing to support that policy's implementation" (1996: 58). Thus, the study of these components of the media as they relate to American institutions and officials is a critical aspect of understanding the workings of our democracy.

While much research has focused on the media's coverage of the president and Congress, considerably less has focused on the important and powerful third branch of our national government, the judiciary. Our purpose in this book is to add to the limited research in this area by providing a thorough analysis of the nature of media coverage of the Supreme Court, the very powerful court of last resort in the United States. More specifically, we present in the following chapters a detailed discussion of how television news covers the Supreme Court. We ask questions such as who reports on the Court and in what context do they operate? How much coverage does the Court get? What are the characteristics of that coverage? What is it about the Court and its activities that affects the likelihood that it will be reported by the national television networks? Answers to these questions lead us to a better understanding of the flow of information between judicial elites and the mass American public and point us toward some possible explanations for the woefully low level of public knowledge and understanding about this critical institution in American politics (see, for example, Caldeira, 1986, 1991; Delli Carpini and Keeter, 1996).

To answer such questions, we have necessarily investigated the substantial literature on the nature of the mass media in the United States. Our study is informed by what we have learned about the workings of the media, and specifically television, as they cover American politics generally and the Court in particular. We are primarily students of the judiciary, however, and our central emphasis is on the institution of the Court – not the institution of the media. As will be evident, our concerns center more on the nature and implications of television coverage for the Court and the American public than around the problems and implications for television.

In the remainder of this chapter, we discuss in greater detail the Supreme Court as a unique institution in our political system, one that has a different relationship with the media than other institutions. We also address the significance of the mass media in American politics, with special attention to television as the primary source of political information for most Americans. Finally, we outline the subsequent chapters of this book to provide an overview of our study of network television coverage of the Supreme Court.

THE SUPREME COURT

When we consider American politics and the necessity of communication between political elites and the mass public, we often focus on Congress and the president. These two institutions are certainly the most visible and obviously political in our national government; they are also the two national institutions to which American citizens are linked directly by elections. Often neglected in discussions about the relationship between the public and political elites is the Supreme Court. The reasons for this are many and often stem from the uniqueness of the Court as an American political institution.

The Court differs dramatically from the other two branches of government. First and foremost, the justices are not elected officials, as are members of Congress and the president. Instead, Supreme Court justices are appointed with life tenure. A second related point is that justices are not directly accountable to the American public; instead, they are able to exercise their authority without the direct pressures and influences of voters. Because justices do not have to run for election (and reelection), they are insulated to some extent from the public pressures that are the stock-in-trade of members of Congress and presidents.

Third, the work of the justices involves primarily the interpretation of law and the Constitution and takes place in a court of law. The implications and public perceptions of such work are many, including the notion that these interpreters be fair and unbiased, neutral in their application of law, treating all who come before them equally; that they do not engage in haggling and do not succumb to the opinions and pressures of outsiders; that they rely on their training in the law to guide them to the best answers to the problems with which they are faced. They are believed to be able to do this because they are insulated from politics and are not elected officials, as the politicians in Congress and the White House are. Moreover, and again related, justices are specialists who speak a language that the average American does not. Typically, they have the best of the best of legal educations and are presumed to have an understanding of the law and the Constitution that surpasses that of most others (perhaps even other lawyers and judges).

Thus, the general perception of Supreme Court justices held by the American public (a perception often buttressed by the justices themselves) is that they are neutral interpreters of our laws and our Constitution, and not part of the political world characterized by the wheelings and dealings of executives and legislators influenced by outside pressures as well as their own political preferences (see, for example, Casey, 1974). In part for these reasons, as well as for journalistic reasons, to which we turn below, the appeal and justification for studying media coverage of the Court have been less than for the other institutions.

Nevertheless, the Court's actual importance in our tripartite system of government clearly renders it worthy of considerably more attention in this regard. Despite its original label as the "least dangerous branch," the Supreme Court has carved a significant and powerful place for itself in American politics for nearly two centuries. Furthermore, and despite the perceptions just described of the practice and purpose of the Court, the justices do not fit neatly into the myth that has arisen around them and their work. While they may be interpreters of law and the Constitution, in so doing, the justices make political decisions on a routine basis. Inevitably, their work necessitates that they choose winners and losers; distribute and redistribute all kinds of goods, including wealth and power, values and rights; and dictate the paths of future behavior by average citizens and elites alike. Such work is, in many respects, no different from the work of legislators and executives.

Additionally, and perhaps even more controversially, the justices engage in judicial review, the practice of declaring acts and actions of other governmental institutions and officials unconstitutional. Generally, this results in a set of nine unelected officials telling, often by the slimmest of margins, a much larger set of popularly elected officials that the action that they have taken is unconstitutional and that it cannot stand. Such action is viewed by some as illegitimate because it violates a fundamental American political value, majoritarianism. Even so, the Court has exercised judicial review in many controversial domains. Armed with this power, the Court has and continues to wield the potential for great policymaking power that rivals, at times, the "political" world of Congress and the president.

The Court is not completely unconstrained, however. Despite their unelected status and relative unaccountability, the justices rely, in part, on a supportive American public. Unlike Congress, with the power of the purse, and the president, with the power of the sword, the Court has no method of enforcing its decisions. Instead, the Court's legitimacy and ability to perform its functions depend largely on its reputation and perceived legitimacy in the public. It must rely, at times, on the willingness of people to go along with its decisions; it generally cannot force them to do so. And, its reputation and the peoples' willingness to follow the Court's rulings depend in large measure on the availability of information about the Court.

Thus, we have good reason to be interested in the information that American citizens have about the activities of this institution. Not only is information about a significant political institution important to a democratic citizenry but, in the case of the Court, such information may be particularly critical as the primary mechanism affecting support, thereby influencing an institution that is not formally accountable via popular elections.

THE MASS MEDIA: TELEVISION

The mass media in the United States play a central role in providing political information to the American public; they serve as the primary link through which the public is informed of the activities of its leaders and are the principal connection between the governors and the governed. As David Paletz and Robert Entman have noted, "Much of what most adults learn about government – its institutions and members, their activities, decisions, defects, strengths, capabilities – stems from the mass media" (1981: 5).

A critical component of understanding the role of the media in American politics is to recognize that while the media are the primary link between elites and masses, they are not merely passive conduits for information. Rather, the mass media play an important role in what we think about, how we think about it, and, indeed, they may even influence what we think (Paletz and Entman, 1981). "Not only do the news media largely determine our awareness of the world at large, supplying the major elements for our pictures of the world, they also influence the prominence of those elements in the picture" (McCombs, 1994: 4).

There is a long history of empirical research that suggests that the media play a very active and influential role in affecting what we know and what we think is important in politics, which may then have implications for our political behavior.[1] Because those who operate within the media industry have the discretion to cover some subjects and not others, and because they have control over how the information is presented to the American public, the mass media act as filters for all of the possible information available. "They may not always mold opinion but they do not always have to. It is enough that they create opinion visibility, giving legitimacy to certain views and illegitimacy to others. The media do the same to substantive issues that they do to candidates, raising some from oblivion and conferring legitimacy upon them, while consigning others to limbo" (Parenti, 1993: 24). In the choices that are made, the media have the potential for enormous power over what we know, understand, and think about our political world.

The mass media are not monolithic, though, and television has emerged as a rather unique form of political communication. Not the least of its special qualities is its pervasiveness; studies have documented for more than twenty-five years that television is perceived by the majority of the public as its "main source" of information, and the advantage enjoyed by television has, if anything, grown as an increasing proportion of the citizenry has been "raised" in a television-dominated environment (Robinson and Levy, 1986: 8). On a daily basis, more than one hundred million Americans view the news on TV, and millions more are likely to gain their familiarity with public issues secondhand through their interaction with television news viewers. "As television has moved to the center of American life, TV news has become Americans' single most important source of information about political affairs" (Iyengar and Kinder, 1987: 112).

Another aspect of television that separates it from most other forms of political communication is that it is a visual medium; "telenews" has the ability to portray events with a sense of realism and emotional drama that other forms of news do not. This characteristic is perhaps a double-edged sword, however, in that visual information has wide audience appeal yet is also vulnerable to even greater sensationalism and superficiality than other mediums. This, in addition to the multitude of commercial constraints, yields a television news format that provides difficulties for its audience. Unlike its print counterpart, television audiences cannot dwell on stories, review them, and digest them in a setting relatively free of distractions; this raises significant questions about television's ability to portray accurately and in sufficient complexity the substance of events.[2] As Congressman David Obey has noted,

The problem is that if the public is encouraged to oversimplify its views . . . because the main source of their information does the same thing . . . it is very difficult to expect that the public is ever going to be in a better position to understand some of the really tough issues that a democratic society has to understand. (Quoted in Moyers and Cohen, 1989)

Because of the isolation and relative public invisibility of the Supreme Court, these characteristics that are associated with everyday television news take on added significance and interest when the focus of the news coverage is the Court. As we elaborate throughout our analysis, problems associated with journalistic resource expenditures, limited access to information not included in the public record, and the absence of sources, combined with the Court's relative disinterest in cultivating the press and its continued refusal to allow cameras in its courtroom, have added to the Court's lower priority status for television news.

TELEVISION AND THE COURT

The relationship between television (and other forms of news media, for that matter) and the Court is a somewhat enigmatic one. On the one hand, the importance of television news is especially apparent in instances when public

knowledge is limited, as it is about the Court. On the other hand, the reporting of Court-related activities has received somewhat mixed evaluations, ranging from very poor to, at best, adequate. While much of our understanding
about this relationship is anecdotal and comes from interviews with justices
and reporters, there has been a smattering of empirical research conducted on
this relationship as well as on the nature of the coverage television affords the
Court. It is within the context of this empirical research that our study of television's coverage of the Supreme Court fits best.

Limited Public Knowledge about the Court

Most Americans receive their political news from television news broadcasts;
if a subject is not covered on the nightly news, then, for all intents and purposes for the average American, it does not exist or has not happened. Thus,
the significance of television cannot be overstated. This is particularly true for
the Court, an institution that is relatively isolated and unknown to the common experiences of most Americans.

Larry Berkson (1978) has characterized two publics that receive Supreme
Court messages: a "continuous public" (composed of attorneys, judges, law
enforcement officers, and lawmakers) and a less attentive "intermittent public." Continuous publics have, in most instances, the greatest need for accurate information, and arguably, they generally "utilize the most reliable channels." It is the unknowledgeable, intermittent publics who are most likely to
depend on the media for the limited information they actually do possess.
When they look to television, they are met by a medium that has been portrayed as having a "lack of interest in what the Court does. Even if a citizen
desired to learn more about the operation and output of the Court, this information could not be obtained by relying on the coverage in the mass media" (Berkman and Kitch, 1986: 250).

And, indeed, there is clear evidence that suggests that the American public is woefully ignorant about the Court. "Research on the attitudes of adults
reveals that there is only a relatively shallow reservoir of knowledge about or
affect toward the Court in the mass public. . . . Few fulfill the most minimal
prerequisites of the role of a knowledgeable and competent citizen vis-à-vis
the Court" (Caldeira, 1986: 1211). The absence of much knowledge about the
Court is strikingly apparent from the results of a 1995 nationwide poll that revealed that, while 59 percent of the respondents could name three of the

"Stooges," only 17 percent could name correctly three of the Supreme Court justices (Morin, 1995).

The significance of this state of public knowledge about the Court and the imperative role of the press in disseminating political information cannot be overstated in light of the argument we have presented about the role of information in a democratic polity. As prominent jurist Irving Kaufman reminds us,

The force of judicial decisions . . . depends on a fragile constitutional chemistry, and it flows directly from popular knowledge and acceptance of their decisions. Courts cannot publicize; they cannot broadcast. They must set forth their reasoning in accessible language and logic and then look to the press to spread the word. (Quoted in Katsh, 1983: 8)

New York Times Supreme Court reporter Linda Greenhouse underscores further the critical function of the press in this domain:

Political candidates who believe that their messages are not being conveyed accurately or fairly by the press have a range of options available for disseminating those messages. They can buy more advertising, speak directly to the public from a talk-show studio or a press-conference podium or line up endorsements from credible public figures. But judges, for the most part, speak only through their opinions, which are difficult for the ordinary citizen to obtain or to understand. Especially in an era when the political system has ceded to the courts many of society's most difficult questions, it is sobering to acknowledge the extent to which the courts and the country depend on the press for the public understanding that is necessary for the health and, ultimately, the legitimacy of any institution in a democratic society. (1996a: 1538)

The degree to which the press, and television more specifically, has been able to spread the word about the Court has been the subject of some anecdotal and empirical consideration and debate. In the following section, we present some of the evidence on this question, establishing the context for the research reported in this volume.

How Does Television Report on the Court?

Perceptions about press coverage of the Court have varied over time. Journalist Max Friedman wrote years ago that

it seems simply inconceivable . . . that the average American editor would ever dare to write on a debate in Congress or a decision by the President with the meager preparation which he often manifests in evaluating the judgements of the Supreme Court

. . . I must declare my conviction that the Supreme Court is the worst reported and worst judged institution in the American system of government. (Quoted in Grey, 1968: 5)

In contrast, and much more recently, Tim O'Brien, Court correspondent for ABC News, has argued that

Max Friedman's observations about the news media and the Court years ago are simply no longer valid; television has changed most dramatically since those days. . . . The *New York Times* and *Washington Post* both have experienced veterans at the Court. The wires similarly are staffed with Supreme Court veterans who provide newspapers around the country with competent coverage. Felix Frankfurter lamented that the Supreme Court doesn't get the media attention the World Series does. It does too! (Quoted in Slotnick, 1991b: 131)

In an effort to come to terms with which view is more valid, several investigators have examined empirically the nature of television's coverage of the Supreme Court.

How Do the Media Report on the Court?

Most scholarly attention to the area of media, institutions, and the American public, as we have noted, has centered on Congress and the presidency. And while there has been some research on the Supreme Court, it has most often focused on the coverage afforded by the print media.

Chester Newland's 1964 study of newspaper coverage of the Supreme Court represents the initial research in this area. From his analysis of the coverage of *Engel v. Vitale* and *Baker v. Carr,* Newland discovered what has since become a scholarly orthodoxy, that stories on the Court focus more on the reactions to the decisions than on the decisions themselves. They "virtually ignored what the Supreme Court had said, and generally even what it had decided, and reported instead on national, state and local reactions and conjecture" (Newland, 1964: 27). This finding was echoed by David Grey, who noted that media coverage of the Court's decisions lacked the penetrating analysis that one would expect of stories on an important political institution (1968: 120).

Much of the subsequent research on newspaper coverage of the Court consisted of specific case studies from which it has been difficult to draw broad conclusions and generalizations or, indeed, even more limited comparisons.

David Ericson's work, however, provided a rare exception. Again from an examination of print media, his comparison of the coverage of the Court's 1974 term by three newspapers (*New York Times, Detroit News,* and *Ann Arbor News*) documented significant differences in the coverage by each newspaper, and, as importantly, generally inadequate coverage of the Court's activities for that term across the three papers (1977: 697).

In contrast, Stephanie Larson (1985) argued that decisions are not all equally newsworthy and therefore not all decisions warrant journalistic attention (see also Tarpley 1984). From an examination of the *New York Times*'s coverage of racial discrimination cases between 1962 and 1977, she found that the *Times* did offer generally comprehensive coverage of these cases. Ninety-nine percent of the race discrimination cases were covered, and almost 90 percent of the articles included some attention to legal issues, impact, case implications or consequences, and the reasoning of case opinions. Larson concluded that "there is no inherent reason that coverage cannot be complete; therefore a lack of comprehensive coverage is a choice rather than an unavoidable situation" (1985: 894). The choice of the media to give thorough coverage to the Supreme Court's decisions depends, according to Larson, on what she termed the decision's newsworthiness.

While research on the print media's coverage of the Supreme Court is somewhat limited, it is much more substantial than research on television coverage of the Court, a subject "that has been almost totally neglected" (Katsh, 1983: 8). A few notable exceptions are research by Stephanie Greco-Larson (1989), who focused on the affect that television might potentially have on public opinion of the Court, and Katsh (1983) and Slotnick (1990, 1991a), Slotnick and Segal (1992, 1994), and Slotnick, Segal, and Campoli (1994), all of which examined the nature of television coverage of the Court.

Ethan Katsh, from his analysis of network news coverage of Supreme Court cases from October 1976 to July 1981, found that television reporting was quite limited generally, with little coverage of some important legal issues. Only 20 percent of the Court's decisions were reported and only half of those were reported by the network's legal expert. Additionally, some subjects were covered more frequently than others; his analysis revealed that civil rights and liberties issues were twice as likely to be reported than corporate, business, or economic issues. Furthermore, television reports gave minimal coverage to aspects of Supreme Court activity other than actual case decisions.

One facet of Katsh's research attempted to examine the amount of television coverage of "important" cases. Perhaps, at the very least, the 20 percent of the cases covered might have been the most significant cases heard and decided by the Court. But, by operationalizing case importance (using *U.S. Law Week* and the *Harvard Law Review*), Katsh found that the cases covered by the networks were not necessarily those that legal experts considered most important (1983: 10–11). Finally, Katsh found that there was no significant difference between the networks in their coverage of Supreme Court activity (1983: 7–8).

While Katsh's study broke new ground on television coverage of the Supreme Court and offered many insights on the nature of that coverage, it was limited by its broad aggregate analysis based primarily on the annotated index of the Vanderbilt Television News Archive rather than on observing the actual news broadcasts. A significant amount of potentially important information about the nature of television coverage could be lost through such an analysis. Slotnick's (1990, 1991a) examination of the coverage of *Regents of the University of California v. Bakke* was an initial effort to overcome some of these limitations. In chapter 4, we discuss some of the results of this study, in combination and comparison with the results of our examination of another prominent ruling, *Webster v. Reproductive Health Services*. Our own work here and elsewhere (Slotnick, 1990, 1991a; Slotnick and Segal, 1992, 1994; Slotnick, Segal, and Campoli, 1994) relies extensively on the utilization of actual videotapes of network newscasts adding, we think, an important dimension to research in this domain. In the remainder of this chapter, we offer a brief outline of what will be found in subsequent chapters in this volume.

PLAN FOR THIS BOOK

The next two chapters in this volume ("The Supreme Court Beat: A View from the Press" and "Television News and the Supreme Court: Opportunities and Constraints") are based largely on the perspectives of Supreme Court reporters themselves, gleaned from personal interviews, as they offer their thoughts on the unique journalistic environment that they inhabit. Chapter 2 explores the parameters of that environment and its broad consequences for coverage of the Court, while considering topics such as the ideal training and background for covering the Court, the journalistic task of Supreme Court reporters, and the nature of the relationship that Court reporters develop with other components of the Court's environment such as the institution's Public Information Office, justices and clerks, interest groups, and other members of the Court's press corps. Chapter 3 places much more explicit focus on unraveling the nature of *television* journalism and network newscast efforts to report on the Court. We examine the strengths and liabilities of television news for covering the Court, paying particular attention to the constraints on reporting brought about by the very nature of the Court itself, as well as those traceable primarily to the working realities of the broadcast news industry. In this chapter we consider the debate over the allowance of television cameras in the Court as well as the broader question of how television coverage of the institution has changed as a reflection of fundamental changes in the nature of television news characterized by the rise and triumph of "infotainment."

Chapter 4 ("A Tale of Two Cases: *Bakke* and *Webster*") offers comparative microlevel case studies of how television news covered two acknowledged leading Supreme Court cases from their inception through their immediate aftermath. The analysis is suggestive of the performance of television news in those relatively rare instances when news broadcasts give the Court extensive coverage and take their "best shot" at reporting a case at its numerous stages and in relatively great detail. In contrast, chapter 5 ("A Tale of Two Terms: The 1989 and 1994 Court Terms") takes a comparative macrolevel approach to how television news covered the Court over the full course of two terms in the life of the institution. The chapter considers news stories broadcast about the Court's docket as well as the considerably less frequent ancillary coverage given to other facets of the Court's institutional life. Special focus will be placed on examining coverage of those cases identified as the "leading" ones of the two terms under study, and considerable emphasis will be placed on documenting the dramatically diminished coverage given the Court by network newscasts in the October 1994 term when contrasted with the October 1989 term. Chapters 4 and 5 both make substantial use of the actual videotapes of newscast coverage of the Court. Consequently, our analysis can address questions and concerns that earlier studies were unable to do in the absence of this rich and critical database.

The data presented in chapters 4 and 5 are suggestive of both the strengths and deficiencies of network newscast coverage of the Supreme Court. In Chapter 6 ("'The Supreme Court Decided Today . . .' – or Did It?") we single out for extensive analysis one distinct facet of the Court's activities, its docketing decisions regarding which cases it agrees to hear, and analyze the manner in which such decisions, when reported, are presented on network newscasts. This is an area that, because of a general lack of understanding of how the Court operates coupled with the realities of broadcast news production, is rife with potential for misreporting. Our analysis is suggestive of just how widespread such misrepresentation of the Court's actions is in this domain, while we also explore the potential consequences of such reporting for public understanding and knowledge about the Court and its policy dictates.

Chapter 7 ("Which Decisions Are Reported? It's the Issue, Stupid!") utilizes the descriptive accounts of chapters 2 and 3, coupled with the empirical analyses of chapters 4, 5, and 6, to develop a multivariate model that seeks to identify and predict the networks' choices about which case decisions ultimately receive scarce airtime and are reported on the nightly newscast. At bottom, the chapter attempts to unravel the characteristics of Supreme Court cases and their context that increase the likelihood of their making it on the news.

Chapter 8 ("Television News and the Supreme Court: All the News That's Fit to Air?") concludes the volume with a summary assessment that synthesizes the data presentation and arguments from preceding chapters. We will return to several themes touched on throughout the book, while also looking forward to assess prospects for change in the interface between television news and the Supreme Court.

The portrait that will emerge from our multifaceted view of television coverage of the Supreme Court will underscore, we think, the substantial distance between the amount and nature of the information about the Court made available to the mass public and the informational needs of the citizenry suggested by the dictates of classical democratic theory. Recognizing that such classical notions of democracy may erect an unattainable metric for judgment in contemporary democratic societies, it appears, nevertheless, that television may fail to offer its viewers sufficient information about the Court to develop the "adequate understanding" that "has long been and still should be a leading aim of the news media" (Schudson 1995: 212). While it is difficult to define that adequacy of understanding, it has been argued that the democratic citizen "is supposed to know what the issues are, what their history is, what the relevant facts are, what alternatives are proposed [and] . . . what the likely consequences are" (Berelson, Lazarsfeld, and McPhee, 1954: 308).

The problematic nature of attaining this level of understanding about the Court, particularly from television news, can be traced in large measure to the mismatch between the two principals examined in this volume, the television news industry and the Court itself. It will be quite clear throughout our analysis that television news and the Court function with inherently different goals, institutional imperatives, and organizational constraints. As Linda Greenhouse has noted:

There exist conventions and habits both within the press and within the Supreme Court itself that create obstacles to producing the best possible journalism about the Court, journalism that would provide the timely, sophisticated, and contextual information necessary for public understanding of the Court . . . the interests of these two vital and powerful institutions, the Court and the press, can never be entirely congruent; the press is always going to want more information than the Court is ever going to want to share. (1996a: 1539)

Greenhouse's observations will be amply supported by the analysis to follow. The television journalists covering the Court will be revealed to be a highly professional (and, at times, expert) group whose best efforts are all too often subjugated to the commercial dictates of the television news industry. The Court, for its part, emerges as an institution that, for good or ill (and we think for ill), cares little about the attention paid to it by the media or the information that the public gleans about the Court from media coverage. The "loser" in such a setting met by "a Court that is quite blithely oblivious to the needs of those who convey its work to the outside world, and a press corps that is often groping along in the dark, trying to make sense out of the shadows on the cave wall" (Greenhouse, 1996a: 1559) is inevitably and ironically the very public that both of these institutions are constituted to serve.

2

The Supreme Court Beat:
A View from the Press

"Unlike anybody else in town, Supreme Court justices don't covet the press. . . . The Court doesn't leak, the Court doesn't spin. The Court is there, and you make of it what you do. . . . It's almost like it's another time, it's another era."

Pete Williams, NBC News

Students of American politics who study the Supreme Court often take as the starting point for their analyses the notion that the Court is a unique and fundamentally "different" kind of institution in our tripartite governmental system, featuring a merging of law and politics that distinguishes it from the American legislative and executive branches as well as from most other national judiciaries. Similarly, many journalists who cover the institution attest to the unique nature of the Supreme Court beat when contrasting it with reporting on the other branches of government. Indeed, ABC News legal correspondent Tim O'Brien suggested that the Court is not, in the final analysis, a "Washington" beat at all: "I don't even think of covering the Supreme Court really as a Washington assignment. . . . [O]ften, unlike any other beat in town, I will not have any shot in my piece from Washington. . . . [I]t's a national beat, but not a Washington beat."

In the following two chapters we will examine the environment in which Supreme Court journalists operate and the world that they inhabit. First, in chapter 2, we will explore the distinctive nature of the Court beat, with particular attention paid to the numerous manifestations of that distinctiveness. We will examine questions such as what type of training and background appear to be most conducive to covering the Court effectively? Does covering the relatively "invisible" Court create a unique publicly oriented journalistic task? Considerable attention will be placed on unraveling the environment in

16

which the Court reporters operate with a particular focus on the Supreme Court's Public Information Office; the relationships between reporters, justices, and clerks; the role of interest groups in Supreme Court coverage; and, ultimately, the relationships among the reporters themselves in the Court's press corps.

Chapter 3 will move from these generic concerns facing virtually all Supreme Court journalists to a much more explicit focus on the opportunities and constraints faced by *television* reporters covering the institution. Along the way we shall see that some of the difficulties faced by those covering the Court are attributable to the nature of the television news industry, whereas others are traceable to the procedures and routines of the Court itself. Particular attention will be focused on the public dialogue over cameras in the Supreme Court, possible reforms of those procedures and norms of the Court that have had an impact on television coverage of the institution, and, most broadly, on the implications of the apparent changes in the nature of broadcast news for the manner in which the Court is covered. All unattributed comments in these chapters, as well as throughout the book, come from personal interviews documented in the appendix.

Some of the inherent difficulties faced by reporters covering the Court have been said to be "built into the system of both institutions." As veteran *Washington Post* reporter and, later, *New York Times* editorial board member John Mackenzie has pointed out:

The Court begins as a mystery, and the reporter or editor who fails to appreciate the fact that certain things about the Supreme Court will remain unknowable . . . simply does not understand the situation. The Court's decisions are the start of an argument more often than they are the final definitive word on a given subject. . . . Secrecy at several levels both protects and obscures the Court and its work. . . . I would suggest that murky decision-reporting may be the reporting of murky decisions as well as the murky reporting of decisions. (Quoted in Devol, 1982: 29)

Supreme Court decisional processes are not open to the reporter's view as they are, at least in part, in other governmental settings. And, as Anthony Lewis has noted, "The process of decision is often more newsworthy than the end result" (1959: 363). Further, while critical judicial decisions are made in private, "What reporters see in the courtroom – all they see – is designed more to elevate than to display the judicial process" (Paletz and Entman, 1981: 101).

These points are all well taken. Nevertheless, as the *New York Times*'s Linda

Greenhouse has cautioned, one may take analogies too far when contrasting the "closed" Court with the putatively more "open" collateral branches of the federal government: "Although some other institutions around this town give the appearance of much more openness, and it's true that a reporter can summon a senator off the floor . . . that only takes you so far. . . . I would argue, having spent a couple of years covering Congress, for instance, that the 535 ring circus nature of that institution, and its ability to be quite secretive when it chooses to be . . . it's not, necessarily, any easier or more open in the ways that count than the Court which, at least, does everything it does . . . on the public record" (quoted in Slotnick, 1993).

Pete Williams, NBC News Supreme Court correspondent, commented broadly and thoroughly on what makes the Supreme Court beat "different" from others he has covered:

Unlike anybody else in town, Supreme Court justices don't covet the press. They don't flaunt themselves. . . . The less attention you pay to them personally, probably the better. . . . The Court doesn't leak, the Court doesn't spin. The Court is there, and you make of it what you do, and it's all in public documents. . . . No reporter that I know has an edge because they have some "in" with one of the justices. That's not the way reporting the Court works. . . . It's almost like it's another time, it's another era. When you go to the Supreme Court . . . every reporter is on his or her own to make of it what they will. . . . That is a huge difference. The second difference is . . . for a television reporter obviously, most of what the Court does, virtually all of what it does, is invisible to us. As reporters we at least get to go into the courtroom when the cases are argued and decisions are handed down, but that's just about all the functioning of the Court we as reporters see, and television cameras can't even see that. So it remains a sort of mystery. There's that building from the outside that looks very imposing with those columns and it looks like some sort of temple, and then you go inside and there's just these fuzzy little drawings that we make. So that is very different.

Williams also pointed out that the substance of Supreme Court reporting renders it an unusual governmental beat as well.

It's the only institution in town where all the stories you write about it, basically, are what it does. You don't write stories about who's up, who's down, who's in, who's out. . . . Very seldom do you see stories about who likes whom and where the power center is shifting in the Court because of who says what behind the scenes. So it is . . . very challenging in that sense but it is also very . . . pure. . . . You get to cover the government function by what it does. And I think that doesn't happen in a lot of the other beats around town.

With news sources and the breaking of stories playing a much lesser role in Supreme Court reporting than in other journalistic beats, and with so much that is being reported available to all journalists equally and, indeed, largely in the public record, it has even been suggested that it is quite possible to cover the institution without actually even being there. As Tim O'Brien has stated, tongue somewhat in cheek, this is part of what makes covering the Supreme Court beat distinctive: "If I have access to the decision, if I have access to the briefs . . . and now that the decisions are on-line . . . I can get the decisions instantly. I can cover the Court without even being there."

In his early examination of press coverage of the Court, Chester Newland framed succinctly the underlying reality faced by those covering the institution: "Journalists must understand that the Court is different and must remain different. It speaks once and is silent" (1964: 15). The consequences of this, according to Carl Stern, a reporter who covered the Court for many years for NBC News, is that "You cannot go to the principal actors and ask them what they meant. You have to try to figure it out for yourself or by talking to other people that have to figure it out for themselves." Stern, head of the Justice Department's Office of Public Affairs at the time of our interview, explained that

anyone who calls in here and asks me why the Justice Department did this or that, I will try to explain it to them. If I don't know the answer, I will go to the relevant decision maker and attempt to find out why we did it and, to the limits that I'm permitted to do so . . . I want the writer to understand fully what we did and why we did it. There is no one in the Supreme Court that can have a comparable role.

For Stern, while this makes the journalist's job more difficult, it remains an absolute necessity for the Court's proper functioning. It is, after all, the Court's words attached to its judgments that are relied on by lawyers in developing their legal arguments. Those words need to be found in one form and in one place only. As Stern notes, "That's why it's so important that the Supreme Court speak only through its opinions."

The whole system would break down if, for example, you had lawyers A and B coming before a court . . . and lawyer A says, "Here's what the law requires because of the Supreme Court's decision in *Schultz v. Schultz,* and lawyer B says, "Well, that's fine, but just a minute. Justice So and So, who wrote the opinion, said at a meeting of the American Political Science Association last month that they really meant something quite different." And lawyer A comes back and says, "Just a second. Justice So and So, who concurred, in *Time* magazine was quoted as saying it means something else." And lawyer B says, "Well, just a second, in *Popular Mechanics* last month, Justice So and So said it meant something quite different." We would never know what the law is. We have to know where we can find it, and you can only find it in the written opinion that the Court had entered into its books, and that's why there is this system, this tradition, this understanding, that they won't amplify on what they've done outside the record. I regard that as necessary for the system to operate. (Slotnick, 1993)

What Stern characterizes as a necessity for the system, of course, can make life extremely difficult for the reporter who must, with dispatch, make sense out of complex rulings often accompanied by several concurring and dissenting opinions that can obfuscate the issues even further. Supreme Court opinions are not written for a lay or journalistic audience, and justices rarely do anything to make them more accessible to such publics. Indeed, some jurists seem to go to great lengths to trump complex legal questions with complexities in their own prose. Justice Felix Frankfurter, for example, was credited with authoring opinions that were "repositories for some of the most exotic words in the English language." Generalizing the point, Berkson adds, "Although Frankfurter's style was uncharacteristically eloquent, it is not unique in terms of those to whom it was directed. Indeed, this lack of concern for the general audience is perhaps the greatest weakness in Supreme Court messages. It places the responsibility of interpreting decisions squarely on the press," where, as Stephen Wasby has observed, "the chances for misinterpretation . . . increase radically" (quoted in Berkson, 1978: 50).

One of the major problems confronting the Supreme Court reporter is the tension that often exists between making a story both intelligible to an audience as well as accurate. There is an ever-present risk of oversimplifying things to the point where important nuances of a critical ruling are lost in translation. An important distinction can be drawn between "inaccurate" and "imprecise" Supreme Court coverage that is also instructive here:

The semantic line between the two terms is . . . thin. . . . But there are differences in connotation that carry considerable implications for coverage of such a complex and technical news field as the law. If accuracy can be defined roughly as "freedom from error" and precision as roughly "exactness or fineness of measurement" then the obvious question can be raised: Is it enough that a story be "accurate" – just free from error? (Clayton in Hiebert, 1966: 189)

Supreme Court reporters are faced with a heavy "burden of interpretation" that cannot be escaped with "objective" reporting or, indeed, even through reliance on the Court's own words. For one can be perfectly accurate in drawing quotations from case decisions, yet "nine times out of ten there is no one quotation – nor any series of quotations that can . . . within the space confines . . . tell . . . what the Supreme Court did and what it means" (Clayton in Hiebert, 1966: 189).

Carl Stern offered several examples of the interpretive dilemmas he faced while on the Supreme Court beat. As a general matter, he asserted, "Covering the Court is difficult and different because it uniquely requires evaluation. . . . [I]n a very large number of cases you're up against one of these 'is the glass half full or half empty?' type [of] situations" (in Slotnick, 1993). One prime case in point was the *Regents of the University of California v. Bakke* case, which we examine extensively in chapter 4. In *Bakke:*

The question was a quota . . . that the University of California at Davis had for the admission of minorities to a medical school. . . . When the decision came, what the Court basically said was that rigid quotas were no good but that race could be taken into account as a factor in admitting students. . . . Well, that decision could have been reported as "Supreme Court Strikes Down Racial Quotas" or it could have been reported as "Supreme Court Upholds Affirmative Action." Either headline, either way of playing it, would have been correct, and yet they sound to some extent as though the Court had done different things. It's a question of judgment as to what you want to focus on. . . . I could give you countless other decisions where you could validly play it one way or another, and it's entirely up to the skills and the intelligence and the experience of the reporter as to how it's going to be played, and that's what makes the Court so very, very different. (in Slotnick, 1993)

The key to how to "play" a case was often sought by Stern in the answer to a basic question, which, itself, at times remained unclear:

The public wants to know . . . who won and who lost. That's what it comes down to, and when you've got a case, let's say the abortion decision . . . the *Casey* decision, where the Court upheld the principles of *Roe v. Wade* but then acquiesced in stringent new restrictions in the state of Pennsylvania, who won and who lost? The foes of abortion claimed they won, the supporters of abortion claimed they won, and they both did win something. How do you play that? How do you tell your viewers . . . who won and who lost? It's not very simple and it's not like covering a fire or covering a plane crash or an election. It requires a certain amount of gutsiness to go ahead and make your call and go with it. (in Slotnick, 1993)

Further, Stern noted, there were times when he and his colleagues would see a case differently and report on it in a different light. A good example was the case of *Rhode Island v. Innis* (1980) where a murder suspect led police to the murder weapon after listening to two officers discuss how tragic it would be if additional deaths occurred as a consequence of the missing gun being found by mentally disabled children who lived near the murder site. The question for the Court was whether Innis had been unconstitutionally coerced into revealing damaging information through a psychological ploy.

Well, the Supreme Court decided about what you would expect. . . . On the one hand, they want to preserve constitutional rights; on the other hand, they are reluctant to turn killers loose on technicalities. . . . And, so, what do they do? They said if this was done intentionally by the police officers as the . . . psychological equivalent of the rubber hose, then it was no good. The statement that was made . . . had to be thrown out [and] he was entitled to a new trial. But they said in this case there was no evidence that it was a ploy. This was just idle chitchat . . . by the officers, and they let the conviction and the sentence stand.

At this point, Stern had a judgment to make:

Well, I called my office and I said to them, "Hey . . . big expansion in *Miranda*. Now not only is the rubber hose out, but even the psychological ploy is out." And they said, "Well, that's funny. AP [Associated Press] is just moving it. They're running this thing as a big cutback in *Miranda*." I said, "Cutback? That's not possible. I'll call you back." So I go next door to Lyle [Denniston, currently of the *Baltimore Sun* and longest tenured Supreme Court reporter]. I say, "Lyle, how are you playing this?" And he says, "Oh, big cutback in *Miranda*." I said, "How do you figure that?" He says, "Well, up until now the officers might have been afraid to engage in any kind of conversation that would extract this kind of statement because they knew it would be in jeopardy in a court proceeding and the whole thing might get thrown out. But now they know that as long as they label it idle chitchat they can get away with it." I said, "Lyle, I understand your point, but to me the larger issue here is that the psychological ploy is out." And I go back to my desk . . . and I call, and they said, "All right, which is it?" "Well," I said, "it's both. It's what question you're asking, it's what you're looking at." And the editor says, "It can't be. It's either a cutback or an expansion." Well, life is not that simple for Supreme Court reporters. I played it that night as an expansion of *Miranda* . . . but here's two reporters who see the case in an entirely different way. (in Slotnick, 1993)

While it is a primary component of most journalists' work (see, for example, Fallows, 1996), Stern's commentary makes it clear that the felt necessity to declare winners and losers can create intractable problems for the Supreme Court journalist. As Linda Greenhouse has observed, "I am often uneasy about the binary won-lost approach to reporting on the Court. To what extent do stories like these, even the most nuanced and sophisticated, mislead readers and risk overly politicizing discourse about the Court and its work?" (1996a: 1551).

COVERING THE SUPREME COURT: WHAT TYPE OF TRAINING?

Scenarios such as the *Bakke, Casey,* and *Innis* cases discussed above point out dramatically the critical importance of having journalists covering the Court who have the ability and the know-how to make informed judgment calls when interpreting complex decisional outcomes. At the same time, they raise the question of what skills and backgrounds facilitate excellence in Supreme Court reporting. Historically, a considerable amount of criticism has targeted the qualifications of Court reporters.

Expanding on the criticism of Max Friedman discussed in the previous chapter, the story is told of Justice Frankfurter chastising the *New York Times*'s James Reston with the accusation that his paper would never consider having a writer cover the New York Yankees with as little knowledge about baseball as Supreme Court reporters tended to have about the Court and the law (in Ericson, 1977: 604). In the mid-1960s longtime Court analyst James Clayton could complain that

the Washington bureaus . . . still think the way to cover the Court is to wait for a bulletin from one of the wire services announcing a major decision, then to obtain a copy of the decision and give it to a reporter to write. . . . As long as newspapers attempt to cover the Supreme Court . . . in this fashion, inaccurate reporting is, upon occasion, a foregone conclusion. (in Hiebert, 1966: 184–185)

As Grey observed, "It is not a subjective judgment to conclude that many reporters appear at the Court without knowing very much about what is going on" (1968: 75).

In some respects, the mid-1960s through the mid-1980s corresponded with a renaissance in professionalism in Court coverage. Some analysts noted an improvement in the preparation and backgrounds of those covering the institution, at least for "national" newspapers and the television networks (Shaw, 1981: 18). Recall, also, Tim O'Brien's assertions that

Max Friedman's observations about the news media and the Court years ago are simply no longer valid. . . . Felix Frankfurter lamented that the Supreme Court doesn't
get the media attention the World Series does. It does too! (in Slotnick, 1991b: 131)

This may be true generally across the nation's leading newspapers and may
have characterized accurately the nature of television news coverage of the
Court at the height of the networks' commitment to covering the institution.
The suggestion that that day has passed, however, will be explored later in
chapter 3 as well as through the extensive data analysis reported throughout
this volume. For now, we return to the central issue of what it is in the preparation, experience, and training of a journalist that offers the potential for excellence in covering the Court.

Broadly, James Clayton has written, one "must know the Court's history
and its place in American government; he must know something about the
Constitution and what it means" (in Hiebert, 1966: 188). Lyle Denniston, the
current dean in length of service in the Court's press corps, adds:

If one does not have an enormous fascination with the substance of the law, it is the
purest of illusions to think that you can go and cover the Supreme Court for more than
one or two terms at the most and get any kind of pleasure out of it, because the Court
is a beat for a student of the Court and not for a transient who simply passes through.
(in Slotnick, 1993)

Just as legal academicians have mused over the necessity of prior judicial
experience for excellence in Supreme Court justices (with numerous examples available to bolster both sides of the argument), commentators and practitioners have addressed the issue of what relevance some legal training
and/or a law degree has for excellence in Supreme Court reporting. Here, too,
examples abound on both sides of the ledger. In a survey conducted in the late
1980s of twenty-four "regulars" covering the Court, Rorie Sherman found
that nine were attorneys including Stephen Adler of the *Wall Street Journal*,
Richard Carelli of the Associated Press, Tim O'Brien of ABC News, Carl Stern
of NBC News, Stuart Taylor of the *New York Times*, and Stephen Wermeil of
the *Wall Street Journal*. Among the prominent and equally well-respected lay
reporters, however, were Rita Braver of CBS News, Al Kamen of the *Washington Post*, Nina Totenberg of National Public Radio, and Lyle Denniston of
the *Baltimore Sun* (1988: 33).

Carl Stern underscored the importance of having "knowledge of what
courts do and what is required by the game of jurisprudence, and if you don't

know that, you could have erroneous impressions and end up doing stories that are either not very helpful or, at best, let's say confused." The "knowledge" that Stern referred to, however, did not necessarily flow from legal training per se: "That's not to say that you have to have a law degree. I'm not saying that. Lyle Denniston knows more law than the rest of us put together. . . . It's not the degree, but it has something to do with knowledge and experience."

Linda Greenhouse, who prepared for her *New York Times* Supreme Court assignment by spending a year earning an M.A. at Yale Law School in a program designed for journalists, emphasized the professional demands of the beat: "When I got here, of course, I found that there was an awful lot of on-the-job training . . . and the book learning from Yale didn't . . . necessarily translate into the job of daily coverage of the Court. . . . [W]hat really matters, or what really matters to editors, certainly, is the background in daily journalism and the . . . nuts-and-bolts craft of turning out . . . stories against a daily deadline" (in Slotnick, 1993). As noted by Stuart Taylor, who has covered the Court for several prominent venues, "I think all things being equal, a good journalist without a law degree is going to do a better job than a mediocre journalist with a law degree" (in Davis, 1994: 67).

With these perspectives in mind, CBS News reporter Jim Stewart suggested that, in some circumstances, legal training might, conceivably, even work against a reporter's effectiveness given the airtime or print-space constraints confronting reporters:

I would certainly hope that it's never true that having a law degree would be a detriment to being a good journalist. . . . A law degree . . . just sharpens your mind . . . so I would hope that's not the case. If, on the other hand, you approach covering the Supreme Court as a lawyer as opposed to a journalist, then you are going to be in big trouble because it is not an exaggeration when they tell you they will take one minute and twenty-five seconds from you. And they don't mean one minute and twenty-six seconds either. And . . . most lawyers would throw up their hands. I don't think they know how to be that concise.

Carrying the argument that legal training may actually be a detriment to Court reporting to an extreme conclusion, Lyle Denniston has suggested that "if a reporter hangs around judges and lawyers too long he begins to smell like them. A journalist has his own smell and he should never trade that aroma for someone else's" (in Davis, 1994: 68). Elaborating on this view, Denniston added:

[T]o my mind the biggest problem we who cover the judiciary now have is . . . the final triumph of that notion that you ought to go to law school before you cover a courthouse for a medium of communication. That is pure . . . 105 percent bullshit. . . . You
do not need to go to law school to cover a courthouse. The law teaches you respect for
order, it teaches respect for tradition, it teaches you respect for hierarchy. And every
one of these values is alien to the proper practice of journalism. . . . I know what I'm
doing. . . . I am a self-confident journalist who would not think of walking into a courthouse to cover it unless I was properly prepared to do so. And that does not mean that
I have a law degree. It means that I am properly prepared to translate what goes on
there for people who don't care three seconds about the substance of the law. They buy
me not as a law review. They buy me as a medium of immediate communication, and
that's all they want from me. (in Hodson, 1996)

Few, if any, journalists have staked out the position that advanced legal
training is a necessity for covering the Court. None, however, is as passionate
in his disdain for such training as Denniston. Some lawyer-journalists have
suggested that their legal training gave them an edge on the beat, albeit not
necessarily for its substantive relevance. In Tim O'Brien's case, a law degree
facilitated obtaining the Supreme Court assignment in the first instance, while
his personal interest in what he is covering has sustained it:

I think what I brought to the beat was a law degree, and that helped me get it. But I
also brought a great interest in the work of the Supreme Court and the issues before
the Court and I think that has been my ticket to success at the Court. . . . You have to
care about what the Court is doing. You have to have a feel for the issues. And I think
you can have that without a background in law.

In Fred Graham's view, his law degree offered a special status that facilitated his relationship with then Chief Justice Warren Burger:

It may not surprise you to know that there are a number of people in the legal profession and especially among judges who can't bring themselves to really accept the fact
that a person who is not an attorney is, indeed, a complete human being. And just the
fact that you have the law degree in some sort of subliminal way makes all the difference in the world in some instances. . . . Chief Justice Burger, you know, really didn't
like reporters at all, and, particularly, he didn't like television. He really didn't like television reporters. He called them all kinds of bad names. And he and I, we had a wonderful relationship and we talked a lot. . . . And he would say to me, you know, "These
reporters do this and reporters are terrible," and I would be looking at him, and here
I am a reporter. And I realized as our relationship went on, that as an attorney he really didn't attach the stigma to me, and so there is something to be said for being a
lawyer. (in Slotnick, 1993)

At the margins, Graham has written, his law degree could be useful in enhancing his credibility:

I learned over the years that the true importance of my law degree was not that it helped me to write knowledgeably about the cases but that it removed the stigma of being a "non-lawyer." The fact that nobody has ever been called a "non-dentist" or a "non-plumber" suggests that lawyers and judges tend to view the uninitiated with more skepticism than other professions do, and the shingle on my wall made them more likely to talk freely with me. (1990: 135)

Further, the degree could be useful within the confines of the news organization as well. As Graham explained, "When I first went to CBS . . . Richard Salant, who was president of CBS News, was a lawyer, and he was very proud of the fact that he had gotten a lawyer to cover legal matters. . . . I pulled my sheepskin off on them. I would say, 'Look, I'm the lawyer here, and I say this is important.' And they would say, 'Oh, well, let's do it.'"

The relevance of what one must "know" to cover the Court relates closely, of course, to the question of what one is seeking to portray and deliver to one's audience. Lyle Denniston proclaims that his readers do not turn to him as a law review. What, then, do Supreme Court reporters and, in particular, television reporters covering the Court perceive to be their job? What is it they are trying to do?

THE JOURNALISTIC TASK
OF THE SUPREME COURT REPORTER

The task for reporters covering the Court begins with determining what portion of the institution's work is "newsworthy." Generally, as Lyle Denniston explained, a story is newsworthy if it's about "an object of contemporary fascination" (in Slotnick, 1993). Denniston, like most specialists covering the Court, can identify what warrants coverage almost instinctively:

After having been in this business now for very close to forty years, I don't wake up at night wondering how I'm going to cover the judiciary tomorrow. I've been doing it long enough that it's not simply a transitory adventure. . . . I'm a professional journalist . . . in the sense that I know what's news and I can tell it when I see it. I'm like Potter Stewart in the *Jacobellis* case. . . . I know what's news. I don't have to consult any muse, I certainly don't have to ask any lawyer, and God knows I don't ask any judge. And what is news to me is what, perhaps, transitorily fascinates the milkman in Hyattsville, Maryland. . . . He has maybe three minutes to read Lyle Denniston's work, however much effort I've put into it. He trusts me not to waste his time with material irrelevant to what fascinated him. So I find myself routinely putting myself in his driver's seat and saying, if I were going to read this story, what would I most want to know about this? . . . What was the outcome? And why did it come out that way [?] in a way that I can understand. (in Hodson, 1996)

In chapter 3 we will examine in greater detail what, particularly, about the Court's work might make it newsworthy for television news. For now we will simply note that, within the confines of what is newsworthy for television, net- work reporters tend to define their task similarly to Denniston's. As Tim O'Brien noted, "I think our job is to take these issues that are so very important and make them relevant to our audience. I think this is true whether it's news- paper or broadcasting." For Fred Graham, it is the "why" that is most interest- ing: "I always felt that average people could understand these complicated legal and constitutional issues if you were able to cast it in terms of 'why.' Why is the law developing? Why is this an issue?" For Carl Stern, "The important thing is impact. Impact. What are the ramifications of the decision? What does it mean to people? That's the important part. . . . Impact, significance, ramifications. That is always what it is about." Pete Williams, too, underscored that "televi- sion places a very high premium on 'What does this mean?'" while emphasiz- ing the centrality of the "human element" in covering Supreme Court stories:

What was the controversy? What was this case all about? You have to have that human element in there. This is a story about a lady, the guy ran over her foot and killed her dog, and the barbecue thing fell on her, you know, started a fire. You have to have all that stuff in there. . . . [T]his started out as a dispute. Who are the people who are mad at each other and why? . . . And then I feel some obligation to . . . rather than just say what the Court said, to say why it is that they said what they said. What did they base that on? . . . But the folks who put the broadcast together always want to know, well, what does this mean? Where do we go from here?

Jim Stewart of CBS News cautioned that, as a journalist addressing a gen- eral audience, he could not attempt to go into great detail or offer analyses analogous to those reporting for specialized publics such as journalists he had witnessed earlier in his career while covering the Defense Department:

[There are] people who follow cases for a specialized audience that I'm not going to ever attempt to compete with in terms of understanding the complexities of the Court.

I find that there is a great deal [more] . . . interest in the interplay among the justices than I care about. . . . I don't want to come off sounding stupid, but I really don't care about how many questions in an afternoon Sandra Day O'Connor might ask, or how she is going to end up being, as she often is, the swing vote, the consensus builder. That sort of inside baseball stuff . . . may be of interest to people who've made a lifetime of covering the Court and intend to record all of that in a book one day, but it doesn't mean anything to an average viewer. Nor, might I add, an average reader. I was in newspapers for twenty-three years, and I think, quite frankly, I would have covered the Supreme Court the exact same way as I do now. I would have picked the cases that I think mean the most to the average American. . . . And you try to find a way to make them be interested in it.

Stewart went on to suggest that, while his audience was not the same as that of the *New York Times*, the broader issue was not, necessarily, who his audience was but, rather, what he as a reporter should be doing:

You've got to remember what you are. You're a reporter. Your first job is to understand what it is that just occurred and then figure out a way to explain that so that others can understand. . . . [W]hen I first started this beat, the trappings and the decor and the great majesty of the Court can sometimes make you feel like, "My God, am I fully understanding what's going on here?" And I would . . . go the next day and read Linda Greenhouse and say, "Oh, my God, she interpreted these three questions that the justices . . . asked, and she has derived from the way they asked those questions and correlated it back to previous decisions and pretty much come to a conclusion of what the Court is going to decide in this case." And I wasn't able to do that. . . . But then I thought, "Well, who the hell am I kidding?" It would take a fool to go on national TV after an arguments case before the Supreme Court and say, "and therefore the decision is going to be probably five to four." Oh, give me a break. That's not your job anyway. Your job is to reflect what happened here and say it in a way that you and I can understand.

Given the Court's relative invisibility and, consequently, the central role that the media, particularly television news, play in informing the public about the Court's work, the question arises of whether journalists feel they have a special "public" function or educative role in covering the Court that may not be present in reporting on more widely seen and understood institutions. From Linda Greenhouse's perspective, it is not the journalist's role, necessarily, that is different but, rather, the setting in which that role is performed:

It's basically the same role of making a government institution accessible . . . but you have to do it differently. . . . I see myself kind of in the role of a translator, not only

translating . . . the legal jargon into ordinary English but sort of putting . . . the cases
in context both in terms of their background and their implications and in what they
say about the ongoing life of the institution. And I think you have to do that on a more
. . . ground-zero basis than you do in covering institutions that are just, by their nature, more accessible and people . . . know more about them. (in Slotnick, 1993)

In Pete Williams's view the suggestion of a public function or an educative
role for journalists covering the Court is a "Wouldn't it be nice?" kind of argument:

Wouldn't it be nice if television said to itself, "Gee, you know, people only get their
news from television, and so we'd better cover the Supreme Court more." It isn't going to happen. And, I suppose, as a matter of social responsibility and all that . . . you
can make that argument. Naturally, as Supreme Court reporters we make that argument. . . . But I don't think it is anything our managers in New York get up thinking
about. . . . And it's too bad, probably, but that's the way it is.

Tim O'Brien is more willing to accept openly that he performs, in part, an
educative role:

I think that we should try to serve an educational function, not just what the Court is
doing, but educate people about the competing interests involved on such matters as
affirmative action and racial gerrymandering and school desegregation and the right
to privacy and free speech and the death penalty. . . . [N]one of them is as easy as you
might think and . . . the more educating we can do the better.

O'Brien noted, however, that the best opportunities to educate the public on
legal issues may arise in the context of covering sensational stories and not,
necessarily, in "routine" coverage of the Supreme Court's docket. Take, for
example, coverage of the celebrated murder trial of O. J. Simpson, warts
and all:

There are a lot of issues that have gotten before the Supreme Court that we really had
to struggle to get on the air. . . . The duty of the police to preserve evidence? The
Supreme Court said in *Youngblood v. Arizona*, "ain't none." . . . [I]t was tough getting
that story on, but it was debated for hours in the O. J. Simpson case and that debate
enlightened the public. . . . [W]hat about the right against search and seizure and the
rule against allowing into evidence material obtained in violation of that right? The ex-
clusionary rule – people think that's a technicality. Watch the O. J. Simpson case, [and]
I think most people see it's not a technicality. It is really very important. What about
the role of race in jury selection? A big Supreme Court issue that people have seen debated on television in the O. J. Simpson case and, I dare say, have debated themselves

around the breakfast table. . . . [T]elevision coverage in O. J. Simpson, yeah, is it a classroom or a circus? It is clearly both, and the benefits of the TV classroom have been enormous in the O. J. Simpson case.

Many journalists range between wishing that they did a better job educating the public and openly accepting an educative role. Standing adamantly against any notion, however, that he had an educative role or responsibility to play in covering the Court is print journalist Lyle Denniston:

It is no part of our obligation nor is it even, perhaps, any part of our opportunity to be the public spokesperson for the Court. We are not part of the furniture of the judiciary. . . . It is highly inappropriate, I think, to assume that when a reporter walks into the courthouse he or she is going to feel that their function is best fulfilled when he has helped the Court explain itself to the public, or have themselves function as a medium through which the Court can be understood. . . . We are covering the judiciary as an arm of government, and we are no more an apologist for the judiciary than one can expect a reporter covering the White House to be an apologist for the president or the presidency. . . . I think we have to . . . get away from the notion . . . that the press, somehow, has an obligation to be useful, to be an educative medium for a complicated institution like the judiciary. First of all, we're not competent to do that. Second, we're not interested in doing that. We are covering the news as news. (in Hodson, 1996)

Denniston's position is not derived from any antipathy to education per se. Rather, it is based on a lifetime of commitment to his understanding of the First Amendment's dictates and his concern that, somehow, a press that "failed" to educate the public sufficiently could find its rights endangered. In Denniston's view, "We do not have to earn our rights."

Many people in this country . . . think of the press . . . the same way they think of the judiciary; as a public institution that is . . . performing a public service. A lot of people will make the argument, and they make it very sincerely and, indeed, with a good deal of passion, that the only reason there is a First Amendment is for you to perform a public service. Absent the proper responsibility in the performance of that public service, you're not entitled to any rights at all.

Denniston takes great issue with this perspective:

I have spent a good deal of my professional life . . . trying to make the point that we just happen to be an institution that has a constitutionally guaranteed right to speak in the same way that every one of you walking up and down the street . . . has a right to speak. And we do not have to pay for that right by fulfilling somebody's objective sense of public service. It is not a right that is going to be withdrawn from us except by the appropriate processes of constitutional amendment or by nibbling away by the judiciary.

Ultimately, for Denniston, the only "check" that legitimately operates on journalistic performance short of constitutional change is a commercial one:

We do not have to perform in a commercial setting in a way that will achieve a Good Housekeeping Seal of Approval from the judiciary or, indeed, from our own readers. Our readers vote with their subscriptions or with their quarters in the box. If they stop voting for us, then we go under. I worked for a wonderful institution, the *Washington Star,* that went under. Not because we were failing in public service. Not because we were failing in educative function. But because times and commerce passed us by. And we will not, in my business, improve what we do in terms of what you, the consuming public, buy, on the basis of trying to earn our rights or trying to earn your respect. That's not what we're about. . . . It's a nice thing, in social value terms, if one of the unintended consequences of quality journalism is that we educate the public now and then. But what I'm trying to stress is, do not think of this as an obligation. Do not lay upon us the burden of justifying our right by the quality of our performance. (in Hodson, 1996)

Fred Graham agreed with Denniston in saying, "I don't think there's a Good Housekeeping Seal of Approval for journalists." He differed somewhat, however, in his perspective on the First Amendment and its implications for journalistic performance:

I would agree in some, perhaps, pristine sense that there is not a responsibility to the courts, perhaps, to a certain level of coverage. But all journalists, I believe, feel there is a responsibility to themselves as professionals and . . . as citizens to do what they do in a responsible way. There is a constitutional right there in the First Amendment, but, of course, it is premised on the fact that the results of that will be socially beneficial coverage. And I know just from my own personal experience now when COURT TV selects the cases that it is going to cover . . . we do have a mix and we have a formula. And the formula is not just necessarily where the most titillating action will be. It's so many civil cases, so many criminal cases, some appellate cases . . . and trial cases. . . . [P]art of the reason for that is to serve some public function in informing and educating the public. (in Hodson, 1996)

THE COURT'S PUBLIC INFORMATION OFFICE

While we have emphasized the unique nature of the Supreme Court beat, it is important to underscore that reporters covering the institution are not completely isolated and on their own when performing their work. Over time, many significant alterations have been made in the relationship between the Supreme Court and the journalists who cover it. Notably, until the late 1920s, reporters did not have access to copies of opinions at the time they were announced, and they were forced to rely in their reporting on their understanding of what they had heard. At that time, proofs of decisional texts became available, but only after rulings were completely read or announced in the courtroom. Now, of course, reporters do receive welcome assistance from the Court's Public Information Office, although, as we shall see, the office is very different from press operations in other governmental settings.

The Court's Public Information Office was formally established in 1935, and, in 1947, a full-time Public Information Officer (PIO) was appointed (Davis, 1994: 30). According to Richard Davis, "The office was a direct response to press requests to the chief justice for assistance. . . . In order to reduce attention to the addition, the Court did not even officially announce the change" (1994: 36). At first, the PIO's job consisted largely of distributing opinions of the Court. In time, the scope of the job increased as additional materials were made available to reporters (such as certiorari petitions, the Court's conference list, orders list, briefs of the parties, and amicus briefs), and the PIO became a source for additional information (such as the schedule of oral arguments and identification of which days would be decision days) (Davis, 1994: 36–49).

Davis underscores some important differences between the Court's Public Information Office and the more publicly prominent press operations in other governmental settings:

Even the title of the Court's press relations arm reflects its effort to disassociate itself with an image of media manipulation. While the title "press secretary" and "press office" have acquired wide acceptance in the parlance of government public relations, the Court prefers the more benign term "Public Information Office." The term connotes a mere conveyance role to the general public without specific reference to the primary mechanism of public knowledge, that is, the press. (1994: 47)

Toni House, who has served as the Court's Public Information Officer since 1982, confirmed the basic thrust of the PIO's job, while linking it more directly to serving the press:

My job is peculiar in Washington because this office doesn't spin, it doesn't flap, it doesn't interpret. Our job is to put the news media together with the information that they need to cover the Court. Most importantly, when an opinion comes down, we put it in the hands of a reporter. That reporter is responsible for deciding what the Court said him or herself. We don't say, "Well, actually, what the Chief Justice meant in this opinion was X, Y, and Z." Our belief, and certainly the belief of the people I work for, is that . . . it's our job to make sure that people get it and then get out of the way. (C-SPAN, 1996)

In discussing House's job, Fred Graham noted its inherent difficulties and, in a sense, her need to play the role of an "honest broker":

She's as helpful as she can be. . . . I sense that she is perpetually caught in the middle between Chief Justice Rehnquist, who either couldn't care less or, to a certain extent, probably has negative views of the media and media coverage. And she is loyal to him. . . . But she also knows that in order to have . . . as full and accurate coverage as possible, she needs to do what she can to accommodate the media, and she does that. And I think she is a wizard at being able to reconcile the two.

For her part, House explained that, while she works for the Chief Justice, she serves the interests of journalists as well:

When I interviewed with Chief Justice Burger I said to him . . . I see the job of the Public Information Officer as someone who really is a go-between, who brings the concerns of the journalists to the Court and the concerns of the Court to the journalists. And that's what we have tried to do here. We have tried to act to be an advocate for the news media to the Court, sometimes successfully and sometimes not. But we certainly feel that's our responsibility. (C-SPAN, 1996)

House's own characterization of the job, which corresponds closely to Fred Graham's assessment of her stellar performance, has not, in Graham's view, characterized the way the office has always worked:

There was one very bad Public Information Officer. . . . Not only did he lie to us, but when we complained to Burger, Burger didn't mind that he lied and probably liked it. That was the way I read it. I went personally to Burger and complained about his guy lying, saying, "Hey, this is not Vietnam. . . . You're not at war, and we're not trying to scuttle what you're up to." And Burger said basically, . . . "Well, you know, he's my Public Information Officer, and I approve of the job he's doing." Toni House has never lied to me, and I've never heard anyone complain she lied to them. . . . [S]he realizes . . . that's such a compromising thing.

Richard Davis has reported that one journalist covering the Court during House's tenure complained, "I don't consider it an information office. It ranges from no information to disinformation. Anybody who understands the English language can't help but be offended by the term 'Public Information Office' at the Court" (1994: 48). This was clearly not a perspective that was shared in any of our interviews. Reporters' wish lists for the Public Information Office all concerned "housekeeping," not substantive matters, and generally centered on things that the PIO had little control over obtaining or disseminating. Thus, some reporters wished they were better informed about and had greater access to off-the-bench appearances and speeches made by the justices, or could routinely receive information about the reasons justices recused themselves from hearing cases. All the reporters recognized, however, that the justices did not answer to the Public Information Officer. As Pete Williams observed, for example, Justice John Paul Stevens never offers a reason for recusing himself, and it would be quite useful to reporters if he did: "And Toni House could go up and say, 'Now, Justice Stevens, you really ought to do this.' And he's going to say, 'Thank you very much, but I just don't do that.' And, so, what can she do?" Tapping the consensus of reporters covering the Court about the Public Information Office, Williams concluded:

They don't spin, they don't tell you why a decision is important. . . . If you go and say, "What are the important cases?" they'll say, "Hey, here are the briefs, read it yourself." . . . They're very good at answering questions about why the Court does things certain ways. . . . They are very good at that kind of institutional question. They are very good at explaining the funky little customs of the Supreme Court. They are very good at helping us with logistical arrangements, where we can put our crew and all that kind of stuff. . . . And they do a very good job of managing the flow of reporters in and out of the courtroom. . . . But I don't know what more they could do.

SUPREME COURT REPORTERS, THE JUSTICES, AND THE CLERKS

We have already taken note that one hurdle facing Supreme Court reporters in their efforts to cover the institution is the relative dearth of traditional news sources. The Court's members and staff all place a premium on secrecy and, to the extent that the relationships between journalists and their sources are often based on mutually beneficial exchanges, journalists are perceived to have little to offer the Court in this regard. This is not to suggest that there is no interaction whatsoever between journalists and the justices but, rather, to underscore that the relationships that do exist do not appear to affect the coverage of the institution or offer much journalistic payback. Fred Graham has written that Supreme Court justices could hardly be considered "news sources" in the journalist's lexicon: "There was an understanding in my dealings with them that all conversations were off the record, and confidential Court business was usually not discussed." While justices might assist the journalist in confirming or denying material for a story, "none played the spin-control game that is routine everywhere else in Washington. None of them tried to manage the news by putting their views, or themselves, in a favorable light" (Graham, 1990: 119). Graham offered a vivid description of the task the Court's reporters consequently faced:

Covering the Supreme Court was like being assigned to cover the Pope. Both the justices and the Pope issue infallible statements, draw their authority from a mystical higher source, conceal their humanity in flowing robes, and because they seek to present a saintly face to the world – are inherently boring. (Graham, 1990: 119–20)

Graham explained that his access to the justices during his tenure at the Court varied a good deal as a result of personality differences. Some, such as Potter Stewart and Lewis Powell, he considered to be close friends. Ironically, Graham developed a close relationship with Byron White, a justice generally known for his hostility to the media:

This happened because he and I were making speeches on the same program in Salt Lake City one day. . . . Byron White is sitting here being introduced, and a huge man from the audience walks up, stands beside him, and starts beating him on the head. . . . And I said to myself, "You know its a shame I'm a reporter. Reporters are not supposed to be involved in events." And then I said, "Wait a minute. I'm not here as a reporter. I'm on the program." (Quoted in Slotnick, 1993)

Freed from his journalistic responsibilities, Graham came to White's aid, and "he and I just got along very well after that" (in Slotnick, 1993). More generally, Graham concluded, "My experiences with the justices was that you didn't talk shop . . . and they didn't tell you secrets. I found some of the justices really were a little lonely. . . . Abe Fortas told me . . . 'The phone never, never rings when you're a justice. Nobody calls you up.' They miss the camaraderie. . . . Lawyers are in awe of them" (in Slotnick, 1993).

The relationships of other reporters with the justices offer variants of the portrait Graham paints. Linda Greenhouse, for example, confessed, "I've never rescued a justice, and I don't have anywhere near the kind of personal relationships Fred describes. I have what I would call a . . . mild social acquaintance with a number of them. . . . [I]f they met me on the street, I think they would recognize me, but it doesn't go beyond that" (in Slotnick, 1993). For his part, Tim O'Brien noted that it "depends on the justice":

Some justices avoid us like lepers, and others you can take to a ball game. I took Harry Blackmun to a ball game. He almost got hit by a foul ball. I went to chase the ball down. I thought his wife might like it as a souvenir . . . and some six-year-old beat me to the ball and forty thousand fans cheered for the six-year-old. It turned out to be very embarrassing.

Carl Stern indicated that, purposefully, his interaction with the justices was "virtually none, almost none":

I have some personal friendships with some. But I went out of my way, and there are reporters who feel differently about this. While I was covering the Court, I never invited a justice to my home. I never tried to engage a justice in conversation at a social event. I gave them wide berth because I felt they would be uncomfortable. I never called one on the phone to ask them something about a pending case or a court decision. That's not to say I never talked to them on the phone at all. There were a couple of instances when I did in connection with particular needs that I had. For example, there was one case that Justice [Thurgood] Marshall heard in his chambers, and I thought he should let some press people attend, that sort of thing. But I never called . . . the justices or the clerks to ask them to reveal something to me in confidence because I felt . . . that would suggest that I'm the kind of person who thinks they are the kind of person who would tell me. And I had too much respect for all the justices to even suggest by implication that I thought they were the kind of people who would tell me stories out of school.

Alone among the reporters commenting on this subject, Lyle Denniston conceded that he would not be averse, necessarily, to using justices as sources and that he had, at times, been told things "out of school." But he also indicated, in this regard, that his interactions with justices had not been particularly beneficial in his journalistic work:

Over the years I have had relationships with the justices such that I can call them on the phone or I can go up to chambers and chat. And those relationships sometimes have involved discussions of cases, and I have been told things that, in tribal normalities, I shouldn't have been told. But, by and large, the relationship that I have with them is, basically, they know who I am and what I'm about, and I know who they are and what they're about. . . . But they are not good news sources, I will just tell you that. You can spend a lot of time talking with a justice and get damn little for the effort. And I suspect that's as it should be. (in Slotnick, 1993)

If the justices are not useful sources for Supreme Court reporters, the question arises, what about their clerks? Here, Fred Graham suggested, clerks may have been a useful source at one time. Later, whether because of his aging or a new environment at the Court in the wake of the publication of Bob Woodward and Carl Bernstein's clerk-attributed book, *The Brethren,* and Warren Burger's aggressive drive for secrecy, the situation changed. Early on, Graham interacted "quite a bit with the clerks because I was more their age and, really, it was helpful":

I had a clerk who tipped me off about Abe Fortas doing so much off the bench on the Vietnam War. This young man was outraged that Fortas was sitting on draft cases and writing opinions sending kids to jail, with indignant opinions about how unpatriotic these kids were. And this clerk knew from things going on around the courthouse that Abe Fortas was on the phone to Lyndon Johnson and they were discussing bombing. It was outrageous. And that was something that I was able to do a story on.

Clearly, however, Graham recognized that going with a story where a clerk served as a source could be journalistically dangerous:

I had . . . one of the clerks tip me off about the fact that they were going to uphold the conviction of Cassius Clay. Well, of course, on the day they were supposed to do that, [John Marshall] Harlan changed his mind, and they didn't uphold his conviction. I would have been wrong if I'd gone with the story. . . . [I]n talking to the clerks it was helpful to get the background of some of the sort of perceptual differences among the justices. . . . In terms of trying to find out who's going to decide what, I was always leery of that. As I got older I found that, because there was an age gap between me and the clerks, I didn't know them as well. Chief Justice Burger really kind of intimidated his clerks. They thought they would be fired if they were seen talking to me. In fact, one of them almost ran away from me at a party, and I kept following him around . . . and he kept backing off and I couldn't resist.

A NOTE ON INTEREST GROUPS
AND THE SUPREME COURT REPORTER

In a setting where the decision-making justices are not routinely available as sources and their press arm, the Court's Public Information Office, provides information but doesn't interpret it, interest groups have made a concerted effort to step into the void and provide their policy spin on the Court's work. Groups and their spokespersons are widely and routinely available today in press-conference and interview settings, often on the public plaza in front of the Court itself, to meet with reporters in preterm briefings, to comment on certiorari grants and denials, to dissect oral argumentation, and, of course, to offer their views on the Court's decisions. As Richard Davis has observed, "In an age of institutional and individual attempts to shape news coverage, the Court's failure to engage in overt activities associated with such attempts – news conferences, photo opportunities, and so forth – creates a vacuum for interest groups to fill" (1994: 100–101).

Finding group spokespersons to serve as sources for stories is, clearly, not a problem for the Court reporter. Linda Greenhouse explained, "I don't make too many phone calls. People call me. Usually the fax machine starts churning out. Usually it's having to fend off phone calls" (in Davis, 1994: 87). Tim O'Brien, who often skips news conferences called by groups, added, "It's amazing . . . the number of interest groups that are holding briefings to mark the great Supreme Court cases coming up and give you their spin on it." The situation can be particularly acute for the television reporter providing coverage in the open Court plaza. As noted by Jim Stewart, "The reaction is never a problem. These assholes line up for two blocks around the building and stand in front of your microphone."

In relying on and utilizing group perspectives, journalists are, of course, adding substantial color and richness to their stories on the Court. Equally obvious, the Court reporter must incorporate group spins in their stories without being unduly manipulated by their sources. As Miranda Spivack of the *Hartford Courant* explained, "You know you have to depend on people who have a vested interest. So you know you have to take what they say with a grain of salt. I figure everybody is giving me their own gloss, and I just have to sift through it" (in Davis, 1994: 90). Tim O'Brien recognized both the importance of interest groups in his work as well as the reality of his differential treatment of them:

We need them in the sense that Congress needs them. The more information we have, the better. Now, not all interest groups are treated the same. Those that can present their arguments in an objective context and without distorting facts, you get to know who they are over a period of time. You expect them to explain their own point of view, which is their own point of view but without distortions. They have a great deal of credibility.

Summing up the views of his colleagues, Pete Williams broadly assessed both the input he receives from groups as well as his cautionary approach to them:

I probably get fifteen faxes a week from someone trying to say, "Hey . . . it's the all-important *Schwartz v. Fern* case. Critical. Essential." If you already think it's important, you say to yourself, "Okay, now I know where this group stands on it." If you don't think it's important, they're not going to change your mind. Look, there are lots of little seminars that go on around town. . . . The Chamber of Commerce has its, and the ACLU has its, and, sometimes, the women's groups have theirs. . . . And Lambda Legal will have theirs, and Pat Robertson's group will have theirs, and the Washington Legal Foundation will have theirs. And I try to go to as many of those that I can because the more I learn about these cases the better off I am. . . . I'm always happy to hear someone's argument about why a case is important. But . . . you then go to neutral arbiters. . . . [Y]ou go to the law professor types and people like that who don't have a dog in the fight, and you say, "Is this case really going to make a difference?" And they'll say, "Not really," or "Yes, it will." So it is good to have the referees around that you can go to.

THE SUPREME COURT PRESS CORPS

The environment in which Supreme Court reporters work can be characterized by many operating realities. The decision makers are not often directly accessible to the media. Everything being reported on is available at the same time to all who wish to report on it. The Court's Public Information Office serves primarily to distribute, not interpret, information, and legions of group spokespersons are ready and willing to occupy the void. In such a setting, relationships among the reporters covering the Court are bound to take on a different flavor from those in other source-dependent, scoop-driven, highly competitive journalistic beats. Indeed, in such a working environment, Supreme Court reporters often find that they provide each other's own best counsel in their daily interactions on the beat.

At the outset, note should be taken that the Court's press corps numbers, at most, about fifty reporters, with only about a dozen or so covering the institution on a relatively full-time basis. The relatively small number of reporters who cover the Court, compared to the scores of journalists who descend on other Washington beats, results in a very collegial beat with a good deal of interaction and exchange between Court reporters and, especially, the "regulars." Among the regulars there is, according to Davis, an even smaller sub-group termed "the elite," whose "designation stems from their seniority on the beat, skill in interpretation and reporting, and, typically, the elite nature of their publication" (Davis, 1994: 63–65). As described by Pete Williams,

there is this little subgroup within the press corps that I'm not a member of because I'm a dreadful television reporter. . . . They go down for this little retreat before the term each year. . . . [They are] the center of the press corps . . . and then the rest of us kind of rotate . . . around those planets.

While there may exist a status differential among Court reporters, it is also evident that the beat is marked by an unusually generous sharing of informa-tion on a routine basis, particularly among the regulars. Tim O'Brien charac-terizes the beat as one in which among television reporters there is, "more cooperation than competition. I think because we all . . . developed an us-against-them mentality trying to get on the air. I don't compete so much with NBC and CBS to get on the air as much as I do with other [ABC] corre-spondents."

The existence of a general "community" of Supreme Court reporters was described by Linda Greenhouse:

There is a community. A small handful of us basically live there, eat there . . . work there. . . . [We are] quite collegial. If somebody finds an interesting case on the cert list . . . they're quite likely to mention it or discuss it at lunch, or swap ideas at lunch about the implications of yesterday's decision or something like that. . . . [T]his is such specialized knowledge, and we . . . have very few people we can discuss it with. And we just find it interesting. We enjoy it. . . . It just pays to have good conversation. (in Slotnick, 1993)

Fred Graham noted that such conversations included "a good bit of help that goes on after an oral argument because we're not permitted to take recorders in the courtroom. . . . [Y]ou can't get a transcript, or . . . when you get one it doesn't have the judge's name to it, and you certainly can't get one on the same day. So people do help each other with quotes."

Carl Stern concurred that there was "a lot of sharing. . . . I didn't know if our editors would be happy knowing about it." He sketched out the broad pa-rameters of the kind of information that was made available to one's colleagues on this uniquely collegial beat:

I would keep a file folder on each case that I was interested in with clippings and briefs and related materials, my own notes, and so on. And I don't think there was ever a decision day that I didn't share with other reporters information that I had if they needed it. The correct spelling of a name, the name and phone number of the lawyer for so and so. I would give them my clippings. . . . And I did this with direct competitors, and, I'm sure, on occasions they did so with me. I never felt that I was in competition with anybody. We would frequently, and this is always a risk, kind of put our heads together and kind of ask each other, "What do you think it means?" . . . I can't think of any press operation that I've experienced or did experience in almost thirty-four years of journalism that was as collegial as the Supreme Court press room.

Given the collegiality and insularity of the Court beat, the question naturally arises of whether it is subject to a charge of "pack journalism," a situation where reporters only cover what their colleagues are covering and where all stories are prone to being interpreted in the same way by all the reporters on the beat. As Fred Graham admitted, reporters "always watch each other and try to find out what's the lead, what interests you." And, of course, as underscored by Linda Greenhouse, "On a day-to-day basis . . . we're working from the same documents and . . . the weekly list of cases that are going to conference . . . the list of cases that are scheduled for argument, and then, when the decisions come down, the actual decisions. And so, if we're in some kind of a race, we all start from the same place" (in Slotnick, 1993).

Starting from the same place, however, does not necessarily mean ending up there. Indeed, reporters covering the Court disagreed universally with any characterization of their work as succumbing to a pack instinct. In the words of Pete Williams,

If what that means is, "Geez, I've sure noticed that there are a lot of reporters hanging out together at the Supreme Court," well, they make us do that because that is where the arguments are so we all have to sort of hang out there. But, no . . . I tend to think that is not the case because you have a lot of peculiar interests. It is interesting to see who will get up and walk out of the room when there is a big case that comes down. Paul Barrett from the *Wall Street Journal* and Jim Vicini from Reuters will get up and get all excited, the hairs will stand up on the back of their neck[s] with some case about the SEC, which the rest of us could care less about and count our blessings that we are not having to cover that story. And . . . if you look at the columns that Stuart Taylor writes in *Legal Times* . . . he is sort of going off in one direction, and Tony Mauro in *USA Today* is going off in another direction, and Lyle is going off in a third direction, and Linda is picking up on some things. So we all tend to write about the big cases . . . we all hang out there together, but there are very different personalities and points of view in that room.

Earlier, we saw in Carl Stern's discussion of *Rhode Island v. Innis* how different reporters can interpret the same case in different ways, belying any conceptions of pack reporting. Perhaps even more noteworthy, for Stern, was his sense of "the extent to which we went in different directions, went our own way" regarding which cases to cover.

I can think of one final day of term . . . when Fred and Tim and I were going nose to nose. . . . Fred went with a story of the Supreme Court [leaving] standing a judgment in a sex discrimination case against AT&T, which, at that point, was the largest settlement that had ever been achieved in a sex discrimination case. And Fred thought that was . . . the Supreme Court event of the day. . . . I chose not to go with that because it was not a decision of the Court – they had simply left standing what another court had done, whatever its importance. Tim went with the story on a Texas death penalty case. For one thing, I think he had some good pictures . . . but it was a very interesting case. On the other hand, I didn't choose to go with it because it only involved a death penalty law in the state of Texas and had no application outside the state. . . . I went with still a third matter, which was the comedian George Carlin. It was the *Pacifica* case, the seven dirty words ruling, and that's not just because it's television . . . but it was a genuinely interesting First Amendment issue as to whether or not a broadcaster could be penalized for using certain words during hours when the FCC said such words should not be broadcast on the public airwaves where they might be heard by children. In my judgment, that was the most important thing that the Supreme Court had done that day. . . . So there you have three different views from three different reporters as to what they thought was the most significant act of the Supreme Court that day that should be reported to their audiences, and generally that's the way it went. Generally, we did not agree on either what was the most important case or what the significance of the case was. (in Slotnick, 1993)

Stern's commentary is most on the mark during the final days of the Court's term when multiple rulings are announced and only a finite number can make it on to a newscast. On such days, unlike slower news days at the Court, there is a considerably greater likelihood that reporters will focus on different cases.

Further, as Lyle Denniston pointed out, an illusion of pack journalism can be fostered by the limited and shrinking universe of what the Supreme Court reporter has available as grist for the journalistic mill:

Every now and then a professor . . . comes waltzing through the press room and spends an hour and goes off and writes a very long and serious article about how reporters in the press room all do the same thing, and when one crow flies away they all fly away, and when one flies back they all fly back. . . . I would like to remind those professors

. . . we are really dealing with . . . a very limited finite body of what is potential news, and so there is bound to be some sameness. The Court is now deciding somewhere around 110 decisions on plenary review. I can remember a few years ago when it was 155, and even when it went up to 170. If you are covering an institution . . . which in its most significant news-making activity only involves itself in 110 incidents per year, it's bound to come out that you're going to cover the same thing, because if we covered every decision with equal intensity, we would still have only 110 stories over a period of 365 news days. But the reality is of those 110 decisions, maybe ten are tax cases, four are labor relations cases, two are securities cases, several of them are state tax cases, and maybe a handful are really significant constitutional cases or major federal statutory cases. So when we get to the decision end of the process, we're always going to be focusing essentially on the same material. . . . [W]e do cover it differently. That's where I think a lot of the perception of sameness breaks down because each of us has a style, each of us has a collection of biases, if you will, or prejudices, or appetites that we serve differently. (in Slotnick, 1993)

Indeed, in Denniston's view, considerably more problematic than the likelihood of reporters choosing to cover the same cases or reaching the same conclusions about those cases that they do cover is the homogenization of the news sought by higher-ups in the editorial process:

One of the agenda-setting phenomena . . . that we do have to live with as reporters is that the Associated Press is usually the first one who gets to speak to our editors. So that when Dick Corelli puts a misguided story on the AP wire, and Dick doesn't very often do that, but when Dick does that at 10:15 in the morning, by the time I get to my office at 12:30 and want to sit down with my editors and tell them what I'm going to write, they already have a perception of what the Supreme Court has done, and they've got that from reading Dick Corelli. So if Dick gets it wrong, and all of us, of course, at times do get it wrong, or if Dick has a slant on it that's different from the *Baltimore Sun* reporter's slant on it, you have already built up an expectation in your editors about what you're going to write before you get there. . . . [S]o I really have to depend upon Dick getting it right, and getting it right in my way in order to make my life easier. Now Dick is not concerned about whether the *Baltimore Sun* is going to follow his lead. Dick is writing for his audience, but it is an agenda-setting phenomenon that is very difficult to deal with on a day-to-day basis. (in Slotnick, 1993)

This phenomenon was addressed in somewhat similar terms by Carl Stern when, after outlining the three different directions that television journalists went on the final day of the Court term detailed above, he lamented, "It's also an example of how in that day and age the desk would pretty much take the reporter's judgment on what was the most important. But it's a different world today."

We will focus more closely on the relationship between television Court reporters and their editors in the next chapter. On the issue of pack journalism, however, Lyle Denniston's words capture with precision the view clearly shared by his colleagues:

I . . . resist aggressively the notion that we're engaged in pack journalism because that comes out of, I think, a flawed perception that since we're all writing about the same thing, we're all writing the same thing, which is not true. (in Slotnick, 1993)

To this point, because of the wide-ranging issues we have been exploring, our examination of Supreme Court reporters and the world in which they work has not, for the most part, necessitated taking into account the differences between broadcast and print journalism. Our primary concern in this book is, of course, to analyze the nature of television coverage of the Supreme Court, and in chapter 3 our focus will move to the unique setting in which television journalists covering the Court operate.

3

Television News
and the Supreme Court:
Opportunities and Constraints

"Over and over again . . . I . . . was obliged to change what the Court had said to meet
the requirements of a producer even though I didn't believe that that's what the Court
had said. It basically got down to a contest every night about a quarter of six between
what I knew the Court had said and what I knew the producer would accept. And then
it got down to a question as to whether we were going to do the story at all."
                                Carl Stern, former NBC News Supreme Court reporter

We have underscored in chapter 2 that the Court presents a unique setting for
reporters covering the institution and, indeed, that some facets of the beat
have important and similar implications for both print and broadcast journalism outlets. It remains important to recognize, however, that all journalistic
venues are not created equal and, clearly, are not the same. In this chapter we
shall examine the inherent strengths and weaknesses of the television medium
for covering the Court. What are the journalistic constraints imposed by the
Court itself as well as those associated with the imperatives of nightly newscasts? What changes have occurred in network newscast coverage of the Court
in past years and what does the future hold for the relationship between the
Supreme Court and nightly newscasts? We shall pay particular attention in
this chapter to the issues and concerns raised for television reporters who
must cover the Court in "the age of infotainment."

THE STRENGTHS AND WEAKNESSES OF
TELEVISION NEWS FOR COVERING THE COURT

The inherent strengths of television newscasts for covering the Court have
been well summarized by Toni House, the Court's Public Information Officer,

who commented, "What television is able to do is put a human face on the decisions when they are allowed to. They go out and put the people who were involved on camera." In Jim Stewart's view, this can "bring a character alive" to help explain what a case is all about: "The set-aside contracts case [*Adarand*] is one in point. You're able to go and find that little small paving contractor in . . . Colorado . . . that really brought heart and spirit to a story that otherwise could have been hard to explain." For Carl Stern, television can offer "the drama of human experience":

Many of these cases involve highly emotional issues in which passions run high. Television is able to convey the intensity of these situations and perhaps even more clearly explain what's at issue than print can. With print you have to figure the words out. So television can transport you to the scene and can tell you quickly what is at issue in a rather simple way.

Foreshadowing what we will later discuss as a generic problem for television coverage of the Court, however, Stern continued, "Of course, many cases are not simple."

In a similar vein, Tim O'Brien noted that television can be an ideal medium for covering events combining human interest with a concern for explaining relevant legal principles – that is, of course, when reporters have sufficient time:

A lot of people think that the Supreme Court deals primarily on abstract legal issues, principles that are beyond [and] don't really affect people, something for academics to debate. And that, of course, we know is not true. In a sense, I found it to be an ideal beat for television. The cases that come up here . . . many of them are almost tailor-made for television. When you talk to the people who bring them and what their stake in the cases are. . . . It does, unfortunately, require time that television doesn't always have to spend. What I've done, and what . . . they [newscast producers] very much like me to do, is to go out and interview the people who bring the cases. That makes the principle relevant. It makes the issue relevant to the viewer. "Ah," I say, "I really have two stories here." I have a human interest story. This person, what happened to this person? Often compelling. Sometimes we do movies on them. And then the legal issue. So I say . . . "Really, you ought to give me time for two stories. You want both. You want the human interest angle and you want the legal significance, so give me time for two." And they say, "Not so fast."

In the commentaries of television journalists such as Carl Stern and Tim O'Brien we see clearly how what television does "best," that is, explain legal principles simply and with a focus on the human consequences of the Court's actions, also plants the seeds of what the medium may do most poorly. Legal principles are not always simple, and a good deal more may be at stake in Supreme Court cases than the consequences of the rulings for the litigants involved. And, as alluded to above, television rarely offers its journalists sufficient time to sort out details and nuance. As explained by Tim O'Brien:

One of my stories, if it runs a minute-forty . . . that might be one column in a newspaper. Barely a column. . . . We can't be as comprehensive as you can in a newspaper simply because we do not have the time.

At times, particularly when really major cases are handed down, the lack of time is joined with a call for immediacy in reporting and instant analysis. Toni House recalled one instance when NBC's desire for a "rush to judgment" from Carl Stern resulted in his on-air refusal to distill the meaning of a complicated decision. Stern was simply not yet ready when the network interrupted regular programming with a news bulletin. As House explained:

The . . . thing that they do that I think is extremely dangerous is that in some instances, most vividly to my recollection is in the abortion opinions, they are so wrapped around an axle about it, they are so hyped on it, they want their people to go on camera at 10:05 [when the decision has been announced at 10:00]. Carl Stern walked out, got on camera, and said, "I can't talk about it. I haven't read it yet." To his everlasting credit. "You're going to have to give me a minute, Tom." Because as able as they may be . . . some of these can be extremely difficult. And the case – I think it was *Webster* where it happened – it was a difficult opinion to try to figure out what happened because, again, they were all over the lot.

Interestingly, some of the major constraints faced by television news reflect the fact that the Court's work is primarily reflected in its words, which, as Pete Williams pointed out, is the forte of print, not broadcast, journalism:

It may be that the print media have an enormous advantage because the Court basically handles the flow of words. I mean it's words in briefs that come in and it's words in opinions that go out. . . . So the print media are kind of well matched to that flow of words. . . . [W]hen it comes to the give-and-take about the law of the case and the sort of core issues, maybe the print media have an easier time of it.

In the sections that follow in this chapter, we shall explore, in greater depth, the constraints on television news coverage of the Court that are imposed by the rules and procedures of the Court itself, as well as those constraints that flow from the imperatives of network television news.

CONSTRAINTS ON SUPREME COURT COVERAGE: SUPREME COURT RULES, NORMS, AND PROCEDURES

Two related areas in which the Court's own rules, norms, and procedures place an especially heavy burden on television are its propensity for issuing multiple rulings, often several important ones, on the same day, and its habit of deciding cases, en masse, at or near the very end of the term. Historically, all Supreme Court decisions were announced during a series of "decision Mondays" with the Court convening at noon. Marginal reforms moved the Court's starting time to 10 A.M. in 1961, a time considerably more conducive to the demands of the news day. In 1965, the exclusivity of Mondays for announcing decisions was abandoned, making newsworthy rulings less likely to pile up on a given news day. While such reforms have been somewhat beneficial, they have not sufficiently alleviated the problems they address in the eyes of Court reporters. Despite the formal demise of decision Monday, rulings are still not spread equally across the news week. Even more importantly, a disproportionate number of the Court's rulings (and the preponderance of its important ones) are announced in June, reflecting the difficulties of reaching decision closure as well as the demands of opinion writing. The empirical realities of these problems have been researched by Stephen Wasby:

Changes in Decision Day practices have not been accompanied by changes in the flow of cases throughout the term. Few opinions can be expected in October, November, and December when oral argument has just begun, but disparities in output between the second three months (January–March) and the last three (April–June) have been considerable. . . . [O]nly a small portion of the Court's output appears by the end of December. Less than half the Court's full opinions have been announced by the end of March. . . . Not only does the Court release most of its output in the last third of the term, but as much as one-third of the Court's entire output for the term is announced in the last six weeks, with more than two-fifths of the opinions appearing in that period in some terms.

In some instances, more than 40 percent of the Court's opinions were released during the last three weeks of the term, while nearly one-fifth were released during the final week of the term (Wasby, 1988: 232–33).

Offering personal evidence of the scope of these problems, Fred Graham recalled a day when "the Warren Court handed down enough decisions and new Court rules to fill an entire 991 page volume of the Supreme Court's official case reports. There was no way for us even to read so many pages, much less write coherent stories about them" (1990: 138–139).

Tim O'Brien labeled such scenarios a "travesty," suggesting that it is not only the reporters and the viewing public who suffer because of it:

For one, anybody who doesn't think the quality of the opinions suffers is mistaken. It clearly does. I mean, why is it that if you have a really big case that's argued in October, it's really complicated, the Court will take nine months and then announce its decision in June? But if an identical case is argued in April, they'll say . . . "We've got to do it by June." . . . And sometimes it just doesn't make sense, and the quality of the opinions suffers. That's the first thing. And then we can't explain . . . to the viewer . . . if there's three or four major decisions on the same day, who's going to read all that? And the Court seems to feel that "[it's] not my job, man," and some of the justices say that should not be any of our concern. "Personally," a justice tells me, "personally, I sympathize with you. But I think it would be wrong to take your interest into consideration."

One reporter who feels that the Court should alter its procedures not, necessarily, to take television's interests into account but, rather, to be more responsive to the public's interest is Pete Williams:

I'm old-fashioned enough to believe we should cover the news and the Supreme Court should do its thing and we should do our thing and that's the way it is. And if the Supreme Court chooses to hold all the decisions until the last day and announce them all at once, then we just have to do the best we can. But if, and I think the Court does care about this a little bit. . . . if the Court really cares about . . . people understanding what they do, and I think that's important, I mean the Court doesn't want to become either so seemingly irrelevant or so mysterious and remote, that's not a good thing. I think it is in the Court's interest to . . . think of themselves as part of the government. . . . [I]f they've got two good cases . . . what's to say they can't do one on Tuesday and the other on Wednesday? . . . I don't see any problem with that. I think sometimes they just say, sort of vicariously, "We'll do it when we damn well please, and this is the way it is." And that's fine. But I'm not sure that the Court loses anything by giving us a chance to take a good bite at each of them and allow folks to let it soak in a little bit. I know that the Court wants to be independent and not appear to take the press into consideration at all, but I don't think these little tiny things would hurt anything and would help everybody.

Other suggestions made by some reporters over the years range from being given advance notification that a decision was to be announced, to some procedure for gaining advance access to opinions. Some have been willing to study opinions in a locked room until their formal announcement has been made. Indeed, in an interview with Stephen Wasby, Chief Justice Earl Warren noted that the television network heads had met with him and "suggested giving reporters the opinion earlier in the day, keeping them under lock and key until the opinion was announced in Court. Warren said the Court 'would be laughed out of town' for doing that, and rejected the idea" (Wasby, 1990).

On other concerns, the Association of American Law Schools (AALS) once suggested that a scholar be on hand to represent the Court in answering questions when decisions are announced (Press and VerBurg, 1988: 256). For his part, Tim O'Brien has suggested that the need for such radical reforms to aid journalists is simply unwarranted:

Reporters regularly assigned to the Court really don't need advance word on what decision is going to be announced. By the time a major ruling is released . . . the regular correspondents . . . have had three prior opportunities to examine the case and the issues it raised: when certiorari was sought, when certiorari was granted, and when the case was argued. (O'Brien, 1991)

Regarding the AALS suggestion, O'Brien added, "considering that the Justices themselves often disagree on what a given decision means, it borders on the absurd to have any official Court spokesman assist reporters in understanding the significance of a decision" (O'Brien, 1991).

Discussing such suggestions from the Court's perspective, Toni House explained, "The Court believes that once it has reached a conclusion it has an obligation to the parties involved to resolve the issue as quick[ly] as it can. And that speaks to not even holding something back for a day." Of the justices she added, "Most assuredly, they do not care about whether it gets on television or not. They just don't."

Evidence that this is the case can be gleaned from an anecdote told by Linda Greenhouse:

One time in an encounter with the Chief Justice, I said to him . . . "Why does the Court do this? Why don't you just spread it out a little more? Not . . . even for our convenience but just so the public will have access to more information about the Court." And he looked at me, I think he was kidding, maybe he wasn't kidding, and he said, "Well, just because we hand it down on a certain day doesn't mean you have to write it on that day. You could just save it for a day . . ." which, actually, from the Court's point of view, I'm sure, makes perfect sense. But from our point of view, of course, makes no sense at all. (in Slotnick, 1993)

Fred Graham has suggested that the full reason for the Court's policy may go beyond House's procedural explanation and the Chief Justice's seeming naïveté about journalistic imperatives. "Do you think that's the real reason? Or do you think they are afraid it [the decision] might come unstuck? . . . It might get out or someone might have another thought." Graham was left to wonder, "I've . . . never understood how Earl Warren, having been a politician, would not consider or did not [consider], I can't tell, means to really improve that."

As a consequence of multiple decision days and the end-of-term decision deluge, Court reporters are left, according to Tim O'Brien, with a "whirlwind at the end of June. . . . All that time you spend shooting the material, you can only do one or two of them." The situation often results in television journalists having to make a tough call regarding how to play their story. Fred Graham explained:

It's a shame and everyone of us . . . has the frustration of having three big decisions come down on a day, and the third one you know deserves public attention, and it's not even going to barely get on the air. And you know that if it had just come down last Thursday it would get the full treatment. . . . On television something you had to decide – let's say that three of them come down – the question is, do you pick one and give it the full bore treatment and really get it understood and get it out there and just tell the other two, have the anchor tell it? Or do you do a story that attempts to tell all three? And I went both ways depending on the nature of the stories and whether I thought I could do it with the brief period of time you had. But it was very frustrating because you just had a feeling that here you go on for forty-five seconds or a minute on subject "A" and then thirty-five seconds of a totally different subject, and who knows if people's minds can shift gears and deal with that?

While the problems Graham addressed could affect both print and broadcast journalists, the likelihood of not being able to present material looms considerably greater for the television reporter, who will generally receive a small window of time to report on the Court's decisions of the day. As Pete Williams observed,

it's sad when, if there's only five or six really good cases that term, and they do two of them the same day. It just breaks your heart because you think, "Wow, I can only do one of these." And if they are both really, really good barn-burner cases, then I will do one and some other reporter . . . will do the other. And that's sort of sad to see that child taken away from you. Or the network will say, "Well, we're only going to do one and which is it going to be?" And you have to make the decision. And it's just sort of sad because the other one begs to be told, but it's just not going to happen. So we just hate that. . . . But it's more of a problem for us in television than it is for the printos, because . . . what it means for the print people is that they will . . . have to do two stories. . . . So we all just hate that like poison, but I think it is worse for us than it is for the print guys.

Several instances of such days when the Court issued more than one important ruling occurred during the October 1989 and October 1994 terms examined in chapter 5. One example, June 27, 1990, proved to be a particularly harrowing day for the network newscasts as they attempted to deal, not very successfully, with three rulings we have operationalized as among the Court's leading decisions of the term (see chapter 5).

The cases decided on that day included *Metro Broadcasting v. FCC*, dealing with an affirmative action program in broadcast licensing, *Maryland v. Craig*, a Sixth Amendment case centering on whether children could testify on closed-circuit television to avoid a potentially traumatic face-to-face confrontation with alleged child abusers, and *Idaho v. Wright*, another Sixth Amendment case concerning whether a doctor could testify at a trial about his meeting with a child abuse victim in lieu of the victim testifying directly at the trial. ABC was the only network to cover all three decisions, however sketchily. Thus, *Craig* aired for 1:50, while *Wright* received forty seconds of airtime, and *Metro Broadcasting* only twenty seconds. On CBS, no coverage was given to the *Wright* decision, *Craig* was covered for twenty seconds, and *Metro Broadcasting* received a mere ten-second mention. On NBC, only the *Craig* case received any mention at all, airing for well under thirty seconds.

This all occurred, we should note, merely two days after the Court had decided *Cruzan v. Director, Missouri Department of Health*, an emotionally laden case first raising the issue of the right to die, and *Hodgson v. Minnesota* and *Ohio v. Akron Center for Reproductive Health*, two cases dealing with somewhat different state laws touching on parental notification and abortion rights. Clearly, all three cases warranted coverage. The networks tended to solve the dilemma by blending the Minnesota case (*Hodgson*) and the Ohio case (*Akron*) without drawing any distinctions between them. *Cruzan* coverage received the most prominence, while coverage of the now "collapsed" abortion cases was substantial as well. On both of these late-term decision days, while things were clearly difficult for the press, they were undoubtedly equally problematic for a viewing public left reeling from the announcement of six prominent rulings, among the term's most important, in a matter of days.

Gaining sufficient airtime for worthy cases is not the only problem facing Court reporters as a consequence of the Court's rules, norms, and procedures. Another, as Carl Stern developed, was the need for reporters to translate greater numbers of opinions and, in addition, more obtuse opinions over time as a consequence of the bureaucratization of the Court and the increased staffing enjoyed by each justice:

When I came to the Court, each justice had one clerk, the Chief had two. I would fire all the rest. . . . It became clerk creep or clerk inflation. They've got too many clerks, so they write these horrendously long law review articles for decisions. . . . It's a reflection of having too much help. Justice [Louis] Brandeis was asked what makes the Supreme Court great. He said it's because we do our own work here. And so it used to be. And the justices wrote relatively brief and compact decisions because they didn't have a lot of help. And that made life relatively easy for reporters, not that that's the only pursuit in life, to have easy time for reporters. But it also meant things were clearer. . . . [J]ust as the Court has reduced the size of its calendar . . . if it were to reduce the number of clerks so decisions would be simpler, less heavily footnoted, less everybody writing their own thing, then life would be immeasurably easier for reporters. And the law, I think, would be immeasurably clearer for the practitioners . . . and the judges who have to apply the law. . . . Today, you have to struggle for hours to read them and . . . each footnote is a sword hanging over your head . . . that may take away from the broad principles being announced elsewhere in the body of the decision. . . . And trying to figure out these coalitions and the parts they joined and the parts they didn't join, you need a nuclear physicist to figure these out. . . . The plain fact is that Supreme Court decisions today look like the periodic tables in chemistry.

THE ISSUE OF CAMERAS IN THE SUPREME COURT

If there is one facet of the Court's rules that, in the public eye as well as in the eyes of many Court reporters, has created the greatest constraints for television journalists, it would clearly be the ban on cameras in the Supreme Court. The refusal to allow cameras to cover oral argumentation and the announcement of decisions flies in the face of the trend in many state court settings as well as the experimental use of cameras in the past by lower federal courts and the current "home rule/local option" approach adopted by the U.S. Judicial Conference for the Courts of Appeals. While many critics of allowing television in courtrooms base their objections on the circus atmosphere associated with trial court settings such as the O. J. Simpson murder trial, the issues and concerns are, understandably, different in appellate court settings and, in particular, in a venue such as the U.S. Supreme Court.

Gilbert Merritt, Chief Judge of the Sixth Circuit Court of Appeals and the Chair of the U.S. Judicial Conference's committee that examined the cameras in the courts issue, summarized the fundamental pros and cons of allowing cameras in appellate courts as developed in his committee's deliberations:

The primary arguments against cameras in appellate courts was that this was a foot in the door, that it will expand from here. A lot of judges are opposed to cameras for a number of reasons. They think it creates a theatrical situation. That lawyers and judges will react to the cameras in an unnatural way by changing their conduct and that this wouldn't be in the interest of justice. (C-SPAN, 1996)

Recognizing that trial and appellate court settings are quite different, Merritt admitted that "the arguments on the one side are not so much that . . . it is bad to have cameras in appellate courts, because there are no witnesses and there are no jurors in the appellate courts. . . . But the argument was more that this is a nose of the camel under the tent argument. A foot in the door" (C-SPAN, 1996).

In summarizing the arguments for allowing cameras in federal appellate courts, Merritt emphasized their putative public benefits:

There were a number of arguments on the other side. One, that cameras have the potential for getting a good bit of information to the public about how the judicial system works. That if they are carefully handled in appellate courts we don't run the risk of the theater entertainment problem. And that the federal judiciary . . . a life tenured institution, unelected, without term limits, needs to justify itself and it needs for the press to understand better how it works and to translate better to the American people . . . the functions of the federal judiciary . . . and that there are reasons why we are life tenured, unelected. . . . And one thing that having some cameras, hopefully under the control of favorable circumstances will do, perhaps, over time, is to educate better the American people about the judiciary. (C-SPAN, 1996)

In a forum sponsored by the American Judicature Society, Judge Merritt indicated his support for the Supreme Court opening its doors to television cameras, emphasizing, once again, the implications for public perceptions:

It would be helpful if the Supreme Court . . . and this is not going to happen . . . would allow cameras there because it would begin to explain and people would watch, and slowly . . . a more informed public would come about. . . . If we're going to communicate effectively with the public, the public now gets most of its news through the television medium, and we're going to have to rethink and reconsider that. . . . [J]udges need to feel some obligation to communicate what they're doing. (in Hodson, 1996)

In contemplating why the Supreme Court remains unwilling to allow cameras, reporters often stressed motivations that were highly personal, which didn't, necessarily, flow from the concerns often aired publicly about the supposed impact of cameras on the delivery of justice. Fred Graham, for example, asserted:

Television cameras are in virtually every other Supreme Court, state supreme court, and many, many trial courts, and it's just no problem. . . . I think there are some control freaks on the Supreme Court . . . and they want to control the system. I think they enjoy their anonymity. I think it must be quite a thrill to have the power that goes with being a justice and to be able to walk down the street and not have anyone harass you. I once saw a very raucous antiabortion demonstration . . . around the corner from the Supreme Court . . . and Harry Blackmun was taking his noonday stroll. Strolled right up and stood and watched, and they were screaming, shouting. No one noticed the author of *Roe v. Wade,* and he padded off after a while shaking his head. (in Slotnick, 1993)

Linda Greenhouse agreed in part, noting that television at the Supreme Court is "going to be a very, very long time in coming":

I think it would require a complete generation shift of the people that are now on the Court. . . . [C]ontrol? Maybe. But it really is . . . a deeply personal feeling. . . . I think the justices are horrified in a deeply personal way by . . . what happens to celebrities on the public stage, especially in Washington. And they just don't want it, and TV brings it. And . . . they absolutely cherish that anonymity. They're kind of bemused by it, but they love it and they're not going to give it up. (in Slotnick, 1993)

Judge Merritt concurred that "they don't want to become celebrities . . . and they don't think it is consistent with the law, with the purposes and functions of the Court as a restrained, nonmajoritarian institution, to join in the sensational celebrity kind of orientation in American society" (in Hodson, 1996).

An argument often raised about camera coverage of the Court underscores that in the sound-bite world of television, there would inevitably be distortion and misinformation cast out over the airwaves. Characterizing newscast coverage of the Court, Judge Merritt opined that "most of the time the sound bite is this. There is a picture of a participant in the courtroom on the stand and a headline reader. An anchor or a reporter tells you in fifteen to thirty seconds what that means, and the picture is used to authenticate oftentimes a false

. . . or inaccurate . . . statement. That is the problem. It's not COURT TV. It's the problem of how it's used in the sound-bite world" (in Hodson, 1996).

Earlier in the forum where Merritt spoke, print reporter Lyle Denniston summarized his position, a stance derived from an adamant belief in First Amendment values of open access:

The judiciary in . . . the federal system now treats the broadcast media as if it had no rights to be present in that courtroom in the only way it can be present because the judiciary does not trust how it will use those rights. . . . Do not assume that we have an obligation to report on the judiciary in the way the judiciary would like, and if we fail in that obligation, then we're going to have our rights taken away from us. (in Hodson, 1996)

Confronted with Judge Merritt's comments, Denniston argued even more vehemently:

When was the last time that a court told a reporter from *USA Today*, "You may not come in my courthouse because your coverage will be too brief or too selective"? . . . But when the judiciary turns to the broadcast media, it says, "Your right of access depends on whether we like what you say about us." And nobody has ever said to me as a print [journalist] when I walk up to a courthouse, "Denniston, you can't come in here unless you give forty inches to this. You can't come in here unless you cover it gavel to gavel. You can't come in here unless you run the transcript." Nobody has the guts to tell me that I can't cover a public institution because of the way I cover it. . . . But . . . the judiciary around this country . . . they sit there on their high-and-mighty bench and decide that if the coverage is not what I'm going to like, you can't even be in the courtroom. And judges need to understand that . . . if television and radio people can't bring their mikes and their cameras, they are not there. They are simply not there. And there is no reason to assume that anybody is going to ultimately tolerate a judiciary that says coverage of our court as a right of access depends upon our agreement with the scope of your coverage. And judges have got to get that straight. It's not their call. It is just not their call. (in Hodson, 1996)

As a practical matter, Denniston's strong First Amendment position can be supplemented by the recognition that venues such as COURT TV and C-SPAN now do exist so that much television coverage of the Court would take on the comprehensiveness that Judge Merritt seeks. Further, as Tim O'Brien observed of cameras in the Court: "They're now unobtrusive [and] television has developed in such a way, the proliferation of channels and networks, that you really can cover the arguments from beginning to end. The equation has changed. Costs and benefits. The benefits are greater than they've ever been before [with] the proliferation of outlets, and the costs have diminished as we've become more sophisticated."

The consequences of the absence of cameras in the Court for television news are, of course, easily stated: "There has been inadequate coverage of the Supreme Court because television reporters have been restricted to the video equivalent of communicating with a quill pen" (Graham, 1990: 107). At bottom, coverage of the Court is less substantial than it might otherwise be, and just as importantly, the nature of Court coverage is different as well. Fred Graham elaborated on these two effects for television news:

If they would permit cameras in courts, there would be much more coverage. The networks will not put, almost literally will not put, sketches on the air. . . . [P]eople are so accustomed to television showing reality, at least real pictures, that it is psychologically jarring to people to suddenly see these crude drawings. So what happens is that this perverts the way a story is covered. . . . [L]et's say the natural focus would be on the wording of an opinion or decision. . . . If you don't want to show a sketch of that justice, normally you would fudge around and put something else in that story rather than what the justice said. So I think the fact that they don't have cameras in courts, first of all, they don't cover as many stories. And I think it does change what they say, what they focus on, because they can get a picture, let's say, of the scene that's involved in the case, so they'll talk about that rather than what the justice said.

As far as the prospects for cameras entering the Supreme Court to cover arguments and decisions in the future, Graham, now the managing editor for Courtroom Television Network (COURT TV), sees both a small window for optimism as well as major obstacles:

I used to think it was going to be just a very few years. . . . I think the personalities and beliefs of the Chief Justice are very important, and we've now had three straight Chief Justices who had very little regard for informing the public. And I think if the next Chief Justice were . . . a more modern person, a person who was more comfortable with modern means of communication. . . . Then I think a process would go on . . . after a justice or two backed out. . . . The fly in the ointment here is Justice [Antonin] Scalia, who . . . is hostile to the media. And he's young and strong-minded. So I really wonder whether Scalia would ever change his mind. . . . [T]his is the sort of thing that the justices tend to want to have unanimity over.

The Court's Public Information Officer Toni House did not offer any reason for optimism, while underscoring the necessity for complete consensus among the justices:

I do not expect to see television in this courtroom for some time to come. When Chief Justice Burger retired, I really thought the time had come. But then other things happened to change the minds of some other people . . . and I just don't expect it. And there's no question in my mind that as long as one justice objects, they won't do it.

Indeed, as House's words suggest, it appears to miss the mark to even talk in terms of a "debate" about cameras in the Court: "There is no debate about cameras in the Court. . . . The Court has steadfastly stood by its policy that cameras are not welcome during session" (C-SPAN, 1996).

CONSTRAINTS ON SUPREME COURT COVERAGE: THE IMPERATIVES OF TELEVISION JOURNALISM

While many of the constraints that affect how the Court is covered on nightly newscasts are derived from rules, norms, and procedures that can be traced to the Court's own doorstep, other circumstances that have an impact on coverage can be seen in the very nature of contemporary television journalism and the way in which the nightly network newscasts are produced. In the heyday of television coverage of the Court the three major networks all had professional journalists who were also attorneys (Tim O'Brien at ABC, Fred Graham at CBS, and Carl Stern at NBC), who followed the Court as a full-time beat. Clearly, much has changed. As Toni House observed:

I don't think we're very interesting to some of them and this is part of their decision. . . . [N]ow there are really only two of them who intensely cover the Court where they really have time to do homework and really keep track of what the Court is doing rather than sort of dropping in when something happens. (C-SPAN, 1996)

Of the "big three," only O'Brien remains his network's legal correspondent today. And, while O'Brien spends more time covering the Court than the correspondents for the other networks do, he, too, recognizes that his professional future may depend on his ability to move beyond a virtually exclusive focus on the Court:

If I'm going to survive at ABC News, it's clear to me that I'm going to have to do a lot of other things besides the Supreme Court. I have to come up with other stories. The Supreme Court will not sustain me at this network. . . . I'm very interested in the Court, it means a great deal to me, and I regret this development. I'm still going to be following it, and any good case I'll still get on. . . . I'll still spend a great deal of time at the Court, but I'm going to have to work longer days.

With the clear change at CBS and the somewhat lower profile the Court beat plays at NBC, one might think that ABC's coverage would be maintained and sustained at a relatively high level, giving the network clear dominance on the beat. O'Brien underscored that isn't the way the scenario is playing out:

I think the network's interest in the Supreme Court is diminishing and the fact that there's no competition doesn't help. You might be terrific, but you're not beating anybody. Competitively, you're kind of shadowboxing: "Say, that was great." But they'd see how great . . . your material was if they could compare it with . . . other networks that were all doing it and they didn't have what you have.

Pete Williams, who covers the Justice Department as well as the Court for NBC, estimated that he spends about a third of his time on Court coverage. Our empirical study of television Court coverage reported in chapter 5 demonstrates that the scope of CBS's coverage has diminished radically in recent years. This has not escaped the attention of the network's former law correspondent, Fred Graham: "In a very distressing way, CBS has gone full circle to where they were when they hired me." Graham explained that until his hiring, nobody paid close attention to the Court, but George Herman served as a "designated reporter," who "had no training. He would wait, and when a story came across on the wires that there had been an important decision, they would send him up. . . . They hired me to prepare in advance and to know and to cover it from a basis of some preparation and knowledge." Now, in Graham's view, CBS's coverage once again resembles the earlier model.

This theme was repeated by both NBC's and ABC's current law correspondents. Pete Williams noted that "there's only two of us that regularly hang out at the Court, me and Tim. . . . CBS has a producer there now. But they don't listen to the arguments as much as we do, so their coverage is declining." Tim O'Brien commented, "CBS does not appear to have any commitment at all," which, he felt, was somewhat ironic because, in the aftermath of Graham's departure from CBS and before Jim Stewart's ascension to the beat, Rita Braver (now the network's White House correspondent) kept the Court at a relatively high profile:

When she was there, they gave her tons of time. . . . I've since come to conclude it's not so much that they cared about the Court – it's that they were promoting Rita. I felt it was the only network to truly treat the Court right, and now it's the only network to truly treat it wrong.

When asked how much time he spent covering the Court, CBS's Jim Stewart admitted, "Not a great deal, to be honest with you. I think we did seven to eight pieces last year. We'll be doing about the same this year." Even more so than NBC's Williams, Stewart's beat covers a wide landscape:

I was on 110 times last year. I covered the Justice Department, law enforcement, law, if you will. And, quite frankly, the events of the day, given Oklahoma City, given the organized crime problem they've uncovered among immigrants, given the immigration problems America has, that is the . . . lion's share of this beat. For me to read every brief, every filing that comes in on every case is a waste of time.

Ultimately, while Stewart admits that something has been lost by the general trend on network newscasts to move away from the utilization of highly specialized correspondents, he appears to defend today's approach both as a matter of sound economics and sound journalistic practice:

Beats are what generate the best stories in journalism, whether it be television or newspaper. That's only common sense. The more you're steeped in your subject matter the better you can explain it and the better you pick up on the nuance and the trends. But it is true across the board for all the networks that I think there has been less of that. To that extent, I think we should be faulted. . . . [W]hen I came to CBS just six years ago, we had a full-time State Department reporter, we had a full-time environmental reporter. We don't have those any longer. And that's a loss. . . . Some days I think we'd be much better off having a legally trained correspondent who carefully watched that because this is important. This is, make no mistake about it, serious business. But at the same time . . . whoever . . . took the job would go fucking nuts before very long because they wouldn't get on the air more than ten or twelve times a year. There is just no way that the events of the day at that Court are going to drive him on the air anymore. So is that a proper allocation of resources? And that's a question every news organization has to ask itself.

Perhaps answering that question for himself, Stewart continued, "I mean, should I go up there and spend every day just to watch to see if Clarence Thomas ever asks a question?"

The answer to that question has also been clearly given, both in our data, presented later in this volume, and in the comments of our interview subjects, all of whom underscored the diminished interest of television news in the Court, which has corresponded to the diminished time that reporters spend on the beat. The reasons for the diminished interest appear to reflect, in part, changes in the Court's behavior. As Toni House commented, "I think the Court . . . is doing things that are less interesting to television." These "less interesting" things can be categorized under a number of continually resonating themes. For one, in an absolute sense the Court is deciding fewer and fewer cases and, consequently, since it is a potential source for news less often, it receives, as a matter of course, less attention. Second, the nature of the questions the Court is visiting has been met with diminishing interest as has its tendency to treat issues, increasingly, by relying on narrow legalisms. This point was hammered home by Lyle Denniston: "There is no such thing anymore . . . as a landmark precedent-setting decision like *Brown* or . . . *Roe v. Wade*. The salami is sliced thinner and thinner and thinner and thinner. In trying to cover a First Amendment case now you almost have to be a Talmudic scholar to slice the differences between the dogmatic principles the Court is going to follow" (in Slotnick, 1993). In addition, television perceives a contemporary Court that appears to be comfortable with its role, one that does not often take the initiative to strike out boldly in new and controversial policy directions. Pete Williams's observations highlighted many of these points:

We are not going through any great upheaval . . . that we are looking to the Court to settle . . . for us. . . . [T]his is a fine-tuning Court. They don't even follow the traditional role of trying to settle all the intercircuit questions. . . . So there's no real focus to the Court right now. They don't seem to be very active [in] reaching out for cases to say, "Oh, that's an interesting one, let's settle that. . . ." This Court doesn't seem to be reaching out just for the fun of it to kind of duke it out.

While also touching on a number of these themes, Jim Stewart added that the networks have become increasingly conservative themselves in assessing the importance of Supreme Court rulings:

We find the pundits are right. This doesn't seem to be an especially aggressive Court. We also have . . . found in New York just not the same appetite for these types of stories. And I don't think that's because we've dummied down to America. I think it's because they have . . . seen that cases are decided on so narrow a legal question that they don't have the impact they thought they would. Years ago . . . we made . . . too much ado of some of the cases that we felt were broad-reaching, sweeping changes in the American landscape that didn't prove to be the case. It proved to be a fine-tuning, a tinkering with the process. I think they're much more careful now about wanting to put that big sticker on a Court decision.

If, indeed, it is the Court's output that is primarily responsible for the institution's diminishing coverage, it is, of course, possible that the pendulum could swing the other direction in the future. This was suggested by Pete Williams:

We've had fewer stories on the air this year than we have in past years and it may just be the quality of the term. . . . Yes, coverage of the Court is . . . declining right now. But that may change. Coverage of Congress was . . . declining too until Newt Gingrich came along, and then it got very different.

Pete Williams's suggestion to the contrary, there are ample reasons to suggest that a significant increase in coverage of the Court, regardless of its output, will not be in the cards. Given the commercial imperatives that drive network newscasts, particularly in an era that Fred Graham characterized as moving from a serious concern with journalistic standards to the age of infotainment (1990: 206–237), this is simply not likely to occur. It is to a consideration of infotainment, its impact on network newscasts, and its consequences for coverage of the Supreme Court that we now turn.

COVERING THE COURT IN THE AGE OF INFOTAINMENT

The very notion of infotainment itself is suggestive of some of the fundamental differences between broadcast and print journalism and the environments in which they operate. Clearly, both newspapers and networks are business enterprises, yet ostensibly the "product" through which newspapers attract their readership is the news. Television news, however, is much less central to the network's operation, and "before network news can be properly analyzed as a journalistic enterprise, it is necessary to understand the business enterprise that it is an active part of, and the logic that proceeds from it" (Epstein, 1973: 78). Entertainment can be as important a requisite for television news as it is for the remainder of the broadcast day. This has important implications for the reporting of governmental affairs and, particularly, for an institution such as the relatively "invisible" Supreme Court, where it can be argued that "proceedings are so dull that it is a public service to keep them off the tube" and where much of what goes on "rocks along at the excitement level of watching cement set" (Graham, 1990: 102).

In discussing the emergence of infotainment in the early 1980s, Graham begins with Eric Sevareid's tongue-slightly-in-cheek comment, "The trouble started . . . when CBS News began to make a profit." In Sevareid's view, "People forget . . . that television news started out as a loss leader. It was expected to lose money." Expectations began to change, however, when CBS News's *60 Minutes* began to show a profit: "Once CBS News became an engine of profits . . . then the goal was no longer quality but ratings. Television news had become a victim of its own success," and, in Graham's view, there was a "fundamental change in values" as "ratings replaced journalistic principles as the guiding force of the News Division" (Graham, 1990: 206–208). The centrality and implications of the success of *60 Minutes* for the movement toward infotainment were underscored further by James Fallows: "*60 Minutes* changed TV journalism for one simple reason: it made money." Prior to the program's success, "the news divisions were subsidized by the rest of the network. Their nonprofit existence meant they always lacked money, but with the money they did have they were more or less free to do as they chose" (1996: 55).

This would change dramatically. While the word *infotainment* quickly became an embarrassment and left "official" usage at CBS, "it remained the underlying technique for presenting the news." At bottom, the approach "boiled down to two new marching orders: First, make the news appeal to the heart by capturing . . . 'magic moments,' and second, make CBS News look, as much as possible, like entertainment TV" (Graham, 1990: 214). These new imperatives changed fundamentally the role of the journalist: "Traditionally, journalists had understood that news was what the public needed to know and wanted to know. Infotainment changed that by making the central focus 'what will keep them watching our network'" (Graham, 1990: 225).

The move to infotainment had important consequences for covering the Court, as Graham related:

They decided that their definition of what they wanted and what was news changed. And they decided that what people wanted to see was very visual, and courts, the Supreme Court, you couldn't show, and so it made it almost by definition . . . not newsworthy. The Supreme Court was not newsworthy. . . . [T]here was very little interest in my superiors.

In Graham's view such a development was not "healthy for the legal system and it certainly wasn't good for the prospects of a correspondent who hoped to make a career broadcasting legal news on TV" (Graham, 1990: 110–111).

This point was brought home when Graham attempted to report on the Court's decision declaring unconstitutional the automatic spending-cut provisions of the Gramm–Rudman deficit reduction law in 1986:

The Court relied on the tortured reasoning that Congress had violated the separation of powers by giving authority to trigger across-the-board spending cuts to the Comptroller General, an official who theoretically could be fired by Congress. To me, the conservative Reagan court had scuttled an innovative effort at fiscal control on a technicality and I thought it important to explain how the Court had tied the logic in knots to agree with the Reagan administration's position. But the grown-ups decreed that I could not utter the words "Comptroller General" or explain the firing problem on the ground that television viewers couldn't handle such detail. My resulting report – that the law was thrown out because it violated the separation of powers – was simple and easy to grasp. It also didn't burden our viewers with an understanding of what had actually happened. I learned that straight news could be harmful to your professional health. (Graham, 1990: 235)

The result of situations such as this for a veteran career journalist such as Graham, whose entry into television news followed a prestigious career in print journalism including service as the Supreme Court reporter for the *New York Times*, was "a severe case of journalistic vertigo":

I became disoriented and off balance because I no longer knew what a story was. . . . Many of us became uncertain and tentative about our work for reasons that had nothing to do with traditional journalism. This disorientation eventually rattled news judgments at all levels of the operation. (1990: 227–228)

Graham observed, "I began to slight traditional stories and I cast about for topics that fit the jazzier mold. My news judgment became skewed" (1990: 233).

Graham learned, too, that even "less than straight" news might sometimes have difficulty seeing airtime when it was focused on the Court. Frustrated at not getting stories aired, Graham admitted that "an increasing portion of my effort went into sifting through the Supreme Court docket in search of whiz-bang fact situations that might make it on" (1990: 236–237). Once he thought he had a "sure winner" in the case of Grendel's Den, a restaurant near Harvard that was denied a liquor license because of objections from the local Catholic parish. The case somehow found its way to the Court:

As Supreme Court cases go, this one seemed made for the age of infotainment. There were boozy college students, a prudish priest, a famous liberal law professor, and a carefully muted question of Church and State. I had cannily concealed the constitutional issue amid scenes of noisy students and aggrieved parishioners; thus, the legal point did not get in the way of a good yarn. To me, Grendel's Den became the benchmark of legal reporting in the infotainment era. "If this one can't make it," I thought, "no Supreme Court case is a good bet." (1990: 236–237)

The Grendel's Den story never made it on to the *CBS Evening News*. The piece was killed, according to Graham, because it was to air on a Friday night and it would not leave the viewers in an appropriate frame of mind to approach the weekend's television viewing (1990: 236–237).

Concerns about infotainment could play as important a role in the stories that did air and how they were played as they could in stories that did not. Graham recounted the scenario "when *Miami Vice* was very popular and our producers at CBS got the idea that the public . . . wanted to see young, good-looking people and . . . they wanted to see a place that was bright and sunshiny and maybe with a little surf out there":

I was covering a . . . decision that had to do with affirmative action among police [and fire] departments. And there were several different police departments that were involved, and I traveled around to the various places to talk to the people . . . who were actually involved in those cities. On the day the Supreme Court decided the case, it was decided at CBS that I wouldn't do the story based on actually having gone to the cities where these disputes arose, but it would be done from Miami. Because Miami had police, although it was not one of the cities involved in this dispute . . . they did have police and they had black police and white police and . . . there were young good-looking people that would be shown and a sunny background and even some water. And so that story was done. It was a Supreme Court decision. Dan Rather came on and said, "The Supreme Court has issued a decision today involving affirmative action in police and fire departments, and now we go to Miami with, whoever the reporter is, for the story." And he did it.

Infotainment also became the order of the day at the other networks and had similar consequences and implications. According to Carl Stern:

It's not just that every week became sweeps week. It's that the individuals themselves were under considerable pressure to produce an attractive show that would achieve high ratings and that would meet certain production values that they had. That's how you got to your eight-second sound bites. Keep the stories moving, moving, fast pace, fast pace, action, action. . . . People who watch news shows are probably not the people who are watching mud wrestling or demolition derbies or Bowling for Dollars, but the producers sure would like to attract some of those people to watch the news shows.

In Stern's case, there were simply things that he was continually discouraged from doing and saying on the air. As he put it, "the *ruling* is the part that counts. Yet that's the only part we can't see or hear." Consequently, "the ruling itself, the very heart of the next day's newspaper coverage, could barely be mentioned." Further, "more often than not, *any* words I used to describe the Court's reasoning were rejected as beyond the understanding of the average Joe. Analogies were substituted, generally from sports or warfare" (Stern, 1993).

The result, according to Stern, is that "what we have today is a sort of a coloring book in which producers design an attractive show. They ask reporters about their color in the boxes. Bring in something. Please hold it to ninety seconds. No sound bites longer than eight seconds. That sort of thing. . . . It certainly made beats like the Supreme Court expendable."

Print reporter Lyle Denniston commented on the state of contemporary television journalism at the Court in similar terms:

They are much more at sea these days than they used to be. They ask a lot dumber questions than Carl ever asked or than Fred ever asked, and they're . . . constantly looking for what I think is the more superficial angle, the more *People* magazine or the more television magazine approach to the law. . . . I think what's happening in television [is] the ensemble concept. . . . [Y]oung, physically attractive males and females will kind of float in and out of a story or a beat and cover the kind of thing much more . . . for their cosmetic appeal than for the depths of their mental perceptions. And I think that's not a problem peculiar to our beat. I think it's a problem peculiar to commercial television generally. (in Slotnick, 1993)

The irony, in Carl Stern's view, is that despite the recasting of the evening news to create greater audience appeal, "the statistics tell us . . . that the network news shows are diminishing in terms of the audience size they reach, and to some extent they have brought that down on themselves because if they are simply an entertainment vehicle or a filler, they have to compete with all the other fifty channels that are available these days to the home viewer."

In his broadside critique of the contemporary news media, James Fallows echoes Stern's analysis:

Mainstream journalism has made the mistake of trying to compete with the pure entertainment media – music, TV celebrities, movies – on their own terms. . . . They are locking themselves into a competition they are bound to lose. If the public is looking for pure celebrity or entertainment, it will go for the real thing. If public life continues to lose its claim on America's attention so – inevitably – will journalism. (1996: 244)

While we have been focusing on infotainment in a critical vein, it is equally important to underscore that it is not only television news' desire to entertain, per se, that constitutes the problem. Rather, it is what appears to be missing from the brew. This point was reiterated by Carl Stern:

It's not just this silly business about happy talk and infotainment. . . . I think TV is entitled to get a little silly if it wants, and if it doesn't meet these Olympian goals we all set for it. . . . That's not the part that hurts. The part that hurts is that at least at bottom there's supposed to be some sort of unwritten contract between people who describe themselves as journalists and the public that they serve that they're going to do their level best to ensure that the public gets the truth, the whole truth, nothing but the truth. And that's not what's happening. . . . Lenin, a peculiar source of information to be quoted at this point, said truth is that which serves. Well, we don't believe that. We believe truth is truth whether it serves or doesn't serve. Well, unfortunately, TV these days, I'm not suggesting that they've become Leninists but, essentially, truth is that which serves the production sense of the people who put the show on the air. And it is a show. It's a show. . . . And that's the loss of it for those who took it seriously.

The news "show," as James Fallows has observed, needs "stars" and operates on the belief that "the delivery system – that is the reporter as an entertainment instrument – is more important than the substance of the story":

I am afraid in television the old value system, where the opinion of your peers mattered so much, is largely gone. Get the ratings and you're forgiven all else. The sin there is not being inaccurate. The sin is being boring. (1996: 278)

It is important to be clear about what Stern, Fallows, and others are charging and what they are not about the changing nature of the evening newscasts that began to take hold through the middle and late 1980s. Clearly, editors and producers have a legitimate and important role to play and often improve the stories that do get chosen for airtime. Carl Stern readily conceded this:

I'm not suggesting that these producers were always wrong. I'm willing to say that more than half the time they were right. . . . As a matter of style or making something more clear or what not, I've never known a reporter who didn't profit from some other person going through their copy and making suggestions. . . . I don't think I ever wrote a script that wasn't improved in some way by a producer.

Further, nobody is suggesting that news producers do not have a legitimate and important professional role to play in making critical choices in putting together the evening news. As Pete Williams explained, "There are more correspondents that want to get on the air than can possibly get on the air in a given day. . . . [A] producer of a nightly newscast is thinking. . . . 'Well, okay, I have those people in the waiting room that want to get on the air. Well, what . . . should we be doing?'" Tim O'Brien admitted that in a reporter's effort to get on the air, a Supreme Court story can often legitimately come out the loser in the contest: "If I have a . . . case that I think might belong on, and I have some editors who might think not, what I'll look at is what's in the lineup, what else are they planning to run. And there are times when I'll say, 'This is an incredibly important story' [and] I looked at what I was competing with and said, 'You know, they were right. They still had bigger fish to fry.'" The Court's Public Information Officer, Toni House, understood that when a case "is competing with another bombing in Israel . . . it is not going to make the air," but she also recognized that there are public consequences: "Because there is such a finite period of time and because the competition for that time can be very fierce, they are likely to miss things that are of real importance to people."

Such a reality may, at times, be both regrettable and, perhaps, unavoidable. There are instances, however, where the dictates of the news "show" create the result. As Carl Stern related, there were times when

you would call them [newscast producers] up at 10:30 in the morning. You know in your gut that this is a story that has got to go. You know your competitors are going to do it, and you know it is going to be all over page one tomorrow. And you can't persuade the producer to go with it because he's got an eight-minute piece booked into the show on pedophile priests that they've been promoting for three days. That's the one that really gets to you. When you know something important has happened and you're not going to be able to tell the public about it. And New York says, "Well, we'll tell it in copy" [news delivered from the anchor desk]. Seldom does the copy tell the story well enough, and frequently the copy is so poorly written or not clearly written that it fails to really convey the importance of the event.

Toni House offered one example of a copy story gone astray:

I spent fifteen years as a newspaper reporter. I really believed, used to believe, in the news media and in their desire to get things right. And I don't think I was here six months and there was an episode . . . where a reporter . . . had been subpoenaed to produce some notes from a jailhouse interview. And it was a Friday, he refused to do it, and he was ordered to jail for contempt. The courts below denied him a stay and he came in here on a Friday afternoon and he came into Justice [William] Brennan. And we all know how Justice Brennan feels about the First Amendment. . . . I'm not quite sure why nothing happened, but nothing happened. So the guy went to jail. Monday morning Justice Brennan issued what we call a chambers opinion in which he said, "I don't believe that four of my colleagues would grant to vote cert in this case, which is why it's denied." But Friday night Dan Rather got on the air and said that Justice William J. Brennan had ordered this guy to jail. Now how far-fetched can you get? I mean I was just horrified. . . . I was flabbergasted. And in that case I think I called Fred Graham and I said, "Fred, how can you let him say things?" I mean . . . it was in no remote way accurate.

The real journalistic problem that developed in the infotainment era as it applied to the Supreme Court particularly (and newscasting more generally) often went beyond such gaffes (if they were inadvertent) and even went beyond the increased propensity to cover only the biggest and most sensational cases that could be made to fit the new approach. As Carl Stern asserted, "If it was simply a matter to be entertaining, I suppose I wouldn't feel so badly about it. But it's worse than that." He continued, "I could live with the fact that they cover only occasionally and that they cover only the cases that seem to be the sizzlers. I understand that. . . . But what I agonize over is distortion and untruth, and quite often I see stories that I believe are . . . conveying to the public an untrue perception of what happened. And that's not done negligently. It's done intentionally, and I think that's unforgivable. I think that is the highest sin in journalism, and I see it all around." In our extended interview, Stern framed the fundamental issue regarding the disjuncture between the Court's action and its portrayal on the air:

You have written extensively about different things that television people did on the air. You reasonably believed that what you heard coming across the television was their thoughts, their analysis, their best efforts to communicate what the Court had done. That is a somewhat simplistic view. And it doesn't take into account the enormous changes that occurred in television journalism in the late 1980s.

These comments, we think, underscore some of the reasons why the serious professional journalists revealed in these pages often fall far short in their coverage of the Court, as documented by our empirical analysis later in this volume. The changes that Stern alludes to are touched on in some of the examples offered by Fred Graham discussed above. They relate to the fundamental altering of the journalistic relationship between the Court reporters and the news producers, and the increasing role the producers took on in determining the very *content* of news reports on the Court. Prior to the triumph of the infotainment approach, reporters' professional judgments held the key to understanding what was sufficiently newsworthy to justify coverage. Fred Graham noted, "In the early years at CBS they relied almost totally on my judgment of what was important. And I used the classic definition of news as what the public needs to know and what the public wants to know, some mix of that." Similarly, Carl Stern stressed:

There was a time when television was a reporter-driven business. Reporters went out on the street, covered certain beats, informed the desk what they had, [and] the best of the day's product was put together into the show. Those reporters wrote the scripts. The scripts were edited for grammar and clarity and so on. But the judgment as to what needed to be said was pretty much left to the reporter. That business died . . . in the mid-1980s.

Newscast content in the age of infotainment became, in a sense, a competition. As Stern explained it, "news is merchandise just as surely as being in the car business or retail clothing. It is a business of merchandising, and the explanation that may satisfy a reporter trying to be precise may not satisfy the producer trying to excite an audience":

At bottom is whether or not you are going to permit an experienced reporter to express their own judgments rather than a remote or vicarious observer's judgments as to what happened. That's the competition. Forget the packaging and all the rest of it. That's the competition. To me that's the bottom line. Are you going to accept the reporter's judgment?

Increasingly, as Stern notes, the reporters lost that competition:

It became a producer's business. Reporters basically were sent out to fulfill the requirements of the producers. And what they reported on the air was what producers wanted reported on the air. And frequently that meant that the voice you heard and the face you saw [were] not using words that he or she would have chosen.

He added that, "It reached a point where . . . none of the producers at NBC . . . were journalists. Again, it's not a sacred calling. It's not a blood brotherhood. But it sure helps."

Fred Graham described a similar working reality at CBS in even harsher tones:

It's hard for nontelevision people to appreciate the fact that people are brought in sometimes in high positions in the television network that are almost idiots. I mean really people who are just incompetent. They don't last long, there's quite a turnover. But for a while you will have almost totally incompetent people.

In such a setting, a basic equation was altered in the television news business. As Stern put it:

The essence of it is that when it comes down to an interpretation, a judgment, of what the event means, the producer had to go with the reporter's judgment, not the other way around. And that's what went wrong. That's what went off the tracks here. In addition, there was a loss of compass with the respect to the fundamental obligations of journalism. There are probably only two really important matters that should be in any journalist's oath to himself or herself. . . . [O]ne, to know what you're talking about, spend the time to know what you're talking about; and, number two, be fair. What else can you ask of a reporter? If they're coherent, that helps too. The plain fact is that this sense of the need to be fair, I don't want to say disappeared, that's not true, but it was certainly diluted by the journalistic practices that began in the late 1980s and that may continue to this day.

A major consequence of these developments for journalists covering the Court became the need to engage in protracted "demoralizing" negotiations to get a story on the air and to get it told in a manner that did justice to the actual event being covered. Fred Graham described the scene at CBS:

The editing process loomed larger and larger. And what happened was, you would write the story in conjunction with your producer and late in the afternoon, say 4:30 or 5:00, that goes to New York. Then there are two levels of editing there, and then they would come back and they would say do so and so. Sometimes the so and so they want you to do is either incomprehensible or flat wrong. And then you have to get on the phone and negotiate that. And quite often you're negotiating. The deadline, of course, is 6:30 for the evening news, and it's 6:00. It was a maddening process and . . . a very demoralizing thing.

The picture Stern draws of what happened at NBC is painted in remarkably similar tones:

Over and over again on a daily basis when I was writing, at least in the latter years of being on the air at NBC, I frequently was obliged to change what the Court had said to meet the requirements of a producer even though I didn't believe that that's what the Court had said. It basically got down to a contest every night about a quarter of six between what I knew the Court had said and what I knew the producer would accept. And then it got down to a question as to whether we were going to do the story at all. Frequently, more often than not, that meant having to . . . just take down the producer's words, the producer having very little knowledge of what the Court had actually done, and going to a microphone and reciting those words. Let me underscore, we are only talking about a phenomenon that developed . . . in the last part of the 1980s and has continued over into the 1990s. But I'm not talking about an isolated incident. I am talking about every report.

Frequently, the subject of the negotiations would revolve around Stern's efforts to quote from the Court's decision or to paraphrase what it had said:

There's many a time . . . that I took . . . if not a verbatim quote at least the essence of what a justice had said and was told by a producer to change it to this or that. And I would say, "But that's not what he said," and they would say, "Well, that's what he really meant." And I would say, "No, that's not what he meant, and that's not correct." And then it came down to, "Do you want to get on the air tonight or don't you want to get on the air tonight?" As you can see by my present circumstance [at the time of our interview, Stern was the Director of the Office of Public Affairs at the Department of Justice], I don't want to get on the air tonight because it reached a point where I no longer believed in some instances that we were accurately describing what the Court had said.

Stern continued, "If a Justice . . . said 'X' and the producer changes it to 'Y,' you can't get there. He said what he said. You can try to make it simpler. You can try to explain it in other terms. But, in the long run, it can't be simply something that meets the satisfaction of some remote figure who's producing the show."

Recall that Stern characterized the journalistic oath to be subsumed by the effort to "get it right" as well as the commitment to be fair in doing so. We have offered several examples where the alterations of producers could lead the reporter to knowingly go on the air without getting it right, and both Fred Graham and Carl Stern admitted that this was, indeed, sometimes the case. Graham noted that at one point, "I refused to do one story. I just said I won't do it because you're insisting that I make it wrong. This is wrong and I won't do it." Graham's action may have had some effect, since "several times after I refused to do the story, they realized that if I felt that strongly, maybe it was wrong and they permitted me to change it." Nevertheless, Graham continued, "there were other times when they required me to say things that were nonsensical or that were inconsistent with other things I had said. And despite my arguments, they insisted, and I did it." Carl Stern offered a similar assessment: "I would occasionally, I say occasionally . . . find myself in a position where I didn't know what I was saying. I didn't know what the piece meant because I was, well, following instructions."

Not only was "getting it right" a seemingly lower priority for the news producers than it was for the Court reporters, so, too, was Stern's concern about fairness. He recounted "a very shattering experience" when he was asked by the Washington producer of the nightly news to look over a legal piece prepared by another reporter. The report "was simply erroneous. It was just wrong. It was misleading. It was unfair in suggesting that the courts were engaged in a practice that they were not. It was ridiculous as a matter of law, but it was just a misunderstanding of the reporter." At the urging of the Washington producer, Stern contacted the head producer for the nightly news in New York:

Well, this fellow profanely practically took my head off. And what did he say to me? What he said to me was, this is a quote, this is not a paraphrase. He said to me, "I've had this fairness bullshit up to here. . . . It doesn't matter whether this story is fair or that story is fair. What matters is that we're fair overall." Well, what does that mean? Does it mean you slant the next story somewhat the other way? Is that like the guy with the one foot in the boiling water and the one foot in the ice water – on average he's comfortable, right?

In the predicament they found themselves in, the reporters could, as Fred Graham's *Grendel's Den* case suggested, practice their art to maximize the possibility of getting on the air. While *Grendel's Den* did not see airtime, cases like it undoubtedly did. The Court received coverage, but the cases exposed may not have been the most important ones and/or the facets of them that were presented may not have been the most legally significant aspects of the case. Alternatively, as Carl Stern's ultimate resignation suggested, the reporter might choose to leave the fray. As Stern put it, "I found more often than not as I went along that I was just as happy not getting something on the air as getting it on the air because it was just too difficult to fight to preserve what you felt was important to say."

As Stern concluded, "It's a different world. As we were reminded over and over again by a producer in the 1980s, it's not a religion. 'It's not the priesthood,' I think is the way he put it. Well, of course, to some it is."

My lament is that, too often, solid, intelligent judgments of people that the networks employ are not utilized to place things into the shows that should be there and to ensure that what is said within those pieces fairly reflects what the participants actually said and did. . . . Again, it's not a lack of intelligence. The people are very intelligent. They are very skillful. It's not that it is over their heads. They have the capability of doing it, or to employ people who are capable of doing it. But they have lost the will to do it. They have lost the will to do it because it is not a priority. It is not identified for them by the people who own and manage these enterprises. It doesn't necessarily sell, and it is what sells in the long run and in the commercial medium that is going to count. The pity of it is . . . that they used to do it. They used to be able to do it. It can be done if there's a will to do it. But it's not going to happen when your principal executive producer is saying, "I've had this fairness bullshit up to here."

THE NUTS AND BOLTS OF COVERING THE COURT ON NETWORK TELEVISION NEWSCASTS

We have utilized the term *infotainment* to characterize broadly the trends in network television operations that had the profound effects on the nature of newscast coverage of the Supreme Court examined above. In actuality, the term was introduced at CBS News in the early 1980s and went out of official use at the network early on, when it proved to be publicly embarrassing.

We have seen, however, in the extended comments of Fred Graham, Carl Stern, and several others that the legacy of infotainment's entrée into network television newscasts remains visible in contemporary network news operations generally, regardless of the nomenclature employed and, in particular, in the status of the Supreme Court as a news beat for television. In the remainder of this chapter we shall explore some of the nuts and bolts of how television reporters cover the Court in the context of the environment we have pictured, a setting marked by constraints imposed by the Court itself as well as those brought about by the general nature of the network news enterprise.

As we have seen, styles of reporting on the Court by television journalists developed largely as a necessary response to the predicament that reporters found themselves in covering a low-priority, visually staid beat. Fred Graham pioneered the approach to coverage that continues to this day as the prototype for television's Supreme Court analysts: "My approach was to go to the community where each dispute arose, take pictures of the scene, interview the people involved, and present the legal question through the stories of the people who raised it." Graham recognizes that this approach seems "obvious now, as it is the way all the networks do it," and he admits that "while it was TV legal journalism at its best, as long as we were excluded from the courtroom it was not good enough" (1990: 107). Earlier, we reported that of the Court journalists for the three major networks, ABC's Tim O'Brien spends the most time on the Supreme Court beat, followed by NBC's Pete Williams, with CBS's Jim Stewart a distant third. Clearly, the fundamental nature of CBS's approach to covering the Court has changed since the tenure of Fred Graham and more closely resembles the situation before Graham came to the beat. As Jim Stewart described it:

The way we have it organized I feel comfortable that we're going to be on top of any major decision because we have an arrangement with the law schools here. . . . [W]e deal mostly with Georgetown and George Washington and Catholic University. [W]e select . . . a third-year law student and they get credit for it and we get the benefit of their work ethic. And they literally live at the Court. We have a small cubicle up there like most of the organizations do. So they come back and file all the briefs. They type up the summaries for us. They actually report to a producer. . . . [A]nd she screens it further. All of which is to say that by the time it comes to me . . . we have synthesized the stuff down to the point where even an idiot like me can follow it. I don't pretend to be a lawyer. I don't pretend to be an expert on constitutional law or any of the other issues. . . . So we're different from the other networks.

These differences are reflected, as we shall document in chapter 5, in the diminished coverage of the Court on CBS News across the two years in our data set.

Supreme Court cases, of course, offer several decision points for possible coverage ranging from the filing of a petition for certiorari through the granting of certiorari, oral argument, and the actual decision itself. Decisional coverage is, logically, the point at which most cases will make it into a newscast since, at that stage, the reporter has the best chance of gauging accurately the case's importance. Stories on petitioning for certiorari or even the granting of certiorari are quite rare since there is a good chance that the case will not pan out down the road in its ultimate decision. Thus, as Pete Williams underscored, spending a good deal of his time on the various facets of the certiorari process is "just not a very productive expenditure of my time. . . . There's already a high homework-to-getting-on-the-air ratio for the Supreme Court, and that would just make it a lot higher." Inevitably, however, there will be isolated cases that do receive coverage through all stages of Supreme Court processing. As Williams noted, "It just depends on how big the case is. . . . [T]he term limits case we covered every step of the way. We covered it when they granted cert, we covered it when it was argued, we covered it when it was decided."

Coverage of oral argumentation, while not as frequent as decisional coverage, is a favored stage of Supreme Court processes for television for a number of reasons. As Toni House observed:

Probably what they do best is oral arguments. . . . [I]t tells the story. Also, it's a drama. It's this side against the other side. The advocates most likely are out front after the argument telling their side. You can quote the justices speaking from the bench. . . . [I]t gives it elements that make it televisable and entertaining.

As a practical matter, there is a strong element of scheduling predictability in oral argumentation that raises its stock for reporters. As Fred Graham explained, "you don't get squeezed out on a day where there are multiple decisions. You know you've got that day. You know when it's coming. . . . So that . . . permits you to lay out your thinking a lot better than on the day of decision." Tim O'Brien indicated that he sometimes preferred to do a story the evening before oral argument was to take place:

We have so little time, I sometimes think it's better spent listening to the people involved in the case and the experts than putting up drawings of justices and questions that they ask. . . . [O]ften . . . I will not have any shot in my piece from Washington, maybe a shot of the Supreme Court only to say this is where the case is going to be argued tomorrow.

We have stressed throughout that because of the Court's relative isolation, coupled with the inaccessibility of the justices to the media, television coverage of the institution focuses almost exclusively on its work output. Little attention is placed on the justices themselves, save for the relatively brief period of their coming on or going off the Court. Pete Williams mused on this seeming irony:

[W]hen . . . it comes time to appoint a new justice, it is the biggest god damn story in town. All the jockeying, who might it be? We crowd around everybody who comes to town. . . . When Stephen Breyer came here the first time, the stakeouts of him walking through Union Station with his broken collarbone. . . . And we pay a little attention to the confirmation hearing . . . because it is a test of the president. And that is why it becomes such a big story. And then there are all these stories about their judicial philosophy. . . . Then they go on the Court and we proceed to ignore them.

The data reported later in this volume corroborate unmistakably Williams's point. Rarely do stories focus on the justices per se, and when they do, it is most often a reflection of reporting on appointment politics and processes. This is not to suggest that stories concerning malfeasance or scandal would not be covered heavily. Rather, it underscores that such information about the justices is rarely forthcoming.

Interestingly, despite the fact that Supreme Court reporters work in a domain where they have less access to decision makers and decision processes than in other governmental beats, the truth of the matter is that they have such complete access to documentary information about what they are covering that they have an unusual opportunity to prepare for stories and are rarely caught off guard by a case decision. When the networks all covered the Court with full-time legal correspondents, their preparation was quite extensive. As Carl Stern described it, "The sort of stuff we did then would be unheard of today for a TV . . . reporter."

For example, at the start of the Court and through the term I would do the conference lists. . . . [T]hat could be doing a couple thousand cases. Why? Because you only know where the Court is going . . . if you have some idea what kinds of cases they are hearing or what kinds of cases they aren't hearing. . . . [A]nd, also, you spot things early. And once you identify those cases that you think the Court is likely to take – obviously, it will be a small list for television that you care about – you would go out and you would start collecting visuals.

If Stern were uncertain about whether the Court would actually hear a case, or if a potentially attractive case remained several stages from the Supreme Court, he might call the network's affiliates and seek copies of any footage they might have "on cases that I thought would come along. There were cases where it would take years."

If I saw an important case that had been decided by a district court someplace and I'd say to myself, "That's an issue that's going to make it to the Supreme Court," I would order the cassettes right then and there from the affiliate so that I'm not calling them two years later when the Court takes the case and they say, "Geez, we washed that stuff a year ago. We don't keep things that long." I would immediately call if I saw a case, if I read about a case someplace that I thought was going to make it up to the Supreme Court. But that's because I was doing this stuff full-time, and I was deeply immersed into it and I cared.

In many respects, the depth of Stern's preparation more resembled what we would associate with a print reporter such as Linda Greenhouse of the *New York Times* or Lyle Denniston of the *Baltimore Sun,* particularly in his focus on cases in their nascent stages, than what we would associate with a network reporter covering the Court today whose interest in a Supreme Court case is unlikely to kick in until after the case has been granted certiorari and appears on the Court's docket. Pete Williams, who characterized the Court as having "the highest homework-to-actually-getting-on-the-air ratio in town," described the winnowing process he goes through in covering cases:

Of the . . . eighty signed opinions we are going to have this year . . . we will keep our eye on . . . fifteen to twenty cases that are potentially of interest to us. So you have to read the briefs in all those cases, you have to call the lawyers, talk to the lawyers, talk to the law school professors. . . . Then we have to in probably ten of those cases go out and shoot a lot of tape.

Williams will also attend the oral argument in the cases that "we are peripherally interested in. . . . I tend not to go to oral argument for every single case. I don't think anyone does that. That would just be a phenomenal waste of time." Regarding his advance preparation, Williams estimated that about half of it does not see the light of day and never leads to airtime and inclusion in a story.

For Tim O'Brien, who spends more of his time covering the Court, the equation is markedly different. Indeed, O'Brien claimed that he "hardly ever" prepared material that didn't receive airtime on some ABC news venue or format, perhaps in recognition of his status as the only "full-time" Supreme Court reporter still employed by his original network:

They let me shoot whenever I want to shoot. I really don't have to clear it anymore. . . . [A]fter the first couple of years they saw that virtually everything gets on . . . because I get a couple of bites out of the apple. I don't usually get it on when it's granted review . . . although sometimes I do, or when it's up for review. . . . But when it's argued I get a shot, when it's decided I get a shot, and there are a number of different shows that are interested. *Good Morning America, The Weekend News, World News Tonight,* sometimes *Nightline, World News This Morning,* the overnight show. So, given the times it's up at the Court, the number of broadcasts we have, a good case will make air six or seven times. I will shoot material on maybe twenty, twenty-five cases in a term and, on average, they make air about 2.8 times.

Good Morning America serves as an especially congenial television venue for O'Brien on the mornings of oral argument, particularly for cases that don't have a strong likelihood of being covered on the evening newscast: "A lot of them will work on the morning news [if] they won't work anyplace else. The program wants to be forward-looking, it doesn't want to be a rehash of yesterday's news. They can say, 'And looking forward today, here's one of the questions the Supreme Court is going to be considering, . . . They love that."

One source of information relied on somewhat by the Court reporters in their preparation is *Preview,* a publication underwritten largely by the American Bar Association, which offers summaries and insights on the issues and arguments before the Court. Maximum use is not made of it, however, because, as Pete Williams explained, "the trouble is it comes out so late. It is always good to read, and I invariably read it if there is a case I'm covering because . . . it is another brain on that case. But I need to know a lot of things before that comes out, so there's just no substitute for reading the briefs." Tim O'Brien acknowledged that *Preview* is a "great asset," particularly in helping to bring an ABC colleague up to speed on a multiple decision day at the Court: "We'll divvy up the work, and I'll have somebody up who's never been to the Supreme Court who's going to be covering, and I'll say, 'Read this, great place to get started.'" O'Brien also suggested that

Preview often has information that we don't have. We could get [it] by going through all the briefs, but, for example, how many states have laws like the one being challenged before the Court and what is the division in the circuits? I used to read the briefs first. Now I tend to read the briefs last. When I am working on a Supreme Court case, the first thing I read is the lower court opinion that's being reviewed because that's actually what the Supreme Court is checking. And then I often read *Preview,* and then I'll read the briefs next.

As a consequence of having so much documentary information on the public record, coupled with aids such as *Preview,* the willingness of interest groups to serve as sources for reporters, and the multistepped processes through which cases proceed at the Court before a decision is announced, television reporters, even today, are rarely caught off guard or unprepared for a ruling. Indeed, Fred Graham asserted that the dictates of preparing footage for broadcasting made him better prepared as a television journalist than he had been at the *New York Times:*

You could almost always look at the case at the time the Court took it, even before, and see pretty much what its potential was to be important. And the ones that showed that potential, you knew that when it was decided it was going to be important news, so you had to go out with your camera well before it was due to be decided and interview all the people and take pictures of the scenes. So I would say that I was better prepared . . . for television, in many instances, than I was at the newspaper, because you can pick up the phone on the day of a decision when you were with the newspaper.

Tim O'Brien, too, underscored that "you can prepare in advance on Supreme Court stuff more than you can on other stories. You know the cases that they're interested in. By the time a case is decided, I really should know it backwards and forwards. I mean I see it when it's coming up, I see it when cert is granted, I see it when it's argued, and then I do it again when it's decided." Pete Williams added that "you'd be crazy" to be caught off guard because "you get so many bites at it. . . . [I]t clears its throat several times before it finally comes at you."

This is not to suggest that the Court reporters know with absolute certainty which will be the "big" cases of the term when the Court's decisions are actually rendered. As Tim O'Brien put it, "sometimes the Court will use small cases to make big statements, and sometimes it will take a major case that doesn't really wash out." Interestingly, O'Brien also noted that with surprising regularity the Court will accept a case for review that, in his judgment, cannot and will not be resolved:

Sometimes I will see a really great case coming up and I'm persuaded that the Court can't answer it. . . . [T]here's a procedural defect in it. And, believe it or not, this is where the Court, I think, screws up terribly. Every year, two or three cases. You'd think with some of the greatest legal minds in the country up there, the great law clerks they have and the justices, it wouldn't happen. But they take a great case, and you see . . . it's moot or the petitioner lacks standing, and you say . . . "Is it possible that they took this case to revise the rules of standing? Why else would they have taken this case? . . ." [A]nd then, a while later, you'll see that it's dismissed as improvidently granted. If it does raise an important issue, I'll try to get it on the air anyway even if it won't be decided, and say, "Here's an issue that the Court would like to address."

Earlier, we alluded to elements of a story that made it newsworthy in the eyes of reporters generally. Now we will turn to the more narrow concern of what makes a case sufficiently newsworthy to receive coveted airtime on the nightly newscasts, an issue we will examine empirically in chapter 7. Interestingly, part of the answer may be dictated by the nature of a case's outcome. As Fred Graham noted, "There are some cases in which if it went one way, big story, but if it went the other way, no story." Carl Stern drew a distinction between statutory and constitutional cases, the latter of which were easier to get on the air, other things being equal: "On the constitutional stuff there are red flags all over it. If this is a case about reading the bible in class or . . . burning the American flag it doesn't take a genius. . . . I always said to myself, half jokingly, 'Does it meet the bar-stool test?' Is this the kind of thing people are going to argue about in bars, saloons? And they're just intellectually interesting. It's something we can really argue about. . . . Those you can spot very easily."

Clearly, the sheer magnitude of some stories alone will get them on the newscast. Pete Williams asserted that "big stories are as television worthy as they are newspaper worthy." Thus, "decisions on term limits . . . affirmative action decisions, the gun in school decisions . . . were as big for us as they were for newspapers. So the big cases are always going to get on television." Other stories that are less "big" will receive airtime when they have "more compelling visual elements . . . or [something] that . . . everybody can identify with."

The story about the little guy in . . . Oregon who wanted to play football but didn't want to take the drug test. That was a sort of compelling little story. Here's this little community, here's this one little family that says, "Wait a minute. Something's not right." And then that touches on a larger national issue. The whole question of . . . drugs and civil rights. . . . It has all those elements in it that seem to add together and work as a television story.

Regarding the importance of visuals for making a case television worthy Lyle Denniston observed, "I used to sit in a cubbyhole between Carl Stern and Tim O'Brien and on big decision days I was always amazed at how much of their conversation focused on the pictures that they had available as opposed to discussing the substance of what the Court had done."

In the final analysis, gauging newsworthiness for the network newscasts involves a fine balancing act. Tim O'Brien assessed some of the elements in the balance:

The case you cover is the one you believe to be the most newsworthy and the most important. Sometimes, you can sacrifice some of the importance if it is an extremely interesting case. And sometimes you can sacrifice some of the interest. It can be a rather dull case, if it is extremely important. But how it affects people generally and its interest to people are both considerations. (in Katsh, 1980: 32)

As Pete Williams has lamented, too often in drawing the balance even interesting cases with the potential for widespread impact do not get on the air. Offering a particular example, he pointed out that "it's very hard to get . . . pure First Amendment cases on television. . . . The lady in Iowa with the antiwar sign in her window, or the woman in . . . Ohio who wanted to pass out anonymous campaign literature. And the little community that prided itself on being sort of special and a little bit snooty that wanted to have no signs." These cases, among others, did not meet the network's criteria.

Some cases do, of course, make it on to the evening news, and rounding out our attempt to understand Court coverage from the viewpoint of the reporters themselves we will try to piece together what happens during the newsday when a television-worthy decision is announced. Perhaps the first imperative noted by several reporters is to actually be in the courtroom when the decision is released. As Pete Williams stressed:

I like to hear what it is that the justice says is important about the case, partly because if I want to use a quote from them speaking it, I can be right there to get the quote. And if they make some gesture. And sometimes they do unusual things, like Ruth Bader Ginsburg reads her whole opinion or something. You just want to be there. . . . And it also provides a little review and it sort of keys me to things to watch out for in the opinion.

Carl Stern concurred: "You've got to sit there and listen to them. Oral announcements are more truncated these days but, in the old days, when Hugo Black was railing against his colleagues . . . or even when Blackmun did some of his famous dissents and so on with passion, you pick up a good sense of the case by listening to oral announcements of it."

Not all of the television reporters enjoy the luxury of "being there" for all of the decisions they cover. Tim O'Brien, for example, often has to file an immediate radio report, which may lead him to obtain a copy of a decision from the Court's Public Information Office as it is announced:

Consider this. . . . The decision comes down at ten after ten and they want something they can put on the air at eleven o'clock. They can record it half an hour after I have the decision, so what I usually do is I read the syllabus, which will say whether the lower court decision was affirmed, reversed, affirmed in part, [or] reversed in part and will summarize why. Then I go to the dissent, read the beginning and end of the dissents or dissent, and then, if time permits, I go back and read more of the majority opinion. Before I go on the evening news, I like to have the whole decision read cover to cover, and usually I can do that but not always.

Carl Stern, too, had to prepare pieces for radio with great dispatch and, looking back, he takes some credit for the syllabus now appended to decisions at the time of their announcement:

When I came to the Supreme Court there was no syllabus, there was no headnote, and it was a terrible time. There was one day . . . when the Court came down with 544 pages of printed decisions in about twenty minutes, and I had to file to radio at 11:00. And all you could do was flip over to the last page and see what the Court said because there was no way to know. And I'd come from Ohio which has a syllabus . . . as black letter law. . . . I had to do . . . six decisions in one spot, and I did fine except on one of them . . . I got it backwards, I got it wrong on the air. That's not supposed to be, and I told Warren Burger that story . . . and . . . Burger ordered the reporter . . . to start putting these headnotes, which they used to prepare after the fact for publication in the bound volume of *U.S. Reports,* to do it ahead of time and to put them out informally with the decision so that people could get a quick summary of it. And that was the result of my conversation with Burger.

Interestingly, to the extent that Court procedures have changed through the years to respond, in part, to journalistic needs, many of these reforms occurred during the watch of staunch media critic Warren Burger. Fred Graham explained:

Burger never conceded that there was a legitimate public interest in such matters as the justices' health, their finances, their reasons for disqualifying themselves from cases, their votes on deadlocked appeals and their off-the-bench activities. Thus, Burger became an enthusiastic reformer of the mechanics of covering the Supreme Court, perhaps in hopes that by facilitating our efforts to cover the formalities we would be less likely to fritter away our energies on personalities and gossip. (1990: 100)

In this sense the Chief Justice sought to bring added efficiency to dissemination of the information already distributed by the press officer. In no sense was the scope of distributed information altered. The irony of Burger's role, however, was not lost on Graham: "It was amazing how enlightened Burger could appear simply by changing some of the musty old procedures that his predecessors hadn't bothered to question" (1990: 100).

For reporters who do not have to worry about preparing an early piece for radio, the drill may be somewhat different. Thus, Pete Williams will contact the news desk in Washington and the appropriate production people in New York to alert them that a decision has been rendered that warrants coverage. Usually, at that time, he will be given the go-ahead. Then, in conjunction with his producer and researcher, he will begin to track down appropriate people to interview about the case, often including efforts to reach the litigants directly:

So those little lines are out, then I proceed to try to read the decision. And I think I have to read the whole thing. I don't screw with the syllabus. I just start with the majority opinion and read right through it, all the concurrings right through until the last words of the dissent. . . . I have to do that. I simply have to do that. Then the calls start coming back.

At CBS, as we have noted, the commitment of reporter resources to and at the Court has been greatly diminished, and, consequently, the procedure for initiating decisional coverage is a bit different. As Jim Stewart described the process, he does not spend time at the Supreme Court waiting for decisions to come down as do the reporters for the other networks:

We have two people there every time decisions are announced. They quickly scan. They call me, I'm listening to them as they're listening to the case as it's announced and called out there. We make a snap judgment on whether these are dog cases or whether these are cases that might have a chance. . . . We know in advance, obviously, cases that we have considered bellwether cases. And if that decision comes down, we immediately hit the red phone and tell New York and start blocking time out.

The routine for information gathering after an initial decision is made to proceed with coverage of a ruling follows a similar frenzied pattern at all the networks. Fred Graham succinctly described it:

A case comes down, the correspondent immediately picks up the phone, calls New York or calls his contact here in Washington and says, "Here's the story. I need someone to get an interview in Los Angeles and someone in Detroit" of so and so and so and so. Then, later in the day, you or your producer call . . . a couple of the groups that filed amicus briefs. What you find out is that so and so here in Washington is going to speak at 2:30 and . . . the opposing side has already seen that and they've laid one on at 3:30. . . . They even coordinated close enough. And I would go there. I knew I was going to see Carl Stern. I know I was going to see Tim O'Brien. So it became fairly ritualized.

In between arranging and conducting interviews or having one's producer doing so, the reporter will often be in contact with the newscast's sketch artist to discuss what drawings are needed. At this juncture, Pete Williams explained:

You start thinking about the graphic elements and you start envisioning what the story is going to be. . . . And then all that stuff starts to come back to you, and they tell you what the people said in the interviews and you choose those things, and the crew comes down and you do your standup. You quibble with them on the script and, finally, get the script approved. And you go in that little room under the Court bench and you voice the track part, and then it all comes together.

If the process as detailed by Fred Graham and Pete Williams seems, to even a limited degree, tidy and ordered, Carl Stern's lengthier description of the day's events reveals the numerous twists and turns between a decision's announcement and its portrayal on the nightly newscasts: "The problem is that you're half a producer and you don't have enough time, really quality time." After hearing the decision delivered and reading the headnote, Stern reported that he would call his office to "give them a quick 'heads up' because the wire copy is going to start coming across, and the wire copy may be misleading or . . . it may do stuff in the order it was handed down." The next step is to arrange for interviews with expert analysts, interested parties, and, if possible, the litigants themselves. Network affiliates can serve as useful intermediaries in instances when the people needed are far from Washington:

> You've got to get things rolling because you've got to produce the piece. It's not just what's going to come out of your head. You've got to get the pictures, you've got to get the comments. So I would probably spend between, let's say 10:20, when I left the courtroom, and roughly noon on the phone trying to crank up different production things. And then I would try to sit and read the opinion . . . while I'm eating my lunch [and] read and write standup copy for a closer because New York is going to want you to do that closer fairly early because things get jammed up late in the day.

There is a bit of irony here because "even though you haven't yet organized the piece or written a piece, they want to know right off the bat how you're going to end the piece." This material was then sent to New York in early afternoon and, hopefully, clearance to move forward would arrive by 2:00, "so you can have a crew at 2:45 or so to come down and do your standupper so you can get back to the building . . . by 3:30 to start working on the actual piece." At this point, the pace would move even faster:

> Then you write a script till about . . . 5:00. You've got to screen the stuff that is coming in, feeds are coming in. You've got to select what sound bites you want. . . . Or maybe, as happened more often than not in my case, I would on the way back to the office stop off to do one or two interviews. Sometimes I wouldn't get back to the office till 4:30.

As airtime loomed closer, the real battles would often begin:

> The copy . . . wouldn't go up to New York till maybe about ten after five and then it would get in a logjam there and now it's 5:40. You're fifteen minutes away from air, and you haven't laid down one picture, haven't recorded one word, and now they're arguing with you. Can't you say this rather than that? Why don't you change this to that? And things are flying all over the place. Frequently you're ad-libbing copy into an open mike trying to get tracked down piece by piece. Sometimes you split the piece and you're doing part of it in two different rooms or relaying pictures that are coming in.

Even when the newscast started, much was likely to remain in disarray and under negotiation:

It was an absolute madhouse. I would say that 90 percent of the pieces that I did were completed within 120 seconds of the show going on the air, or the show was already on the air but it just wasn't up to my piece yet. . . . It's an absolutely crazy business, because you are half producer, you're interviewer, you're everything. But you do it because you think it's important to do it. But it's important to do it right and . . . it became for me increasingly more difficult to do it in a way that I believed was right.

SUMMING UP AND LOOKING FORWARD

In chapters 2 and 3 we have taken an extended look at the world in which the Supreme Court reporter operates with a particular focus on the job of a network television correspondent covering the Court. We have relied mostly on the reporters' own perceptions of what their jobs entail and how they define their journalistic as well as their public responsibilities. Our exploration has examined the resources at the Court reporter's disposal including consideration of the roles played by interest groups, the Court's Public Information Office, the justices themselves, and the Supreme Court journalist's own colleagues in performing the job. We have paid considerable attention to the uniqueness of the Supreme Court beat, while exploring the constraints imposed on journalists by the institution of the Court itself as well as by the nature of the television news business. Much of our focus has been on changes in the television news industry that culminated in the 1980s in what Fred Graham characterized at CBS News as the triumph of infotainment over news substance. Along the way we have explored several possible reforms that have been proffered from many sources, including reporters themselves, to help facilitate "better" coverage of the Court that would, it is argued, lead ultimately to a better informed public. Special attention was placed on the issue of cameras in the courtroom.

The portrait that emerged from our consideration of the task of the television Supreme Court reporter is quite a sobering one. Their job is quite complex, and in the absence of visual access to the decision-making process and routine interviews with the decision makers, they must find alternative ways of convincing their superiors that airtime is warranted. Once gaining valuable airtime, they must present as much as they can in an attenuated time frame.

Tim O'Brien admits that, as a consequence, television news can be a "head-line service" with very little in-depth legal reporting:

If you are really concerned about quality news reporting on the law, you should not be watching television. . . . Every line is a headline on television. And we sometimes wind up just reading headlines when we read Supreme Court stories and that is frustrating. (in Katsh, 1980: 42–43)

Much more recently, however, O'Brien added, "Well, things are relative."

I think we do a reasonably good job. It could be a hell of a lot better, but given the restrictions that we have inherent in the nature of the business and the restrictions imposed on us by the Court, problems that we have, I think we do a reasonably respectable job. But it could be better, of course.

We will return to an assessment of the quality of Supreme Court reporting on the network news in our concluding chapter. Before we get there, however, we will add a detailed empirical dimension to our analysis that will help us to more properly assess what the reporters, themselves, have told us. Our analysis will include detailed case studies of how two extremely prominent Supreme Court cases, the *Bakke* affirmative action case and the *Webster* abortion case, were covered on network newscasts. In addition, we shall analyze two full years of Supreme Court coverage, the 1989–90 and the 1994–95 Supreme Court terms. In particular, we shall focus on how television news covered the Court's leading cases in those two Supreme Court terms. We shall also consider in depth how television has handled one particular facet of Supreme Court case processing, certiorari decisions, in reporting on the Court. Finally, prior to reaching our summary assessment of network news coverage of the Court we shall attempt to develop a model that helps us to understand better the kinds of cases that do receive valuable and scarce television airtime as compared and contrasted with those that do not.

4

A Tale of Two Cases:
Bakke and *Webster*

"One of the more unfortunate things about the *Bakke* case is that it became the vehicle for educating, or should I say miseducating, the public about affirmative action. The public learned about affirmative action almost, literally, for the first time through . . . ten-second sound bites on television, with people polarized against one another."
Eleanor Holmes Norton, while a member of the Equal Employment Opportunity Commission (in Blackside, 1989)

"[F]ollowing *Webster*, some network reporters suggested a lockup, giving each reporter five minutes . . . to study the decision . . . so they could all report the decision more responsibly."
Tim O'Brien, ABC News

On June 28, 1978, the Supreme Court issued its much anticipated ruling in the case of *Regents of the University of California v. Bakke.* Allan Bakke, a white male, claimed that he was discriminated against by the medical school at the University of California at Davis (UC-Davis) because of his race. The celebrated case marked the Court's first full-scale effort to address the legality of publicly promulgated affirmative action programs, in this instance in the context of admissions processes at a professional school. More than a decade later, on July 3, 1989, the Court issued its decision in the similarly anticipated case of *Webster v. Reproductive Health Services,* dealing with the constitutionality of several provisions of a Missouri law that regulated and restricted a woman's right to obtain an abortion. This time the Court was not working on a clean slate, however, since it had revisited the issue of abortion rights many times in the wake of the landmark *Roe v. Wade* ruling in 1973 overturning a Texas antiabortion statute. What made *Webster* noteworthy, however, was the distinct possibility that it would be the vehicle through which the Court overturned the historic *Roe* ruling.

Neither the *Bakke* nor *Webster* decision turned out, in hindsight, to be the definitive ruling that many anticipated. In *Bakke*, the Court's majority invalidated a specific affirmative action program while, at the same time, a different majority coalition remained supportive of affirmative action efforts per se. The confusing hybrid ruling was likely to be misunderstood by many while pleasing few. Clearly, it settled little in the public and constitutional battles over affirmative action. For its part, *Webster* did not prove to be the death knell for *Roe* that was anticipated by many. To be sure, Missouri's restrictive regulations of abortion were upheld. The Court, however, split five to four on the various facets of the Missouri law, and while some justices called for overturning *Roe*, a majority could not be mustered to explicitly overrule that landmark precedent. Indeed, somewhat ironically, the fundamental freedom of choice protected by *Roe* survives today and seems less in danger of being overturned than it did at the start of the 1990s.

In subsequent analysis in later chapters we shall draw a picture of how network newscasts broadly portray the work of the Court by examining all stories broadcast during its October 1989 and October 1994 terms. Our macrolevel view of television news coverage will include discussion of general news treatment of the Court, coverage focused on its docket, and special consideration of how each term's leading cases were presented. We have suggested that, for many reasons, the Court is not a governmental venue favored by television newscasts. Most Supreme Court cases fail to be sufficiently newsworthy, in light of the constraints of network news, to receive substantial coverage or, more often than not, any coverage at all. Obviously, however, not all cases are created equal. The *Bakke* and *Webster* cases, for reasons amplified below, represent exceptions to the general rule, and in this chapter, we examine television news coverage of the Court in two instances where the medium took its "best shot." Before we examine television's handling of these two prominent cases, they will be placed in appropriate context and we will comment further on why these two decisions were isolated for extended analysis.

THE *BAKKE* CASE

Focusing on *Bakke* as an example of television coverage of Supreme Court policy making warrants some justification since the decision is more than two decades old. Nevertheless, the subject matter of affirmative action remains as controversial today as when the case was decided and, indeed, the nature of the *Bakke* holding itself has remained a factor in the issue's continuing evolution. Ample testimony to the issue's currency can be seen in state efforts such as the California Civil Rights Initiative of 1996 (Proposition 209) that banned affirmative action in governmental programs (including programs such as those at issue in *Bakke*), as well as by the issue's broader prominence in the 1996 presidential election where clear differences between Bill Clinton and Bob Dole were revealed in the presidential debates and throughout the campaign. That the *Bakke* case was both newsworthy and rife with importance was clear to contemporary analysts. While the decision would not, necessarily, be definitive, it would be a touchstone for future development of the law in the affirmative action domain.

Clearly, the final character of the law on preferential racial treatment would likely not be known for many years; it would depend on a succession of judicial, bureaucratic, and legislative actions on different kinds of preferences reflecting a variety of contexts and circumstances. Nonetheless, few doubted that the judiciary's contribution would be anything less than substantial, and perhaps decisive. *Bakke* gave the Court the opportunity for a precedent-setting ruling that could establish the framework for subsequent policy resolution of the controversy (Sindler, 1978: 162).

The importance of television news in a democratic polity for understanding public knowledge about and reaction to *Bakke*, as well as the broader issue of affirmative action, was noted by Eleanor Holmes Norton, then a member of the Equal Employment Opportunity Commission:

One of the more unfortunate things about the *Bakke* case is that it became the vehicle for educating, or should I say miseducating, the public about affirmative action. The public learned about affirmative action almost, literally, for the first time through . . . ten second sound bites on television, with people polarized against one another. As a result, what is really a quite complicated concept . . . became depicted as an element of unfairness. (in Blackside, 1989)

Bakke arose in the context of a Court that had successfully sidestepped the constitutionality of affirmative action in the earlier case of Marco DeFunis, which the institution's gatekeeping rules allowed to be declared moot. Public attention to the issue ripened after *DeFunis*, and expectations developed that *Bakke* could be the most important Supreme Court ruling since *Brown v. Board of Education* in 1954. Like *Brown* and *Roe v. Wade*, which had been decided only a few years earlier, *Bakke* could be the case by which an entire judicial era became known.

In light of *Bakke*'s potential importance, the national media focused on it very early in the litigation's development. For example, in early 1975 the *New York Times* covered a California state trial court judge's announcement of his intended decision, noting that a potential legal landmark was in its formative stages (Sindler 1978: 222). As the case worked its way up through California's legal system and appeared to be headed for the U.S. Supreme Court, this theme was often repeated. Joel Dreyfuss and Charles Lawrence III noted, for example, that "reporters have grown fond of referring to the *Bakke* case as 'perhaps the most important Supreme Court decision since *Brown v. Board of Education*'" (1979: 234). In a similar vein legal scholar Ronald Dworkin observed that "no lawsuit . . . has ever been more widely watched or more thoroughly debated in the . . . press before the . . . Court's decision" (in Sindler, 1978: 2). Indeed, when *Bakke* was ultimately announced, even the normally insulated Court took notice that the ruling was much anticipated. As noted by pivotal Justice Lewis Powell, "Perhaps no case in my memory has had so much media coverage" (in Sindler, 1978: 292).

Clearly, the press was well aware of the role it might play in fostering understanding or misinterpretation of the Court's ultimate ruling in *Bakke*. Indeed, a CBS/*New York Times* poll in October 1977, a half year before the decision's announcement of the decision, was suggestive of how important the media could be in framing the affirmative action issue. The poll revealed a public that opposed "quotas" in jobs or admissions for minorities but that could support ill-defined "special consideration" for the best minority applicants (Sindler, 1978: 15–17). In a public setting fraught with ambiguity and ambivalence about affirmative action, the public's posture toward the issue could be uniquely affected by the media's message regarding the unfolding *Bakke* litigation. To the extent that the Court itself was divided and its reasoning complex, which was the defining reality of the *Bakke* decision, the media's interpretive role could loom even larger.

Recognizing that *Bakke* was not business as usual, Fred Friendly, former head of CBS News and leading media analyst, went so far as to urge "that the Court provide a one-week alert before the decision day on *Bakke* so that the newspapers and broadcasters could ready their ablest staff to handle the decision and could budget enough space and air time to ensure ample and accurate coverage" (in Dreyfuss and Lawrence, 1979: 291). While no such notice was given, it remains clear that in *Bakke* reporters did go to special lengths in their preparation. Dreyfuss and Lawrence noted, for example, that at oral argument "the reporters from major publications had pooled to pay the expenses of an unofficial reporter and they chafed at the wait for a transcript" (1979: 201–202). *Newsweek* reported that added efforts and plans came into play as the anticipated decision day neared:

NBC, for example, began on May 1 to station two camera crews equipped with microwave transmitters for instant transmission at every Court session. Public broadcasting stations recruited scholars . . . two months ago for its post-*Bakke* analysis. Many leading constitutional authorities received calls from reporters wanting to know where they could be reached for interviews at the moment of judgment. On the evening of the decision, all three commercial networks and the public television system produced news specials – with NBC and PBS running them in prime time. (July 10, 1978: 31)

Arguably, *Bakke* represents the "best of all worlds" for examining news coverage of the Court since so much effort went into getting this important and newsworthy story "right." On the other hand, "getting it right" in this case would not be easy or, perhaps, even possible. For the *Bakke* decision was a complicated one, with multiple opinions and no clear majority. The decision was not readily accessible to a lay public, and it was a particularly vexing one for the media, particularly television news, to cover. Indeed, ABC's Tim O'Brien mused on how television might have portrayed the ruling in news bulletin format:

The decision of the Supreme Court of California is affirmed . . . in part, and reversed in part. Justice Powell announced the Court's judgment and filed an opinion expressing his views in the case of Part I, II-A, and V-C, in which Justice White joined; and in Parts I, and V-C in which Brennan, Marshall, and Blackmun joined. Brennan, White, Marshall, and Blackmun filed an opinion concurring in the judgment in part and dissenting in part. White, Marshall, and Blackmun filed separate opinions. Stevens filed an opinion concurring in the judgment in part and dissenting in part in which Burger and Stewart, and Rehnquist joined. Film at 11! (1990: 341)

THE *WEBSTER* CASE

If *Bakke* presents us with the opportunity to examine television coverage of a highly anticipated ruling in which the Court was expected to break new ground while opening up an area of emotionally laden and highly divisive litigation, *Webster* suggests the other side of the equation. Unlike the affirmative action issue in *Bakke,* for which the Court could draw little guidance from its earlier rulings or from other courts, the fundamental issues surrounding abortion rights had been addressed by the Court in *Roe v. Wade* in 1973 and were revisited in numerous guises in the decade and a half that passed between *Roe* and *Webster.*

Much of *Webster*'s prominence as a newsworthy event derived from the political context in which the case emerged. First, the case reached the Court during the transition between the Reagan and Bush administrations, a time when the new president was bent on demonstrating that he was firmly in the right-to-life camp, reversing a "softer" stance he held on the issue when opposing Reagan for the 1980 Republican presidential nomination. During Reagan's two terms in office, his strident opposition to abortion had played well for his presidency. He was a vocal supporter of a constitutional amendment to overturn *Roe,* and he was equally committed to the appointment of federal judges, including Supreme Court justices, who held strong pro-life and anti-*Roe* positions. As noted by Barbara Hinkson Craig and David O'Brien, "Reagan's denouncements of the Court's abortion rulings were stronger than any of his predecessors. . . . His language was typically impassioned and moralistic, particularly in comparing the battle over abortion to that over slavery" (1993: 170).

In 1986, in a Justice Department brief in *Thornburgh v. American College of Obstetricians,* the Reagan administration, for the first time, called explicitly for the overturning of *Roe* in actual litigation before the Court. On one level, *Webster* can be seen as Reagan's next and parting shot at *Roe* as the Justice Department convinced William Webster, the Missouri Attorney General, to repeat the *Thornburgh* attack on *Roe* verbatim in the state's own brief in the case. Initially, "Webster's legal strategy was to defend Missouri's law as 'nothing more than regulating abortions within the parameters allowed by *Roe v. Wade.*' But he was persuaded to repeat word for word . . . the language Charles Fried had used in his *Thornburgh* brief demanding *Roe*'s reversal" (Craig and O'Brien, 1993: 187). When Bush took office, *Webster* served as a "gut check" for the new administration as the president formulated his stance in support of Webster's anti-*Roe* argument and offered independent support to Missouri through the Justice Department's own amicus brief and participation in oral argument. Quite naturally, examination of the implications of the presidential transition made the *Webster* case an attractive focal point for television news scrutiny.

What made *Webster* particularly "special" and, consequently, television worthy, however, was the real possibility that it would be the vehicle through which *Roe* was overturned. During the Reagan years, William Rehnquist had become Chief Justice and Justices Sandra Day O'Connor and Antonin Scalia had joined the Court. It seemed to many analysts that the newly configured Court was just one vote away from overturning *Roe*. That "one vote," many thought, came to the Court in 1987 when Anthony Kennedy replaced Lewis Powell, who, until his retirement, had been the pivotal swing vote in the precarious balance upholding *Roe*. Indeed, just a few weeks prior to Kennedy's confirmation the Court had split evenly four to four in *Hartigan v. Zbaraz*, an abortion case dealing with a law requiring parental notification for teenagers seeking abortions. Thus, with Kennedy now on the bench, *Webster* became a perfect vehicle through which to focus on the possible demise of *Roe*. Susan Behuniak-Long summarizes the unusual degree of interest generated by the case:

With the 1988 appointment of Justice Anthony Kennedy to fill the vacancy left by Justice Lewis Powell, a reversal of *Roe v. Wade* was possible. Court watchers tallied a 4–1–4 lineup. Expected to support *Roe* were Justices Harry Blackmun, William Brennan, Thurgood Marshall, and John Paul Stevens. The original dissenters in *Roe*, Justices William Rehnquist and Byron White were expected to be joined by Justices Antonin Scalia and Kennedy. With Justice Sandra Day O'Connor viewed as the swing vote, *Roe* was now subject to a 5–4 reversal. When the Court agreed to hear *Webster* . . . the time was ripe for a major abortion decision. Such anticipation led to the unprecedented number of amicus briefs. (1991: 261)

Indeed, if further justification is needed for our choice to focus on the *Bakke* and *Webster* litigation settings as two instances in which case studies of television news coverage can underscore how the medium reported on unusually prominent Supreme Court decisions generating unusually rich news coverage, it may be found in the widespread and similar level of interest group involvement in these two cases. As Craig and O'Brien have noted:

The politics of interest-group litigation and how it had changed since *Roe v. Wade* was registered in the record number of amici curiae briefs filed in *Webster*. Together, seventy-eight amici briefs were filed in *Webster*, representing a broad range of interests, thousands of individuals, more than 300 organizations, and various coalitions forged over conflicting interpretations of law, history, science, and medicine. The total was twenty more than that filed in the previous Court record holder, *Regents of the University of California v. Bakke*, the only slightly less controversial 1978 reverse-discrimination case in which 120 organizations joined in fifty-eight amici briefs. (1993: 204)

The central role that groups and their spokespersons would play in network newscast coverage of *Webster* was mirrored in the unusual aggressiveness with which their views were being brought to the attention of the Court itself. Indeed, a good deal more was being brought to the attention of the justices than suggested by the record filing of amicus briefs alone.

While the Court was deliberating *Webster* during the 1988–1989 term, interest groups on both sides of the abortion issue placed advertisements on television and radio to influence public opinion and to encourage expression of that opinion to the justices. Pro-choice groups ran full-page advertisements in major newspapers directed at the justices. Both sides initiated letter-writing campaigns to the Court. Telephone calls and mail to the justices reached more than forty thousand daily prior to the *Webster* decision. In contrast, the Court normally receives a thousand letters daily (Davis, 1994: 26).

The normally insulated Court was not immune from the public prominence the *Webster* case had obtained and the attention that, consequently, was being focused on it. Indeed, when the *Webster* decision did not take the definitive step of overturning *Roe*, Justice Scalia lamented somewhat ironically in his concurrence:

We can now look forward to at least another Term with carts full of mail from the public and streets full of demonstrators urging us – their unelected and life-tenured judges who have been awarded those extraordinary, undemocratic characteristics precisely in order that we might follow the law despite the popular will – to follow the popular will.

Clearly, much like *Bakke* before it, the *Webster* case created an unusually newsworthy litigation setting for the network newscasts. For its part, the media viewed *Webster* as one of those "special" cases that, like *Bakke*, warranted immediate news bulletin treatment on decision day thereby increasing the difficulties reporters would face in reporting on the decision accurately. As ABC's Tim O'Brien noted, cases like *Webster* have led to suggestions from reporters that they receive an early view of the ruling prior to its public release, as a means of enhancing the prospects for accurate reporting: "Following *Webster*, some network reporters suggested a lockup, giving each reporter five minutes (or some other agreed upon amount of time) to study the decision . . . so they could all report the decision more responsibly. It is exceedingly rare, however, that decisions are deemed so important that they merit interrupting regular programming" (in Slotnick, 1991b: 133).

BAKKE AND WEBSTER:
HOW MUCH COVERAGE

The logical place to begin our exploration of network news coverage of *Bakke* and *Webster* is through utilization of several measures tapping the sheer amount of attention the cases received. Clearly, at the broadest level, coverage of these cases belies criticisms that portray television as unconcerned with the Court. Indeed, during the time period under study (from the first stories broadcast on each case through the decisions' aftermaths well into the subsequent year's Court term) a relatively large number of stories (60) focused on some facet of each of these cases.

The networks used various types of pieces in their *Bakke* coverage, with straightforward news stories reporting on actual events in the case's development emerging as the most frequent type of story (29, 48.3%). An additional twenty stories (33.3%) combined a news report with an elaboration on some elements of the case in a combined news/feature format. Six stories (10.0%) did not report on any specific newsworthy event transpiring in the case and could be characterized exclusively as feature stories. Five commentaries were included in *Bakke* coverage, two of which occurred on the day of oral argument, with one broadcast on decision day.

Webster coverage revealed a somewhat different pattern with only eight stories (13.3%) classified strictly as news reports and seven (11.7%) exclusively as features. The predominant approach to *Webster* coverage combined a news/feature format (45, 75.0%) underscoring baseline differences between the *Bakke* and *Webster* settings that would be manifested in several ways in the coverage the cases received. *Bakke,* with its central focus on the emerging issue of affirmative action, was, indeed, a "new" news story that engendered coverage of many newsworthy events in the unfolding of this novel litigation. *Webster,* on the other hand, was a case situated in an ongoing stream of litigation that, in some respects, was simply one manifestation of a larger political and social struggle of many years' duration where central battles were often occurring well outside of the litigation setting. Consequently, when significant events in the *Webster* case occurred, they often became the backdrop or means of entrée to a combined news/feature story elaborating on the broader picture beyond the *Webster* litigation.

These differences are reflected further in the relatively equal number of *Bakke* stories run by the networks (ABC: 21, CBS: 20, NBC: 19), when contrasted with the greater divergence in *Webster* coverage (ABC: 25, CBS: 19, NBC: 16). Arguably, network coverage of *Bakke,* with its substantial focus on the case itself, took on some of the elements of pack journalism (as explored in chapter 2) in reporting on the case's unfolding. Obviously, there are certain key events in the case's development that one would expect to be covered by all three networks. The similarity in the flow of *Bakke* coverage, however, goes well beyond such occurrences. Thus, while *Bakke* stories appeared on at least one network news program on thirty different days, on only fifteen of these days did a story appear on only one network. A full third of the time when *Bakke* stories aired (10 days), they appeared on all three networks.

Among the days *Bakke* was addressed on all three networks, some were quite predictable. These included reporting on the granting of certiorari, oral argument, and the announcement of the case's decision. On seven other days, all three networks ran *Bakke*-related pieces. These included stories on the Justice Department's amicus brief writing process and its filing, same-day stories on the U.S. Civil Rights Commission's posture on affirmative action, "day-after" pieces elaborating on the decision's implications, stories focusing on *Bakke* in the context of other pending cases, Allan Bakke attending his first day of medical school, and same-day stories relating *Bakke* to the granting of certiorari in the Court's next major affirmative action case, *United Steel Workers v. Weber* (1979).

The flow of *Webster* coverage across the networks can be cast in somewhat different terms. It should be underscored, however, that some of the differences in the networks' attention to *Bakke* and *Webster* may, in some respects, be more apparent than real and reflect stylistic differences among the networks and contextual differences in the two case settings. Our viewing of the newscasts revealed that while ABC, for example, might run a piece on an antiabortion rally and place it in the context of *Webster,* another network might cover the same protest on the same day without drawing the *Webster* connection. The ABC piece would become part of our data set while the other network's would not. Thus, the most meaningful distinctions between network coverage of *Bakke* and *Webster* may be found most clearly in stories focused directly on the unfolding of the key decision points in the cases themselves.

Pieces touching on some facet of the *Webster* litigation ran on thirty-nine different days, with a single newscast broadcasting a *Webster* story on a clear majority (24, 61.5%) of those days. On only five days (12.8%) that *Webster* made the evening newscasts did stories run on all three networks. These included the obvious focal points of the Court's granting of certiorari, oral argument, decision day, and aftermath stories the day following the Court's ruling. Interestingly, all three networks ran stories on June 29, 1989, anticipating the end of the Court's term and awaiting the *Webster* decision. When the decision was not announced as expected, that in and of itself became the subject for journalistic speculation. Despite the fact that a schedule for releasing decisions is never announced by the Court, anchor Peter Jennings told ABC viewers that the Court had "postponed" the *Webster* ruling, while NBC's anchor Tom Brokaw took note that "in an unusual move, the Court extended its session until Monday, and everyone now is wondering what's going on." The anchors then turned to their Supreme Court correspondents to amplify on the "meaning" of the story that wasn't.

Additional observations can be made about the flow of *Bakke* and *Webster* newscast coverage in meaningful periods of the litigation processes the cases followed, as documented in Table 4.1. First, both cases received some coverage prior to the Court's granting of certiorari to them. In *Bakke,* ABC ran a twenty-two-second story reporting that the University of California planned to appeal a reverse discrimination case to the Supreme Court. NBC reported the same news event on the same day in the context of a lengthy (4:45) feature providing an overview of the case. CBS ran its first *Bakke* piece, a lengthy overview (3:45) on the day the certiorari petition was filed. Thus, while the case received little early attention, two of the network's first stories were quite comprehensive ones. The preponderance of *Bakke* stories (61.6%) were aired prior to the actual decision, and more than a third (38.3%) were broadcast before oral argument. Thus, when decision day arrived, the *Bakke* case should not have been an unknown event to an attentive television viewing public.

Some facets of the flow of *Webster* coverage followed a similar pattern while clear differences also emerged. Only two of the three networks (ABC and CBS) aired pieces prior to the granting of certiorari and none covered the case prior to the filing of a certiorari petition. ABC's initial piece was a short, anchor presented news piece reporting the Justice Department's position favoring a certiorari grant in *Webster* and stating its desire to have the case serve as a basis for the reconsideration of *Roe.* The following day (11/11/89) CBS

Table 4.1. *Network news stories, by period in litigation process*
(percentages in parentheses)

	Bakke	Webster
Lower court processes	2 (3.3)	0 (0.0)
Certiorari petition filed/petition vigil	1 (1.7)	2 (3.3)
Certiorari granted/case being prepared	20 (33.3)	14 (23.3)
Oral argument/decision vigil	14 (23.3)	15 (25.0)
Decision and aftermath	23 (38.3)	29 (48.3)

weighed in with a lengthier (2:10) news/feature elaborating on the government's support for review of *Webster* and the role that the case played in the Reagan-Bush presidential transition. Like *Bakke*, the *Webster* case should not have been an unknown news event when decision day came, as more than a quarter (26.6%) of *Webster* stories aired prior to oral argument and more than half (51.7%) were broadcast before the Court's ruling.

The large number of stories in *Webster*'s wake, when contrasted to *Bakke*, reflects key differences in the two case settings. The *Bakke* decision was followed by several stories examining its legal meaning and its role in generating future litigation, but the complex and confusing ruling did not have the immediate political fallout that followed *Webster*. Consequently, when *Webster* upheld Missouri's restrictions on abortion while not overturning *Roe*, newscast coverage of the case (as it had in *Bakke*) examined the new litigation likely to follow. In addition, however, in light of the leeway states now appeared to have in the abortion arena, considerable newscast coverage turned to the ongoing battles of well organized antiabortion and pro-choice forces in numerous state legislatures over new efforts to restrict abortion while also focusing on the implications of *Webster* for state electoral contests.

Other measures of the amount of coverage *Bakke* and *Webster* received further document the relative degree of importance given to the stories. For example, while many (28.3%) *Bakke* stories were less than thirty seconds long, the majority (51.7%) aired for more than a minute and a half, relatively expansive airtime for network news pieces. One of five *Bakke* stories enjoyed a leisurely length of more than three minutes. On decision day, ABC devoted 16:41 to *Bakke*-related coverage while NBC (14:51) and CBS (14:34) gave the case nearly equal emphasis. These figures represent extraordinary coverage, for, as

Herbert Gans has noted, "When events that journalists deem to be world-shaking take place . . . the normal daily format may be set aside, with 8 to 10 minutes or more given to one story" (1979: 3). Story length, it should be added, has greater implications than simply denoting the prominence that news producers place on events. As John Robinson and Mark Levy have found, "longer stories are better comprehended no matter where they are placed" (1986: 191).

While *Webster* did not fare quite as well on these measures, it remains clear that it was not treated as an ordinary news event. Thus, while a majority of *Webster* stories (51.7%) aired for less than half a minute, 40 percent ran for longer than a minute and a half, and 15 percent were more than three minutes in length. On decision day ABC again led the networks with 13:40 coverage, with CBS (13:00) and NBC (11:00) also giving remarkable attention to the case.

In addition to broadcast length, story placement is another dimension of network newscasts that holds a key to the perceived importance of a story as well as the likelihood that it will be comprehended. "The news program is structured like a newspaper," Gans has noted. "The day's most important story is the lead, and the first two sections are generally devoted to the other important hard news of the day" (1979: 3). Story placement has also been linked to comprehension of the news, as viewers generally remember initial stories, and it is also common for viewers to remember stories placed late in broadcasts (Robinson and Levy, 1986: 180). In particular, according to one study, closing stories are consistently among the best comprehended (Robinson and Levy, 1986: 191).

On all of these dimensions the data reveal that coverage of *Bakke* fared quite well. *Bakke* was the lead story ten times (16.7%) and an "up-front" story (broadcast prior to the second commercial break) 60 percent of the time. *Bakke* closed a newscast twice (3.3%) and aired during the newscast's last section seven times (11.6%). In addition to being the lead story across the networks on decision day, *Bakke* opened two network newscasts when the Justice Department filed its brief in the case and when oral argument was heard. *Bakke* was an integral part of CBS's and NBC's lead coverage of the certiorari grant in the followup *Weber* case, and a focus on *Bakke* was part of CBS's lead coverage of related affirmative action cases about a week after the decision was handed down.

In some important respects, coverage of *Webster* was even more prominently featured on network newscasts. Thus, the case was the opening story on sixteen (26.7%) broadcasts with stories generally airing (61.7%) prior to the newscasts' second commercial break. *Webster* was the lead story across all three networks when the Court granted certiorari in the case and on the day of the Court's decision. ABC and NBC opened their respective newscasts with *Webster* coverage on the day of oral argument, while CBS opted to report the death of Lucille Ball before turning to its oral argument story. Both ABC and CBS led with aftermath stories on the day after the *Webster* ruling. Interestingly, *Webster* opened newscasts when NBC reported the "postponement" of the Court's decision (6/29/89) and when ABC anticipated and speculated on the nature of the ruling (7/2/89), now expected the following day. *Webster* also played a role in lead stories on CBS (1/22/89) and ABC (1/22/90) covering the anniversary of *Roe v. Wade* as well as in postdecision stories focusing on antiabortion initiatives in a special session of the Florida legislature (NBC, 10/10/89) and congressional action on federal funding for abortions (ABC, 10/11/89).

One final measure of the perceived importance of *Bakke* and *Webster* was the manner in which they were reported. In only eleven instances (18.3%) was a *Bakke* story delivered exclusively by a newscast's anchor. The majority of reports (56.7%) were offered by the anchor and a news correspondent specializing in the story. On decision day six correspondents joined the anchors on ABC's and NBC's *Bakke* coverage, while four correspondent's joined Walter Cronkite on CBS. Similarly, only eight (13.3%) *Webster* stories were broadcast exclusively from the news anchor's chair. The vast majority of stories (76.7%) joined the anchor with a specialist news correspondent. On decision day, six correspondents joined ABC's anchor Barry Serafin in reporting on *Webster*, while CBS and NBC both utilized four correspondents in addition to their news anchors to deliver the story.

The data offer substantial evidence that both *Bakke* and *Webster* were considered unusually important stories by the network newscasts. Examination of the sheer amount of coverage these prominent cases received only tells a part, albeit an important one, of the story. In the remainder of this chapter we shall examine the nature of the newscasts' coverage of these two leading cases.

BAKKE AND *WEBSTER:* WHAT KIND OF COVERAGE

Perhaps the most important concerns analysts have demonstrated in examining television news center on the questions of what a viewing public can learn and what remains hidden about the prominent events covered in a newscast. To the extent that television is and remains the public's primary source of news and information about politics and government, any evaluation of the state of public knowledge is inevitably constrained by what the public can know, that is to say what information they have received over the airwaves. When we consider information about the activities of the relatively invisible Supreme Court, television news may often be the sole source of information for many. With that in mind, much of our coding of television stories about *Bakke* and *Webster* attempted to tap several facets of their substantive content.

As in nearly all legal controversies reaching the Court, *Bakke* had a litigation history. Such a history helps to establish the critical issues in the litigation while also suggesting possible resolutions of them. In *Bakke*, a California court record existed from 1974 through late 1976. Initially, a trial court judge had found the UC-Davis program to be unconstitutional as applied to Bakke but did not order it dismantled. Rather, he ordered the university to reconsider Bakke's application without regard to race. Ultimately, the California Supreme Court issued a six-to-one decision upholding trial judge F. Leslie Manker. In a sweeping opinion Justice Stanley Mosk utilized a heightened "strict scrutiny" standard of review for the UC-Davis program and found that, under the Fourteenth Amendment's equal protection clause, the special admissions program was unconstitutional. The case was remanded to determine whether Bakke would have been admitted absent the special admissions approach. In a stinging dissent, Justice Matthew Tobriner argued that strict scrutiny was unnecessary to assess "benign" racial classifications and that the compelling goals of the Davis program were being sought appropriately through rationally related means.

The details of these pre–Supreme Court proceedings were not expected to be a central component of *Bakke* coverage on the network news. Nevertheless, the California court processes created a rich background on the fundamental issues in the case and a proximate "winner" at the state level. Any thorough and accurate presentation of *Bakke* in the Supreme Court ought to have included some consideration of the case's history and a recognition that this was not an issue springing out of the blue, full-blown, on the Court's doorstep.

Yet this is an impression that network news viewers easily could have received. Using a liberal measure of whether a story made some reference to *Bakke*'s lower court history, we found such a reference only ten (16.7%) times, and only once on ABC News. Virtually all such references occurred early in television's treatment of the case since presumably, at that point, there was little else to focus on. Indeed, the case history prior to reaching the Supreme Court was alluded to only three times following oral argument and, understandably, was never mentioned once the Supreme Court rendered its ruling. When the case history was mentioned, it was generally through oversimplistic and sketchy presentations indicating simply that Bakke had won in the court below. Such reports did not capture the richness and impact of the full-scale legal controversy that had transpired in California.

The treatment of *Webster*'s lower court history can be characterized in similar terms. Missouri's statute placing important constraints and restrictions on freedom of choice in abortions was passed into law in April 1986 after a three-month legislative battle. A class action suit in federal district court was filed by an abortion clinic, Reproductive Health Services, and several colitigants seeking a declaratory judgment that many provisions in the law were unconstitutional. About a year after the statute's passage, its principal provisions (including a preamble declaring that life begins at conception; a requirement that, after fifteen weeks, abortions be performed in hospital settings; a requirement that doctors perform viability tests on fetuses; a prohibition on the expenditure of public funds or use of public facilities to perform abortions; and a prohibition against public employees counseling a woman to have an abortion except in an instance where it was necessary to save her life) were declared unconstitutional by District Court Judge Scott Wright. Wright's decision was immediately appealed to the U.S. Court of Appeals for the Eighth Circuit where a three-judge panel affirmed all facets of the lower court ruling save one, its finding overturning the state's choice not to fund abortion procedures.

Reference on network news stories to any facet of this lower court history in *Webster* occurred in only six (10.0%) instances (never on CBS News), failing to meet even the minimal attention such historic context played in the *Bakke* setting. The last mention of the lower courts' handling of the case occurred in NBC's coverage of oral argument. All attention to the lower courts' decisions was cursory, simply indicating that Missouri had appealed the earlier judgments.

The relatively ahistorical and acontextual reporting in *Bakke* and *Webster* should not be seen as surprising since, as James Fallows reminds us, "For TV purposes, the ideal world is one in which whatever is on the screen at this moment is entirely engrossing." All news events are, in this sense, fungible, and equally important, "because they are all supposed to claim our attention in the brief *now* during which they exist." With a focus on the current "spectacle," this "flattening" effect, which "is natural to TV . . . is at total odds with some of journalism's fundamental roles. In the real world, events have a history. Part of the press's job is to explain that history, although that goes against TV's natural emphasis on the *now*" (1996: 52–53). Clearly, in *Bakke* and *Webster*, television news did not often "do its job" of placing the cases in appropriate historical context.

Discussion of the litigation history and context represents just one of many substantive foci that television can bring to covering Supreme Court cases. Our coding of *Bakke* and *Webster* news stories also included an effort to assess whether any case-related facts or specific substantive information were provided about the litigation. At bottom, what specific legal issues did the cases raise? Here television fared somewhat better. Indeed, more than half (55.0%) of the *Bakke* stories were coded positively on this dimension, although the cynic would take note that a full 45 percent of *Bakke* stories lacked specific content about the nature of Bakke's claim or the factual scenario underlying it. Interestingly, the longer the *Bakke* story was in the news, the less specific factual information was presented about it. Thus, more than three out of four (82.6%) *Bakke* stories broadcast prior to oral argument in the case included some factual information about the litigation. Beginning on decision day in *Bakke* through the case's aftermath only about one in five stories (21.7%) contained such factual information. It appears that, over time, the case took on a life of its own, apart from the set of facts that had brought it about in the first instance.

Once again, the picture is even bleaker when attention is focused on coverage in *Webster*. In some respects the "facts" in *Webster* were less complex, more accessible, and more easily reportable than those in *Bakke*, amounting simply to allegations of the unconstitutionality of the provisions of the operative Missouri statute. While we were quite liberal in our coding, accepting any reference to the fact that provisions of a Missouri law were being challenged in the case, only slightly more than one in four stories (26.7%) met our criterion. And, as was the case in *Bakke*, attention to the facts of the case dissipated the longer the story was in the news. Thus, more than a third of the television news stories broadcast about *Webster* through the eve of oral argument (37.5%) and of those aired from oral argument through the eve of the Court's decision in the case (40.0%) contained some factual information about the litigation. While all the network newscasts on decision day referenced the facts of the case, not a single one of the twenty-six *Webster*-related stories broadcast in the decision's aftermath included a reference to any of the facts of the actual litigation. Most importantly, during the period when the Court's decision was finally known, the public had little substantive information to help inform their understanding of what the Court had actually done.

Television is, of course, a visual medium, and our analysis included consideration of what viewers "saw" when *Bakke* and *Webster* stories were broadcast. Included was consideration of those visual images related to the coverage of the cases themselves, and, consequently, the "talking heads" of news anchors and correspondents, interview subjects, and all press conference settings were eliminated from consideration. Examination of the most frequently appearing visuals associated with *Bakke* and *Webster* aptly illustrates some of the difficulties associated with television news coverage of the Supreme Court, an institution whose decision processes take place far from the public eye and one that does not allow cameras in the courtroom to record oral argumentation or the announcement of its decisions.

In *Bakke* coverage the most frequently utilized visual was a sterile picture or drawing of the Supreme Court's building, an image present in nearly four out of ten (38.3%) stories. Nondescript college campus scenes served as a backdrop in more than a quarter (26.7%) of the stories, suggesting that the case had something to do with education. Allan Bakke's visage appeared in fifteen (25.0%) stories, either through an artist's drawing, a photograph, or an "action" scene of his efforts to avoid cameras. (*Bakke* coverage may have been even more difficult for television reporters than many other Supreme Court cases since the main protagonist refused to be interviewed and remained a very private person throughout the litigation process.) Also shown with some frequency were pictures of court documents and scenes of protest activity related to the litigation, both of which occurred in ten stories (16.7%). Interestingly, Supreme Court justices remained relatively invisible players throughout the coverage, with drawings and pictures of them not appearing until the time of the case decision and its aftermath.

The visuals most associated with *Webster* coverage create a similar mix of the relatively innocuous and nondescript as well as some case-specific images. *Webster* was treated in many respects, as we shall see, as a clash of diametrically opposed interests in American society. Thus, it is no surprise that the most frequently appearing visual in case coverage did not focus on the Court per se but, rather, on political demonstrations on one side or the other of the abortion issue. Scenes from such demonstrations, with their attendant action and drama, were present in nearly three out of four (73.3%) *Webster* stories. The next most frequently utilized visual, pictures or drawings of the Supreme Court building, appeared in more than half (53.3%) of the stories. While issue-related graphics were present in several (11.7%) *Bakke*-related stories, such presentations appeared to be considerably more adaptable to *Webster* coverage and appeared in twenty-four (40.0%) of the stories. Thus, television viewers frequently saw graphics such as those outlining the provisions of the Missouri law under attack in *Webster*, public opinion polls on the abortion issue, characterizations of the status of abortion rights in the American states, the prospects for state legislative initiatives in the wake of *Webster*, and several other illustrative presentations. "Team photos" or drawings of the Supreme Court's members or some subset of them appeared in seventeen *Webster* stories (28.3%), underscoring that, unlike in *Bakke*, the track record of the justices on the abortion issue combined with personnel changes on the Court since earlier abortion rulings fostered journalistic efforts to portray the Court's division and, possibly, its ultimate decision in the case. Next in frequency of appearance, scenes from hospital and clinic settings, appeared in fifteen stories (25.0%), playing the role of scenic backdrop in *Webster* that campus scenes had earlier played in *Bakke*.

ADDITIONAL PATTERNS OF NEWS COVERAGE: THE *BAKKE* CASE

In addition to a concern with visuals, analysts of newscast coverage of the Court have suggested that story development focuses on the actors involved in ongoing litigation and, in particular, the individual litigants the unfolding case drama revolves around. *Bakke* was no exception. The case's protagonist, Allan Bakke, was referenced in nearly nine out of ten (86.7%) stories, more than twice as often as UC-Davis, his faceless institutional opponent, which was referenced in less than half (40.0%) of the stories. The central focus on Bakke himself (despite his concerted efforts to avoid the celebrity status the case brought with it) actually increased substantially over time, with UC-Davis identified in only ten stories (27.0%) broadcast from the time of oral argument through the case's decision and aftermath. Quite clearly, the *Bakke* case was treated by television news, in large part, as a story about the plight and fate of Allan Bakke. Personalizing the case through a central focus on Bakke resulted, in part, in frequent repetition of case themes that were quite sympathetic to his claim. Thus, for example, seventeen stories (28.3%) noted Bakke's charge that a quota system was in place at UC-Davis that reserved seats for specified minorities. An equal number of stories took note that minority students with lower test scores than Bakke had been admitted to the medical school while he had not. Often, the messages presented were far from subtle and, in some respects, overstated the case or were factually wrong.

Thus, for example, CBS's Fred Graham reported that "Bakke's lawsuit rocked the statewide university system after the medical school was forced to concede that Bakke was better qualified than the students admitted under the nonwhite quota, and that if he had not been white he probably would have been admitted" (12/14/76). On ABC News Howard K. Smith asserted even more bluntly, "Soon the . . . Court will rule on the *Bakke* case, the young white man who lost admission to a medical school to less qualified minority candidates" (6/19/78).

To be sure, some information was presented to the public that was sympathetic to UC-Davis and the thrust of affirmative action. For example, ABC's Tim O'Brien reported that less than four of one hundred doctors were black, while the demand of blacks to get into medical schools was higher than ever before (9/19/77). Twice (on ABC and CBS), viewers would learn that not only were lower-scoring blacks admitted before Bakke, but many lower-scoring whites were admitted as well. Yet only rarely were news viewers subjected to perspectives such as those offered by ABC's Howard K. Smith on a commentary piece:

It's a thorny case, but it must be said that common and often sensible accepted practice opposes Bakke's case. Colleges have rarely accepted students strictly on the basis of grades. Above a given high grade for all, they have sought a mix of students they judged favorable for the whole college climate. . . . In the *Bakke* case, it should be noted, he was passed over not only by a few blacks, but by thirty-six whites with lower grades than he had. The inclusion of those few blacks seems amply justified in a nation where 91 percent of medical students are already white and where we're trying to break down three centuries of segregation. With deepest sympathy for Mr. Bakke, I would decide against him. He invokes standards, namely grades, that have never been decisive to enrollment, and it's contrary to the national interest that they should now suddenly be made decisive. (9/26/77)

Few *Bakke* stories, however, viewed the case with such a sense of its complexity. The fact that whites were admitted with standardized scores below Bakke's would seem to be as relevant a fact as the reality that lower-scoring blacks were admitted. Yet broadcast references to the lower-scoring black admittees outnumbered references to lower-scoring whites by nearly nine to one. Bakke had been rejected twice by UC-Davis, suggesting, perhaps, that more was going on with his application than simply "reverse discrimination." This fact was mentioned only three times in network news stories. Indeed, during a two-year period Bakke had been rejected by twelve medical schools and had not received a single acceptance (Dreyfuss and Lawrence 1979: 9). This fact about the *Bakke* litigation was mentioned in two stories, both on NBC. The overwhelming impression left by the news broadcasts was extremely sympathetic to Bakke. Of the fifty-five substantive thematic case references we coded in *Bakke* stories, all but ten (18.2%) could be characterized as pro-Bakke in their orientation.

Utilizing the personage of Allan Bakke to focus on the issue of quotas and "less qualified" minorities was understandable for the network newscasts. The issues contained drama and controversy and, clearly, represent what television news seeks the most of and does best. Furthermore, divergence in standardized scores was an easy topic for journalists to portray in the news format. As Dreyfuss and Lawrence noted, "Considering the vague and ambiguous quality of most of the issues in the case, the numbers had a comforting solidity" (1979: 110). Yet to the extent that such reporting suggested that blacks admitted under the UC-Davis plan were "unqualified" (and, on balance, the reports appeared to do just that), news coverage misreported and misrepresented an important fact in the case. Indeed, Bakke's attorney Reynold Colvin simply did not pursue the claim that minorities admitted under the affirmative action program at UC-Davis were unqualified:

By the rules of litigation, therefore, in the absence of effective challenge at the trial court stage the "basic finding that everybody admitted under the special program was qualified" was established as the fact situation binding on the appellate courts, state and federal. (Sindler, 1978: 61–62)

Clearly, this basic "fact situation" went generally unreported on the network news, with seemingly important implications for public understanding of the *Bakke* case. As noted by Dreyfuss and Lawrence, "Many . . . preconscious assumptions can be found in the reporting on the *Bakke* case. 'Less qualified minorities' is a term that was not supported by any evidence . . . but that term followed the case from its early days to the morning of the Supreme Court's decision" (1979: 159).

In addition to the primary focus on Allan Bakke, television's fascination with the political angle of the case was also substantial as the Carter administration, through the Justice Department, struggled to define its position on the affirmative action issue in its amicus brief. Media interest in the government's position resulted in the Justice Department and its key officials serving as a focus in nearly one out of four (23.3%) *Bakke* stories, mostly during the period following the granting of certiorari (when the government brief was being prepared) and following the case decision (when government strategy for future litigation was developed). Similarly, the Congressional Black Caucus and its leader, Parren Mitchell, emerged as prominent players in one out of four (25.0%) *Bakke* stories, with references to the caucus particularly frequent as it sought to influence the government's amicus preparation.

The focus on the case in the context of this political story began about two months prior to oral argument, and reports fluctuated with what were, apparently, fluctuations in the administration's position. Thus, on August 23, 1977, John Chancellor reported on NBC that the Justice Department would probably argue on behalf of "reverse discrimination" even though this position works against some whites. The next day Tim O'Brien told ABC's viewers: "Preferential treatment has been likened to starting one controlled forest fire in order to bring another raging one under control. The Carter administration apparently accepts that philosophy." By September 12, 1977 (one month prior to oral argument), O'Brien was suggesting that "after weeks of haggling" the Justice Department brief endorsed affirmative action, but not UC-Davis's specific affirmative action program. In a considerably more "pro-Bakke" light, CBS News anchor Walter Cronkite stated, "President Carter apparently is going to come down against quotas to assure minority educational opportunity. . . . The Justice Department plans to support a California white man's argument before the Supreme Court that he was discriminated against because quotas for blacks kept him out of a California medical school. The Justice Department brief . . . reportedly says that race may be one of the factors the school considers in admitting students, but that rigid quotas violate the constitutional rights of whites." In all three network reports on September 12, the analysis focused on efforts by the Congressional Black Caucus to bring the brief closer in line with its anti–Bakke/pro–affirmative action stance.

One week later, the Justice Department brief was filed, and all three networks covered the story with CBS and NBC utilizing it to open their newscasts. The reports all documented the political struggles that preceded the final brief and characterized the outcome of these struggles. As reported by ABC's Tim O'Brien, "Only a week ago the administration opposed the specific California program but then came pressure from the Congressional Black Caucus which was pleased with the finished product" (9/19/77). CBS News opened its telecast with a strong and unequivocal statement by anchor Walter Cronkite: "The Carter administration today strongly endorsed the consideration of race as a factor in helping blacks and other minorities gain admission to colleges" (9/19/77). In the report that followed, Fred Graham outlined the nuances of the brief, noting that the Justice Department had shifted its support from Bakke after intense lobbying efforts by civil rights advocates, "and the final draft came out strongly for affirmative action" (9/19/77).

Coverage by NBC News of the filing of the government's brief was extensive and rife with political reportage from coanchors John Chancellor and David Brinkley as well as correspondents Judy Woodruff and Carl Stern. Alluding to the political machinations in the brief-preparation process, Brinkley commented, "Since the White House position on this touchy question could be politically and socially explosive, there was a good deal of discussion and argument over there before they settled on what they would say to the Court" (9/19/77). Developing further the White House angle, Judy Woodruff continued:

As soon as the public became aware of the original Justice Department brief, Cabinet members . . . screamed bloody murder. They spoke out against it . . . and there were loud objections from members of the president's own Domestic Council staff and from blacks and from civil rights organizations. The president agreed with them, and the Justice Department was directed to rewrite the brief as strongly as possible for affirmative action without going so far as to endorse racial quotas. (9/19/77)

So as not to let the political implications of the government's shift go unnoticed, Woodruff paraphrased a White House official who noted that the case "had enormous implications for the country as a whole and for Mr. Carter's political base. He said, 'If the brief had been filed as it was originally written, we'd be in bad shape.' It was clear that he meant with black voters" (9/19/77).

The networks' fascination with the government's amicus brief and its development was quite understandable. At bottom, it allowed reporters to cover a Supreme Court case in a fashion that eliminated many of the liabilities associated with reporting on the Court. By focusing on the White House and the Justice Department, sources could be used, political implications teased out, and drama heightened. This was now a story with a plot, intrigue, shifting tides, and winners and losers, angles clearly more suited to television coverage than legal arguments and actual court proceedings.

While the government brief story had much to say about politics and processes within the Carter administration, it could be argued that viewers of the news received an inflated picture of the government's role in the case and of the importance of the brief for the Court's ultimate judgment. In an effort to develop pieces that resulted in "good" television news, the networks had partially transformed a Supreme Court story into a presidential one. It even appears that the substantial attention focused on the brief may have had some consequences for executive branch–Supreme Court relations. According to Sindler, "Chief Justice Burger told Solicitor General [Wade] McCree that the entire Court 'was offended . . . by the numerous news leaks of early drafts of the brief [and] that the justices felt the resultant uproar had subjected them to improper public pressure when they were about to hear oral argument' in the case" (1978: 248).

Television's focus on the Justice Department's brief-writing troubles illustrated a broader contextual political focus that was present in a substantial number (41.7%) of *Bakke*-related stories, as the case was used to explore what might transpire in other affirmative action settings and what role the government might play in subsequent litigation. In addition, the case was often used as a baseline (23.3%) through which other cases being reported on could be better understood, particularly in the period after the *Bakke* ruling. *Bakke*'s service as a "divining rod" for examining other cases is somewhat curious since the decision itself had left so much unresolved about affirmative action, even in the context of medical school admissions programs, the specific setting of *Bakke*. Nevertheless, the prominence of the ruling and the extensive media attention to it rendered *Bakke* a natural link for television news efforts to examine the ongoing developments in this complex litigation setting.

Of considerable interest, outside of the aforementioned attention to the Justice Department and the Congressional Black Caucus, little television play was given to the extraordinarily rich and diverse structure of interest group support for Allan Bakke and UC-Davis that the case generated. More than one hundred organizations sponsored or endorsed amicus briefs in *Bakke*

(Sindler, 1978: 242), and the fifty-eight briefs filed represented the most the Court had ever received (Craig and O'Brien, 1993: 204). For the most part, however, the politics of group involvement in the *Bakke* case did not receive much treatment from television news, in stark contrast to the coverage that the *Webster* abortion case received, as we shall document. Only during a lengthy CBS News report (3:40) on the day before oral argument could a viewer gain some sense of the complex group struggle that was taking place under the litigation's surface. In his report, Fred Graham took note that more than 160 groups were involved in amicus briefs in the case, and on-camera interviews with representatives from the American Jewish Committee and the Leadership Conference on Civil Rights served to frame the opposing interest-group positions. Graham concluded, "The issue has created some strange constitutional bedfellows with normally liberal Jewish groups lining up with such conservative organizations as the Young Americans for Freedom in support of Bakke and with black groups uniformly against him" (10/11/77).

Finally, it should be underscored, our examination of the actors and the roles that they played in the presentation of the *Bakke* story on the television news reveals that Supreme Court litigation, in many respects, may not proceed as a story focused squarely on the Supreme Court. Indeed, all nine justices were identified only in stories broadcast on decision day, while only six additional references were made to individual justices across all other days the case was covered.

ADDITIONAL PATTERNS OF NEWS COVERAGE:
THE *WEBSTER* CASE

In many respects, the patterns of coverage and the actors featured in television news reporting on *Webster* can be seen as graphically different from the treatment accorded *Bakke*. Detailed consideration of *Webster,* however, reveals that it, too, was covered in a manner that best structured the story line for television newscasts. First, it should be noted that *Webster* did not present the networks with a central dramatic figure, such as Allan Bakke, around whom a "plot line" could be anchored. Consequently, newscast attention to the actual litigants in the case was relatively minimal. Broad references to the fact that the case involved Missouri or Missouri legislation appeared in sixteen stories (26.7%). William Webster, Missouri's Attorney General whose name appeared on the lawsuit was, unlike Bakke, not known for his aversion to television cameras or coverage. Nevertheless, mention of Webster (who lacked any "human interest" link to the case) only surfaced in six (10.0%) stories. The primary litigant on the other side, Reproductive Health Services, a nonprofit clinic, also failed to provide a central focus for case coverage and was identified in only eight (13.3%) stories. Some attention was cast on B. J. Isaacson-Jones, the clinic's director, in seven (11.7%) stories, but she was generally presented as a spokesperson for the broad pro-choice position without being tied directly to the *Webster* litigation setting.

In the absence of television-worthy litigants (like Bakke) around whom *Webster* could be presented, the case became a vehicle through which television portrayed the ongoing societal battle of two well-organized political forces, the "pro-life" and "freedom-of-choice" camps in the American polity. Our analysis included an effort to gauge the primary substantive focus of each *Webster* story, and six (10.0%) were found to center predominantly on demonstrations featuring pro- and anti-choice forces airing their views both before and after the *Webster* ruling. More graphically, five out of six (83.3%) *Webster* stories included some consideration of the group activities and support systems activated on both sides of the litigation, with the group struggle generally far overshadowing attention paid to the specifics of the *Webster* case.

Thus, for example, on the day of oral argument NBC's Tom Brokaw led off the evening's newscast with dramatic flair:

A historic day at the Supreme Court. . . . This is one of those days that may deserve bold print in the front of future history books. The day when two powerful but opposing forces converged on the U.S. Supreme Court. One determined to change the nation's abortion law, the other equally determined to keep it as it is.

Describing the scene with commensurate color, Carl Stern, too, underscored the group struggle and drama the *Webster* case reflected on the day of argument: "In a frenzied eleventh-hour effort to preserve abortion rights pro-choice demonstrators massed illegally on the courthouse steps. . . . The Supreme Court mail room has been averaging fifteen thousand letters a day" (NBC News, 4/26/89). Lisa Myers concluded that "the only thing on which both sides agree is that regardless of what the Court decides, the abortion battle will escalate. They say it's like the Civil War. There is no suitable middle ground" (NBC News, 4/26/89). ABC's Tim O'Brien reported that "the Supreme Court appeared to be under siege this morning [with] opponents of abortion shoulder to shoulder with abortion rights advocates chanting" (4/26/89). Days later Scott Pelley reported in his coverage of abortion demonstrations, "The protests come as the Supreme Court considers a Missouri case that could overturn the 1973 ruling legalizing abortion. . . . [W]hatever the Court decides, it is not likely to settle the issue in the streets of America" (CBS News, 4/29/89). As the calendar moved closer to the expected decision day, NBC's Jim Cummins underscored further that a ruling would not be likely, by any means, to settle the issue:

The President of the Unitarian Church today declared his congregation's willingness to defy the Supreme Court if the Court reverses its 1973 decision legalizing abortion. . . . Universalist Church members will be ready to take women anywhere they have to, to obtain safe abortions. In the meantime, members of a group opposed to abortion say they're also willing to defy the law of the land and continue clogging jails if they have to. (6/24/89)

On the eve of the decision, ABC's Tim O'Brien reported from the Court, "This is the eye of the storm. . . . Tranquil tonight but a ruling is expected tomorrow on abortion – a ruling many believe is more likely to elevate this highly charged debate than it is to solve it" (7/2/89). And, on decision day, it was confirmed that the Court merely contributed to but did not bring to an end the ongoing political struggle. In the words of ABC News anchor Barry Serafin, "Only one side was declaring victory after today's ruling, but both sides were declaring war" (7/3/89). The next day, CBS's law correspondent Rita Braver added, "The passions unleashed by yesterday's abortion decision exploded today on the streets of America" (7/4/89).

Numerous "one-shot" players representing several national organizations and their local affiliates found themselves featured and interviewed on the national news in discussions of the abortion debate. More prominently, several key players emerged as animated protagonists appearing often on newscasts to fill the void left by the relatively mundane *Webster* litigants. Indeed, the most frequently appearing player in *Webster* stories was Kate Michelman of the National Abortion Rights Action League (NARAL), who, while not a direct party in the litigation, was present in one out of three (20) *Webster* stories. Other spokespersons in support of the pro-choice position were, as noted above, B. J. Isaacson-Jones, Molly Yard of the National Organization for Women (NOW) (9, 15.0%), and Norma McCorvey (the "Jane Roe" of *Roe v. Wade*), who appeared in six (10.0%) *Webster* stories. (McCorvey, it should be noted, has since altered her abortion stance and, more often than not, is found among the pro-life forces in ongoing television attention to the abortion issue.)

The primary opposition to the freedom-of-choice position was most often articulated by Susan Smith, National Right to Life Committee spokesperson who appeared in nine stories (15.0%), Randall Terry of Operation Rescue who appeared in six (10.0%), and prominent pro-life doctor and National Right to Life Committee head John Wilke who appeared in five (8.3%) newscasts. Also playing an important "supporting" role in *Webster* coverage was President Bush, whose appearance in nine (15.0%) stories buttressed the attack on *Roe*. Frequent stand-ins for the president included Attorney General Richard Thornburgh (4, 6.7%), Chief of Staff John Sununu (3, 5.0%) and former Solicitor General Charles Fried (3, 5.0%), who presented the government's position in oral argument in *Webster*. Frank Susman, who argued the case for Reproductive Health Services, appeared in five (8.3%) stories.

Significantly distinguishing *Webster* coverage from that of *Bakke* was the more prominent role played by the members of the Court. Thus, all nine justices were referenced in four stories (6.7%), while individual justices appeared on news reports with some frequency. Sandra Day O'Connor led the way (9, 15.0%), followed by Anthony Kennedy (8, 13.3%), Antonin Scalia (7, 11.7%), Harry Blackmun and William Rehnquist (4, 6.7%), and Byron White (3, 5.0%). There are a number of reasons why greater attention was placed on the justices in *Webster* than in *Bakke*. First, *Webster* arose in the context of a line of cases in which several justices had staked out well-defined positions on abortion, and, consequently, the justices served as actors on whom the drama centered and predictions about the case outcome could be fashioned. Second, some justices held particular interest for journalists in *Webster* because of their identification with *Roe* (Blackmun) or their gender (O'Connor). Finally, personnel changes on the Court, particularly the recent appointment of Anthony Kennedy, gave the media new opportunities to speculate on the possibility that *Roe* might be overturned.

Of further note, in addition to illuminating battles in society and battles on the Court, *Webster* also became a catalyst for examining ongoing struggles in the political arena. Indeed, 80 percent (48) of the *Webster* stories placed the case in a political context, and more than one out of four stories (17, 28.3%) were coded as focusing primarily on the political implications of the case. Thus, *Webster* was often utilized to illuminate electoral contests among candidates (particularly in state elections) who differed on the abortion issue as well as a motivating force behind new efforts in several state legislatures to curtail the scope of freedom of choice. Such a focus surfaced in some of the earliest *Webster* stories such as in a CBS News piece reported by Susan Spencer weeks before oral argument. Spencer noted, "Both sides do agree that if the Court overturns *Roe v. Wade*, the battle will be fought in fifty state legislatures almost constantly. In other words, no one sees an end to this highly emotional fight" (4/7/89).

Utilization of a political context was particularly evident in the wake of the Court's decision, which appeared to throw much of the responsibility for defining the scope of abortion rights back to the states and to the ballot box. NBC's Jaimie Gangell reported in her day-after story that "activists on both sides . . . have vowed to make abortion a key issue in state and local elections. . . . [P]oliticians predict confusion as each state now tries to shape its own laws and cover elections, as each side targets political races with a whole new sense of purpose" (7/4/89). On CBS News, anchor Connie Chung took note that "pro- and antiabortion forces. . . . took to the streets believing now more than ever before the issue is a political one to be fought at the ballot box." The story included NARAL's Kate Michelman, who announced, "We can no longer depend on the Court to protect our rights. It now depends on our votes. And we intend to take that message immediately into the political races we are targeting for 1989." New Jersey's gubernatorial election was illuminated as a prime battleground, as correspondent Richard Roth added, "Garbage disposal and transportation, and the high cost of insurance were the issues people were asking about and politicians were talking about in New Jersey's gubernatorial campaign until the Supreme Court spoke on abortion" (7/4/89). The race between a pro–choice (Jim Florio) and a pro–life (James Courter) candidate was a primary focus in four stories on the national news tied to the *Webster* ruling.

Later in the summer, a special election to fill a vacancy in California's State Assembly was characterized as "a referendum on abortion rights" by ABC News anchor Sam Donaldson, with correspondent Bonnie Strauss adding that "abortion will be the center of thousands of legislative contests in 1990" (8/8/89). As the regularly scheduled general election drew nearer, CBS anchor Dan Rather introduced a story on state abortion battles by noting, "Beyond the abortion policy split in Washington, the battle over abortion law is being waged now state by state and increasingly as a political campaign issue – all a consequence of last July's Supreme Court ruling making it easier for states to impose new abortion restrictions" (10/13/89).

In addition to *Webster*'s implications for electoral contests, substantive legislative battles in the states became a prime postdecision focus. Two days after the decision, NBC's Lisa Myers reported that "pro-choice activists are discouraged about the short-term political outlook. They realize that quick action to restrict abortion is likely in a number of states. . . . Both sides predict a long and difficult battle in almost all states, and they agree that the situation in most states will be chaotic" (7/5/89). When Pennsylvania became the first state to consider new restrictive legislation, Dan Rather took note of "new fallout from the U.S. Supreme Court's ruling last July, making it easier for states to restrict abortions. . . . The state legislature [in Pennsylvania] . . . will be the first in the nation to consider new and sweeping abortion restrictions. The first, but by no means, the last" (10/3/89). Florida Governor Bob Martinez's actions became the focus of several stories examining his efforts to seize the leeway that *Webster* appeared to create by calling a special legislative session to write a new restrictive abortion law. Indeed, NBC News treated the story as its lead on October 10, 1989.

Rounding out the substantive foci that dominated *Webster* coverage, eight stories (13.3%) centered on anticipating the ruling and, as amplified below, joined numerous other stories in including a predictive component in forecasting the case's outcome and implications. An additional six stories (10.0%) placed *Webster* in the context of the anniversary of *Roe v. Wade*, drawing the obvious connection between the two cases. Thus, in observing *Roe*'s anniversary a few weeks after certiorari had been granted in *Webster*, CBS's Lynn Brown reported, "This year's anniversary comes at a crucial time in the abortion controversy. The Supreme Court has agreed to hear arguments on a Missouri law that could restrict or even reverse the 1973 decision" (1/21/89).

At bottom, *Bakke* had served primarily as a palate for examining one man's quest for justice and a presidential administration's difficulties in articulating a position on the broader issue the case represented; *Webster* served broadly as a vehicle through which to examine ongoing political battles in the legislative arena and at the ballot box, an opportunity for two large-scale and well-organized political interests to wage their policy struggle, and a case setting through which the Court might resolve its own differences and alter the delicate balance of power on the abortion issue. In large part, these differences reflected the relative state of maturation of the underlying substantive issues and the political context in the two cases, with *Bakke* representing the Court's first attempt to grapple with the merits of a controversial frontier issue of enormous importance in the American polity, whereas *Webster* reflected the Court's continuing attempt to deal with an issue that had a relatively long litigation history and that was part of a long-term policy controversy in American politics.

"SPIN DOCTORING" THE NEWS: THE *BAKKE* CASE

Much of what the public might glean about a Supreme Court decision's importance, implications, and impact could be influenced by predictions and assertions made on network newscasts. Our analysis included consideration of such speculation about *Bakke* throughout all facets of its processing and revealed a rich array of such observations by interview subjects in twenty-seven stories (45.0%) and by newscasters themselves in thirty stories (50.0%) touching on the case.

When news reports contain predictions about a case's importance as seen through the eyes of interested parties, it is likely that the viewing public will take them with a grain of salt. Nevertheless, viewers were subjected to numerous perspectives underlying *Bakke*'s importance and, in many instances, making dire predictions about untoward consequences that could follow from the ruling. A sample of predictions about *Bakke* made by various interested parties offers a flavor of what the viewing public was told as the case progressed:

An adverse decision . . . will have horrendous impact on affirmative action programs not only in terms of education but in a spillout into other areas. (Parren Mitchell on NBC News, 9/12/77)

"If the *Bakke* case is upheld, qualified blacks will be bypassed." In their view and those of millions of others in their environment, there is no middle ground in the *Bakke* case. It is to them like the plug in the dam separating a white and black America, and if *Bakke* is upheld by the Court, they fear racial gains of the era will be swept away by a white society now ready to withdraw from its earlier commitment. (ABC News, quoting UC-Davis medical student Tony Chavis, 10/3/77)

I think it's very hard to see how an affirmance of the California court could fail to impair and certainly cut way back, perhaps destroy, affirmative action programs of all kinds. (Archibald Cox on NBC News, 10/12/77)

Curiously, until the actual day of the ruling only Reynold Colvin, Bakke's attorney, was heard as a cautionary voice on the pending case. On the day of oral argument, he was quoted on both ABC and NBC News:

We have never taken the position that this is a landmark case or the most important case of any kind. We believe this is a case where an individual's rights have been deprived. We think the United States Supreme Court can affirm the California decision, protect Mr. Bakke's rights, and that it can do so without making tremendous changes in the progress that has been made in this country. (10/12/77)

On decision day (6/28/78), a wide-ranging set of outsiders' perspectives on *Bakke* was presented across all three networks. Included were the views of Colvin, the president of the University of California system, UC-Davis medical students, Carter administration officials Griffin Bell and Joseph Califano, legal experts Philip Kurland and Robert Bork, interest group spokespersons, principals from other pending affirmative action cases such as Brian Weber and a Kaiser Aluminum spokesperson, and a myriad of civil rights leaders including Parren Mitchell, Jesse Jackson, Coretta Scott King, Benjamin Hooks, Julian Bond, and Joseph Lowery. Interviews and commentary on the meaning of *Bakke* ran the policy gamut from A to Z and, all told, twenty-one different players were called on across the three networks to comment on *Bakke*'s meaning and implications.

It is noteworthy, perhaps, that some of the most "restrained" *Bakke* commentaries came from the case participants themselves. Allan Bakke had gone to great pains to steer clear of media attention throughout the litigation process, and decision day would be no exception. On ABC, Bakke's "pleasure" with the ruling was alluded to, while in a brief CBS telephone interview Bakke stated simply, "I'm pleased with the decision, and that's all I intend to say about it. My own personal life is private, and I intend to keep it that way." As he had throughout the litigation, Bakke's attorney Reynold Colvin refused to amplify the importance or the policy consequences of a case he continued to characterize as that of an individual seeking redress of a grievance.

For David Saxon, president of the UC system, the task was one of damage control and accentuation of the positive. He conceded that the UC-Davis Medical School would have to alter its admissions processes, but he underlined that other schools would have to change less drastically or, indeed, not at all. Putting the decision in its best light, he declared:

I think the most important thing about this decision is that it overrules the California courts with respect to the affirmative use of race. That is a great victory for those who are seeking to provide through affirmative action greater social justice than has been possible in the past. (ABC News)

For the U.S. government the task was one of assessing the ruling while avoiding the confusion surrounding the preparation of the Carter administration's vacillating amicus brief. The government's measured support for the *Bakke* ruling reflected its unsettled posture throughout the litigation process as Attorney General Griffin Bell stumbled through similar terrain in his comments on all three networks: "I think the bottom line was to confirm what we thought the law was. It confirms our position and what we've been doing about affirmative action programs. The president was pleased that the affirmative action position that we took was upheld" (ABC News).

The reception to the *Bakke* ruling in the civil rights community received, understandably, extensive coverage across all three networks, and on each newscast a mixed portrait was painted of the decision's meaning from a civil rights perspective. Jesse Jackson's sweeping comments on ABC News would emerge as the most distraught and ideological in tone among the civil rights spokespersons surveyed:

I think that between the punitive effect of Proposition 13, rising unemployment, and now the *Bakke* case, the black community really has its back up against the wall, and it must come out with a commitment to massive, disciplined struggle.

Coretta Scott King was asked on ABC News how Martin Luther King Jr. would have viewed the decision. She replied, "I'm disappointed, and I'm sure he would have been disappointed. . . . [B]ut I don't feel that it's a total defeat."

Emphasizing the Court's broader holding on affirmative action, Congressional Black Caucus Chairman Parren Mitchell noted, "Obviously we would have preferred a decision not in favor of Bakke. I think that we would be remiss as members of this caucus to push the panic button, to give a false interpretation of this Court decision, so that it becomes our job to get the gospel out around this country that affirmative action has, in essence, been upheld" (ABC News). Vernon Jordan added, "This decision struck down the process by which Bakke was denied admission, and that is all. It is a limited, narrow decision dealing with the process at the University of California at Davis."

Spokespersons for other interests beyond the American civil rights leadership would also have their say on the meaning and implications of *Bakke* on the evening newscasts. A radical view of the ruling was offered by a black UC-Davis medical student: "Obviously . . . we won't have a minority admissions program. We won't have any kind of . . . program . . . to enlist and recruit students from lower socioeconomic backgrounds any longer" (ABC News). More positive assessments of the decision were offered from more conservative reactors. The American Jewish Committee's Sam Rabinove noted, "It has been our view that quotas have tended to undermine and discredit legitimate affirmative action," while Clifford White of the Young Americans for Freedom went further to say that "the decision was only the first step toward elimination of affirmative action programs" (CBS News). Balancing that perspective, Walter Cronkite reported on the same newscast that the Association of American Medical Colleges was "relieved" to have a decision and guidelines. The association was reported to have said, "We are pleased that the majority of the Court accepts the use of race as one element in the selection of students."

Given the myriad of voices that viewers heard on decision day, it would be remarkable for anyone to have come away from the decision with a clear understanding of what the case actually meant. Yet, in several respects, the complex nature of the *Bakke* holding did, indeed, make this a reasonable and acceptable posture.

While the views of interested parties in *Bakke* could play a role in how the case was perceived by television viewers, it is, perhaps, even more important to assess the predictions and assertions made by the network newscasters themselves. Their reports, unlike those of many interviewees, might be perceived as more credible and untainted by the viewing public. Analysis of what the newscasters said about the case demonstrates clearly that television journalists did, indeed, play the role of "spin doctors," often making sweeping statements about the case and its potential importance.

Interestingly, some of the earliest assertions made by reporters proved to be the most balanced and cautious. For example, in the first piece from CBS News (12/14/96) Fred Graham forecasted accurately that a defeat for UC-Davis need not spell the end of affirmative action: "If the university loses in the Supreme Court, they will probably create a new quota system for disadvantaged students, including whites, but with some sort of edge given to nonwhites." While the words *quota system* were, perhaps, ill-chosen, the Graham piece foreshadowed the legitimacy of approaches such as the Harvard Plan (discussed at length in the *Bakke* decision) for admission. Graham would repeat his prophecy of moderation the day before oral argument when he predicted with stunning accuracy the decision and the likely impact of the ruling the Court would render more than eight months later:

Many observers now believe that the Supreme Court is most likely to take a middle ground: upholding affirmative action . . . but declaring unconstitutional rigid quotas which exclude all whites. If so, this could lead to years of litigation to determine which affirmative action programs are legal and which unconstitutional. (10/11/77)

The tone of many newscaster assertions about the *Bakke* proceedings would prove to be considerably less temperate. For example, Howard K. Smith introduced an ABC News story (8/24/77) by stating, "The case now before the Court is considered to be as important to civil rights as the 1954 decision in which the Court outlawed separate–but–equal school facilities." The analogy being drawn to *Brown v. Board of Education* would be repeated on six additional *Bakke* stories. Picking up on Smith's theme, Tim O'Brien continued, "His suit has touched off a major debate and threatens the future of thousands of similar minority programs across the country."

On October 12, 1977, the day of oral argument, newscaster predictions about the case loomed quite large. Harry Reasoner opened ABC's newscast: "One of the most important civil rights cases in two decades, the Allan Bakke reverse discrimination suit, was argued before the Supreme Court today." Correspondent Tim O'Brien reported the presence of "an overflow crowd for what could be one of the most important civil rights cases ever," while his colleague Tom Jarriel concluded, "This is one man and one school and one case. But the decision of the justices . . . could determine the national attitude towards promoting minorities in all aspects of life." Howard K. Smith's commentary placed the case in its broadest and most expansive context:

What they finally rule in this case will deeply affect the root nature of our society. . . . One can recall no harder decision to make in the Court's whole record. One can only pray for courage and wisdom above their norm in the nine honest men who know they're deciding, as much as Jefferson did, what kind of nation we want to be.

CBS News's oral argument coverage included Walter Cronkite's assertion that *Bakke* could lead to the Court's "most important civil rights ruling in two decades." Eric Sevareid's commentary continued, "The nine judges must try to resolve a historic dilemma, and whatever the resolution, historic consequences will flow from it. . . . Today's *Bakke* case was as inevitable and is as significant as the school desegregation cases of the early '50s."

Oral argument was the lead story on NBC News, and several prognosticators mirrored what was being said on the other networks. Law correspondent Carl Stern noted that "by daybreak there were hundreds of people waiting to hear what may be the most important civil rights case since segregation was outlawed in the 1950s." Coanchor John Chancellor's comments were cautiously expansive:

The question is, and nobody's sure, will the *Bakke* case make it to that Hall of Fame of great cases which changed the interpretation of the Constitution – cases like *Dred Scott* or *Marbury v. Madison,* or *Brown v. Board of Education* which changed the face of integration in this country.

Whatever network one was watching on the day of oral argument, it would be impossible to be blind to the strong possibility that something of extraordinary importance was happening at the Supreme Court that could have enormous and untold consequences for the future of American society.

Interestingly, two networks (CBS and NBC) pulled back somewhat from their oral argument posture less than a week later when the Court sought briefs addressing the application of the Civil Rights Act to *Bakke.* In both instances, the stories were reported cursorily by the news anchor and lacked prominence on the newscast. Thus, Walter Cronkite concluded a twenty-second piece touching on several Court-worthy news items by adding, "The justices also indicated that their forthcoming ruling in the *Bakke* reverse discrimination case may not be the landmark which had been expected. They ordered all parties in the case to submit written arguments as to how the 1964 Civil Rights Act might apply. This suggests the ruling may be based on law, not the Constitution" (CBS, 10/17/77). This legal distinction, without an accompanying explanation, was likely to be lost on most viewers.

NBC News also reported the Court's action through anchor John Chancellor on a minute-long potpourri spot labeled "Briefly":

The Supreme Court is asking for comments on the idea that the *Bakke* reverse discrimination case might come under the Civil Rights Act of 1964. If that's a clue to the Court's thinking, its ruling in the *Bakke* case might be less sweeping than some had hoped. (10/17/77)

This speculation was wedged between mention of the government's refusal to ban saccharin and a comment on the failure of chimp heart transplants in humans.

Few additional *Bakke* stories between oral argument and decision day speculated about the case, with some simply raising expectations that a decision would be handed down shortly. When decision day (6/28/78) arrived and the

Court's ruling was both less expansive and definitive than might have been expected, newscasters were forced to pull in the reins a bit. On ABC News, Tim O'Brien commented, "The ruling is not likely to be regarded as a defeat for minorities. While the Court is placing limits on the kinds of affirmative action programs it will uphold, the principle of giving special consideration on the basis of race has withstood a substantial challenge." Looking ahead to the pending *Weber* case, however, Betina Gregory erroneously speculated, "The *Bakke* decision may not displace quotas in the job field, but it apparently threatens them. The Supreme Court has yet to rule in this area, but legal experts say that the *Bakke* decision has started a trend towards striking down laws that require specific racial quotas or even laws that require specific numbers of jobs to be set aside for minority group workers." Not only was the *Weber* outcome (as well as the immediate future of affirmative action litigation) forecast incorrectly, but the report confusingly mixed the issues of private voluntary programs and governmental mandates.

The "last word" on the meaning of *Bakke* in ABC's decision day coverage came in the form of a commentary report by Howard K. Smith that put the day's events into much-needed perspective. Smith asserted that confusion in reporting inevitably flows from confusion in the Court's decision itself:

Never was explanation so needed as in the *Bakke* ruling of today. Of the nine members of the Court, six had differing opinions. . . . In this case theoretically everybody should be happy. Bakke, a clearly high-grade candidate wins admission . . . yet it remains all right for future Bakkes to be rejected in favor of . . . blacks who have suffered from past discrimination. The case is resolved, but the principle on which depends our achieving a race-neutral America remains confused. However, the Court will have plenty of chances to think some more about that. . . . Today . . . the Court said simply we are just as confused as you ordinary humans are.

The underlying theme of CBS News's speculation about *Bakke*'s meaning was that it left much unresolved and would lead to considerable litigation. Fred Graham commented, "The result of today's decision is that affirmative action programs at universities are illegal when they use rigid racial quotas. . . . But such programs can be legal when they give nonwhites an edge so long as race is not decisive in ruling out white applicants." As a practical matter, Graham added, "These principles are difficult to apply in practice, and they will apparently also apply in such areas as employment and the granting of government contracts. So there will apparently have to be many more court cases before a definitive line can be drawn between those affirmative action programs that are legal and those that are illegal." NBC's decision-day coverage continued on a similarly cautious, speculative tone. Correspondent Carl Stern reported that "what happened at the University of California may not end special admissions programs, but it will redefine the rules."

Decision day also brought with it the use of legal experts who added their voices to the assessments being made in the case by partisans, interested parties, and network correspondents. While in no sense "disinterested" observers, constitutional law professor Philip Kurland of the University of Chicago was interviewed on ABC and CBS, and Yale Law School's Robert Bork was also heard on CBS. While NBC eschewed the use of "outside" legal counsel, they did interview their own law correspondent, attorney Carl Stern, about the decision's importance. The general posture in these efforts was to synthesize the lines in the story, underscore that the story was not over, and bring a voice of caution to the overall assessment. Kurland's effort on CBS did the trick nicely:

This, like several other decisions of the Supreme Court, has been exaggerated in its importance and the expectation of its conclusions. The press and the bar and the academics have built this up into the closest thing to the delivery of the Ten Commandments that has occurred since that time. It should not have been expected that it was going to be that. One of the problems was, of course, that the partisans have exaggerated the expected results if it went one way or the other. The proposition that this has dealt a death blow to all affirmative action programs is, I think, nonsense. The government invited this kind of overbroad reading by coming in and saying that if the Court ruled in favor of Bakke, some seventeen or eighteen governmental programs would go down the drain. I expect that they don't take that position anymore, and they shouldn't have taken it in the first place.

Robert Bork added, "On the whole it's a decision which is unstable, and the struggles that come afterwards are likely to be much more important than the decision itself."

After decision day, speculation about the importance of *Bakke* tended simply to suggest that it had implications for future litigation. Amplification of the case's importance was eschewed and, instead, a moderating tone prevailed. Note, for example, the comments of NBC's John Chancellor at the conclusion of the Court's term:

The Supreme Court is now on vacation after a busy session. The *Bakke* decision got the headlines, but what may have a more lasting impact is the Court's decision that police can get a search warrant without a prior Court hearing to search a place where no crime has been committed for evidence of a crime committed somewhere else – for example, maybe search a newspaper office. (7/7/78)

The final journalistic predictions about *Bakke* in the time frame under study were pronounced when the *Weber* case was granted certiorari (12/11/78). At that juncture ABC's Tom Jarriel stated, "It's believed the Court's ruling in this case may have even more far-reaching effects than the *Bakke* decision of last summer." Tim O'Brien added that *Weber* "involves employment, and more people stand to be affected. In the *Bakke* case the Court upheld the principle of affirmative action, but it gave little guidance as to what specific kind of program it would allow. So the real issue in the *Weber* case is not whether employers may give preference on the basis of race, but when they do it and how they may do it." In a similar vein Walter Cronkite noted in a CBS News lead story on the *Weber* certiorari grant that "the decision could be far more reaching than the *Bakke* ruling, striking down rigid racial quotas for school admissions." David Brinkley offered a similar introduction on NBC's lead story on television's new featured case: "The *Weber* case it's called, and it may come to be more famous and more important than the *Bakke* case since, of course, far more people work than apply for graduate school."

In a sense, speculation about *Bakke* had come full circle, and a new emotionally laden case was gearing up to take its place. In the period leading up to the *Bakke* ruling much speculation by newscasters served to heighten the drama and the possible importance of the case. Television was doing what it does best. When the decision was announced, it failed to live up to much of its advanced billing. At this juncture, television news did not miss a beat. While admitting that *Bakke* did not live up to expectations, it was, nevertheless, utilized to place the remaining issues and cases in appropriate context. When certiorari was granted in *Weber,* speculation about that case's importance mirrored the image of *Bakke* past. The cycle was beginning anew.

"SPIN DOCTORING" THE NEWS: THE *WEBSTER* CASE

Even more so than *Bakke,* the *Webster* case provided unusual grist for the media's speculative mill, both with regard to prognostications from interview subjects as well as television journalists themselves. For, unlike *Bakke, Webster* arose in the context of an issue area surrounded by substantial case law and the clear possibility that the Court's landmark decision in *Roe v. Wade* was about to be overturned. This possibility was played out in a setting with well-organized interest groups eager to utilize the media to "sell" their position to the public and, perhaps, the Court as well. Speculative comments about the case and its implications from interview subjects were included in more than half the stories (53.3%), while newscasters made such observations in more than three quarters (76.7%) of the stories broadcast. In nearly nine out of ten stories (87.0%), we found explicit reference to the possibility that *Roe* would be overturned in *Webster*, clearly the dominant theme in framing the case's importance on network newscasts. In addition to stories about the fate of *Roe*, interview subjects (much like the newscasters) offered their thoughts on the likely legal impact of *Webster*, its broader human impact, and the role that it would play in legislative battles and ongoing electoral contests in the states.

Among the interview subjects consulted on newscasts, NARAL's Kate Michelman weighed in most heavily and often on the precarious status of the *Roe* precedent, referring to *Webster* as "without a doubt the most serious threat to reproductive choice in America in decades" (ABC News and CBS News, 1/9/89). Among those concurring with Michelman was Sarah Weddington, the attorney who had argued *Roe* before the Supreme Court: "I am quite concerned about the Missouri case because until I can count five votes on the U.S. Supreme Court in favor of *Roe v. Wade*, I am going to worry" (CBS News, 1/21/89).

Coming at *Roe* from the opposite camp, Attorney General Richard Thornburgh responded to a query about his expectations in *Webster*: "My guess is that they will return the regulation of abortion, like many health and safety questions, to the states" (ABC News, 1/22/89). Interestingly, just as Bakke's attorney had been a voice of moderation in his speculations in the earlier case, Michael Boicourt, an Assistant Attorney General working on *Webster* for Missouri, was less willing to call for an expansive holding and saw no need to overturn *Roe*: "We don't believe that any of the statutes we're asking the Supreme Court to review really affect or impede the availability of abortion to such an extent that there is any reason to suggest that result" (ABC News, 1/9/89). As decision day neared and outside expertise was sought to predict the Court's holding, Boicourt's position would be echoed by Robert Bork: "Justice O'Connor has written opinions recently saying that you don't overrule wrong decisions unless it is absolutely essential to reach the correct result in this case.

Now you can uphold the Missouri statute in whole or in part without over-turning *Roe v. Wade*" (ABC News, 6/25/89).

Many individuals were utilized on broadcasts to comment on the case's potential human and political impact as well as its likely legal consequences. The human drama fanned by *Webster* was tapped most graphically by reactions to the ruling broadcast on decision day. On ABC News (7/3/89), viewers were told by Patricia Ireland of NOW that "this decision which I hold in my hand is dangerous, it's divisive, and it could be deadly." Norma McCorvey, "Jane Roe" from an earlier day, noted that "poor women are going to be suffering again as they were before the 1973 decision." Judith Witticomb, the founder of Reproductive Health Services, the clinic involved in *Webster*, opined, "This is literally the beginning of war. And this is going to become our Vietnam of the '90s. The people will take to the streets. The people will make their voices known." After decision day, some coverage continued to center on the human impact of the ruling, a focus best pursued in an extended story (4:10) on CBS News six weeks after *Webster* (8/15/89). The story centered on the realities, not legalities, of the post-*Webster* environment. As Bob Schieffer reported, "Even without changes in state law, doctors are coming under increasing pressure from antiabortion groups, and it's becoming increasingly difficult for women in some parts of the country to get an abortion." Underscoring the thrust of her report, Susan Spencer added, "As the battle heats up over new restrictions, even more doctors are likely to decide abortion is too hot to handle and, in rural America at least, that option may be left, as it once was, only to those who can afford to travel and pay." On NBC News, Lisa Myers documented that the Missouri legislature was having unexpected difficulty in the wake of *Webster* in passing even more restrictive legislation while, as a practical matter, women in Missouri were experiencing great difficulty in traveling to neighboring Nebraska to obtain more readily accessible abortions. Myers commented, "Both sides predicted that the Missouri law would have profound consequences. But as it turns out, what was predicted and what has actually happened are very different" (1/20/90).

The prospects for state legislative battles brought on by *Webster* discussed earlier were referenced in stories broadcast well before the actual decision, such as in news consultant Harrison Hickman's forecast on NBC's coverage of oral argument (4/26/89): "I don't think people have really been able to fathom the magnitude of lobbying and political unrest and political pressure.

It will clearly be the most dramatic social issue they've had to handle at the state legislature level since civil rights."

Most discussion of the legislative fights to come by interview subjects, however, came in the context of decision-day coverage where the debate was framed by the opposing sides. As noted by John Wilke of the National Right to Life Committee, "We invite the states, and we'll be working with them, to pass new legislation at the invitation of the Court. . . . We are smiling, our thumbs are up, and we feel that a new era is dawning" (CBS News, 7/3/89). On the same newscast, Planned Parenthood's Roger Evans was not smiling as he contemplated the message that *Webster* was characterized as sending to the state legislatures: "They said, 'Go further and go further until you present us with a case where we have to explicitly overrule *Roe.*'"

Newscasters, too, offered a number of comments about what the decision meant for state legislatures. On CBS News Susan Spencer commented in great detail:

Just the last two years at the state level some 250 different bills on abortion have been introduced. But given today's nod from the Supreme Court, that could soon seem like nothing. The fifty state capitals are the new battleground now and, within hours of the ruling, the battle had been joined. . . . Some of that new legislation is likely to be even more restrictive than the Missouri law as antiabortion groups test the limits of the Court's ruling. . . . [We] could see a patchwork of laws around the country, potentially fifty different sets of rules and regulations in fifty different states. One side calls that democracy. The other side calls it chaos. (7/3/89)

In addition to taking the battle to the floors of state legislatures, the *Webster* litigation was also credited with moving the fight to the polls by those interviewed on evening newscasts. Here, again, Kate Michelman of NARAL often served as the prognosticator, both before and after the Court's ruling. Michelman noted on an ABC News piece previewing *Webster* that if *Roe* were overturned, "there would be a political firestorm all across the country. Social chaos. This would be a dominant issue in every state legislative race, 7,461 of them all across the country" (4/25/89). The next day, Michelman asserted in NBC's story on oral argument, "The cards are going to change on this issue. It's no longer going to be acceptable for a politician to be antichoice. He or she will lose his or her seat" (4/26/89). Michelman also echoed these themes on decision day: "To politicians who oppose choice we say, 'Read our lips.' Take our rights, lose your job" (CBS and NBC News, 7/3/89). In the wake of the ruling she added, "When the pro-choice majority begins to vote and begins to flex its political muscle, the antichoice forces won't know what hit them, and politicians won't know what hit them either" (ABC News, 7/4/89). "We can no longer depend on the Court to protect our rights. It now depends on our votes. And we intend to take that message immediately into the political races we are targeting for 1989" (CBS News, 7/4/89).

Newscasters, too, were ready to point out the likely impact of the *Webster* litigation on electoral politics, especially after the decision had been rendered. On decision day, ABC's Chris Bury opined, "The two sides agree on very little but this. Abortion will now become a dominant factor in every campaign for every seat in the statehouse" (7/3/89). In a similar vein Lisa Myers reported after the ruling that

within minutes it was clear that abortion is likely to be the dominant issue in state races this year and next. . . . Pro-choice forces will try to convert the anger and fear generated by today's decision into political power in upcoming elections. . . . For sixteen years, the Supreme Court enabled state legislators to duck the issue. Today, that ended. Both sides agreed that abortion may now become the most emotional and divisive domestic issue since civil rights. (7/3/89)

In the lead story from CBS News the day after the ruling, Connie Chung underscored that "candidates for office now have reason to fear their political lives will rise or fall on the abortion question" (7/4/89), a theme present in many news stories.

Decision day, as we have seen, gave numerous players (thirty all told, including twenty who appeared on ABC and three – Molly Yard of NOW, John Wilke of the National Right to Life Committee, and Randall Terry of Operation Rescue – who held forth on all three network newscasts) an opportunity to comment on some facet of the ruling and its implications. These included predictions about the human, legislative, and electoral toll of the case as well as a good deal of discussion of the case's implications for the state of abortion law. While *Roe*, per se, was not overturned by *Webster*, interview subjects were virtually of one voice in their characterizations of the ruling and the landmark precedent's vital signs. Randall Terry was clearly the most graphic in his proclaiming, "I am convinced *Roe* will fall by the end of this presidential term, and child killing will be driven back to hell where it came from" (CBS News). Antiabortion activist Andrew Puzder, a key player in drafting the Missouri legislation, delivered the same message in less strident tones: "When a state can constitutionally recognize the simple medical scientific fact that human life begins at conception, legalized abortion cannot last very long" (NBC News). Succinctly stated by Missouri Right to Life's Loretto Wagner, "Today's ruling signals the beginning of the end of legalized abortion in this country" (CBS News).

Lending added credibility to these perspectives from clear partisans in the abortion struggle were the comments of legal experts Lawrence Tribe (on ABC) and Paul Rothstein (on CBS), neither of whom could be accused of being spokespersons for the antichoice position. Tribe opined, "*Roe v. Wade* is alive in name only. The fundamental principle of *Roe v. Wade,* that women should be able to decide whether and when to have a child, when to end a pregnancy, that principle survives as a hollow shell." A similar message was offered by Rothstein:

The bottom line: this decision means that the time during which the states can regulate pregnancy and regulate abortion is moving back in the pregnancy earlier and earlier. . . . They went as far as they could to narrow *Roe v. Wade* without reading it off the books, and [in] the future we'll watch with bated breath to see if it disappears entirely. . . . Their current thinking will lead them in that direction.

Across all three network newscasts on decision day, the only player who refused to place *Webster* in its most expansive light but, rather, counseled caution was Planned Parenthood's Faye Wattleton, whose comments were only aired on NBC: "The Supreme Court did not overturn *Roe v. Wade* today. The Supreme Court sent very mixed signals as it forewarned us that they will consider these questions in further depth in the fall."

As we noted in our consideration of *Bakke,* while a good deal of the spin a case receives on the network newscasts will come from numerous actors approaching the case from their highly partisan perspectives, greater credibility may be granted by viewers to what they are told by the newscasters themselves, who are likely to be perceived as more objective sources of information about the case. Here, as in *Bakke,* newscasters traveled the same roads in their commentary and speculation as did their interview subjects, with particular attention paid to the precarious state of the *Roe* precedent and, at times, an effort to predict the decision's outcome.

Viewers of evening newscasts were alerted throughout all stages of the litigation process that *Roe* was in danger, starting with the lead stories on all three networks when certiorari was granted (1/9/89). ABC's Peter Jennings noted that "when the Court makes up its mind, the impact on the nation's abortion laws may well be definitive, even to the point of altering the Court's landmark decision in *Roe v. Wade*, which legalized abortion almost sixteen years ago." Somewhat more dramatically, Dan Rather commented on CBS that "the explosive, sometimes violent debate over abortion is moving back to the nation's highest court. . . . This could lead to a narrowing or even a reversal of the high court's sixteen-year-old decision that made abortion legal." On NBC Carl Stern opined, "For sixteen years antiabortion groups have been working to get the Supreme Court to say it was wrong about abortion, and that time may finally have come." It should be noted, however, that Stern's coverage of the case was well tempered throughout its processing. Here he added, "Of course, the justices may still decide not to change anything at all."

Additional recognition of the possibility of *Roe*'s demise was aired by all three networks in the context of coverage of the ruling's anniversary and, subsequently, in stories previewing and covering oral argument in *Webster*. In the wake of that argument NBC's Maria Shriver covered an abortion demonstration: "These latest protests end a week in which the U.S. Supreme Court heard an appeal that could overturn *Roe v. Wade*, the landmark decision legalizing abortion" (4/29/89). As the end of the Court's term neared and the *Webster* ruling was anticipated, speculation was again focused on *Roe*. On ABC, Carole Simpson took note that "activists on both sides of the issue are eagerly awaiting a new Supreme Court ruling that could . . . overturn the historic *Roe v. Wade* ruling that legalized abortion" (6/10/89). Previewing the remaining rulings the Court was expected to announce before its recess, ABC's Tim O'Brien underscored, "But by far the most awaited decision is the Court's abortion ruling, the first opportunity in more than sixteen years . . . to overrule *Roe v. Wade*, the landmark decision effectively legalizing abortion" (6/25/89). Speculation about the fate of *Roe* continued as the networks covered a "nonstory," the Court's failure to hand down *Webster* on the day that it was anticipated. According to Peter Jennings:

All over the country today countless people were waiting for the Supreme Court to issue its ruling on abortion. They're going to have to wait a little longer. The Court has postponed, at least until Monday, ruling on an abortion case from Missouri – a case which could be used to significantly alter the status of abortion in the country as a whole. (ABC News, 6/29/89)

Beyond generalized speculation about *Roe*'s possible demise, newscasters were also ready to speculate about the likely division of the justices in *Webster*, a task that was presumably "easier" in this case setting than it had been in the relatively clean legal slate presented by *Bakke,* where little, if any, relevant case law existed. As early as the day of the certiorari grant in *Webster,* CBS News correspondent Rita Braver took note that

Reagan appointees Antonin Scalia, Anthony Kennedy, and Sandra Day O'Connor are considered highly likely to vote to overturn or modify *Roe v. Wade,* siding with William Rehnquist and Byron White, who voted "no" on the original decision. Only three of the justices who supported *Roe v. Wade* are still on the Court: Harry Blackmun, William Brennan, and Thurgood Marshall. John Paul Stevens, appointed by Gerald Ford, is considered likely to stand with them. (1/9/89)

By the time oral argument was heard, Braver's tune was slightly modified. Counting the same four votes in support of *Roe,* she was now a bit less certain of the range of views in the opposition, while noting, "O'Connor could be the swing vote." Ultimately, Braver appeared to side with those forecasting *Roe*'s survival: "But, for now, most experts are predicting that the Court will neither uphold nor overturn *Roe v. Wade* but, instead, will modify it in some way giving the states leeway to regulate more aspects of abortion" (4/26/89).

On NBC, Carl Stern's early coverage engaged in similar head counting and speculation about *Roe*'s prospects:

Not since the civil rights turmoil of the 1950s has the Court been so conspicuously at the center of a storm. For the first time in sixteen years there is genuine uncertainty about . . . whether women will retain the right to choose to have an abortion. . . . The Supreme Court has been asked before to overturn its ruling, but the two dissenters in 1973, William Rehnquist and Byron White, have never mustered the five votes needed to change the law. Now, changes in the Court's membership may have given them the votes. Antonin Scalia has been sharply critical of the reasoning underlying the *Roe* decision. Both he and the newest justice, Anthony Kennedy, were chosen in part for their perceived hostility to *Roe.* And Sandra Day O'Connor has said that the ruling may have become unworkable now that medical advances have made it possible for a fetus to grow outside the mother. Thus, there could be five opponents now, a prospect that horrifies the abortion rights movement.

After carefully laying out *Roe*'s precarious position, Stern moderated his tone, suggesting that it had a good chance to survive:

The abortion ruling paved the way for other Court decisions on women's rights and rights of privacy. A reversal of the *Roe* decision might affect more than just abortion. That is one reason for skepticism that the Court will overturn *Roe.* Historically, the

Court has never gone backwards after declaring a fundamental right. The Court's conservatives are most likely to be respectful of that tradition. (4/9/89)

In his coverage of oral argument, Stern added that "there was no indication that the landmark abortion decision of 1973 was in serious danger" (4/26/89). Finally, speculating broadly about the decision when it was not announced when expected, Stern's story opened the evening's newscast:

It could be that the Supreme Court's print shop is running behind or the justices want the case reargued next term. . . . The justices have been writing their decision since the end of April. There's some speculation that Justice O'Connor is writing the crucial one favoring more state control. But one expert says that could produce a Court split in several factions, none of them absolutely controlling. . . . *Roe v. Wade* was actually heard twice before the Court decided in favor of abortion in 1973. On Monday, the Court will announce whether this one, to roll it back, will have to be argued a second time. (6/29/89)

Viewers of ABC News were treated to several forecasts about *Webster* in the coverage offered by law correspondent Tim O'Brien. First, in coverage of the certiorari grant, O'Brien discussed the implications of personnel changes on the Court while laying out his view of the decisional options faced by the justices:

Three of the seven justices who voted to legalize abortion sixteen years ago have been replaced by President Reagan, and the new justices have the potential to turn that seven-to-two vote around five to four. But the Rehnquist Court . . . has a wide range of options. It could reject the Missouri law. It could reject *Roe v. Wade* completely and allow states to ban abortion again. Or it could just modify *Roe v. Wade*, greatly enhancing the power of the state to regulate abortion, to make it more difficult again, just as the state tried to do here. (1/9/89)

A few weeks before oral argument, O'Brien went further in offering his take on what the Court was likely to do in words that proved quite prophetic:

The Supreme Court has historically been reluctant to reverse itself and may not overrule *Roe v. Wade*, even if a majority believes it was wrongly decided. . . . While some modification of *Roe* is a distinct possibility, a complete about-face is widely thought to be unlikely and unnecessary to decide this case. Even if it did happen, abortions would not automatically become illegal again. It would be up to individual states. Many would still allow abortion. And most women, especially those who can afford to travel, would still have access to them. (4/9/89)

When the day of oral argument arrived, O'Brien's coverage took on a much more dramatic tone, yet he ultimately concluded with a moderating prediction of what the case's outcome would likely be:

People from all over the United States had begun lining up yesterday in hopes of getting a seat for what could become an historic argument. . . . The outcome could easily turn on the views of President Reagan's three appointees to the Court. Justices Scalia, Kennedy, and O'Connor dominated the questioning but provided no clues as to how they might vote. . . . Should McCorvey's landmark victory now be reversed, each individual state would decide for itself whether to permit abortion. Court scholars say the justices are more likely to chip away at *Roe* making it more difficult in some states to get an abortion. (4/26/89)

The day after oral argument, O'Brien aired a relatively lengthy (2:10) feature story describing the Court's decisional processes, utilizing the *Webster* case to develop an example. In the process he continued the effort evident on all three networks to count heads on the case:

Rehnquist . . . a dissenter in *Roe v. Wade* . . . is a likely vote to overrule it tomorrow morning. . . . William Brennan, Thurgood Marshall, John Paul Stevens, and Harry Blackmun, the justice who wrote *Roe v. Wade,* are all expected to vote to reaffirm it. Byron White, who dissented with Rehnquist in 1973, [is] a likely vote to overrule it. It would take the votes of all three Reagan appointees to overturn *Roe v. Wade.* Sandra O'Connor and Antonin Scalia have both criticized the decision, but it's unclear whether their misgivings are sufficient to overcome the Court's historic reluctance to overrule itself. Should the vote be split four to four, the future of *Roe* and, to some extent, of abortion in the United States, would fall to the last justice, Anthony Kennedy, a conservative who has never decided an abortion case before. (4/27/89)

O'Brien's final predictive effort came in a story reporting on the seeming delay in announcing the *Webster* decision. The report speculated on what was holding up the case and relied, in part, on unidentified "sources," an unusual element in a story covering the Court:

The Court did not publicly explain what's holding up the ruling, but sources tell ABC News that Justice Harry Blackmun is writing a bitter opinion, that he has asked the Chief Justice for more time until Monday to complete it. That is significant because Blackmun is the author of *Roe v. Wade* and is the Court's main defender of abortion rights. The opinion that has so distressed Blackmun and other members of the Court is said to have been written by Justice Sandra O'Connor, a frequent critic of *Roe v. Wade,* but, again, she has never revealed any inclination to have it overruled.

At this juncture, O'Brien moved to the "bottom line":

It's widely believed the Court has declined the administration's invitation to overrule *Roe* and that abortions will remain legal in every state. But to what extent may states regulate the procedure? That's the key in this most controversial case. The Court's language and rationale will be crucial and what this eleventh-hour struggle, we're told, is all about. (6/29/89)

Interestingly, all three network newscasts covered the Court's nondecision in *Webster* on June 29th, with only NBC treating the nonstory cursorily. This occurred despite the apparent efforts of the Supreme Court's Public Information Officer, Toni House, to steer the networks away from investing substantial resources on the Court on that day:

I think we did a very good job . . . when we knew pretty well that *Webster* wasn't going to come down. I had a television cameraman standing on the credenza in back of me filming our not releasing the *Webster* decision. I tried to say to people, I don't know anything, but my gut tells me it ain't over till [it's] over. And you people are predicting out loud, in public, that *Webster* is going to come down on Thursday, and I'm telling you that you could be embarrassed. And they were. So then they had to write stories about why it didn't come down, which were wrong. You try to warn people off something – negative guidance. I don't think we did know, but we had a strong sense the elephants were still moving around, as one of the law clerks used to say. (in Davis, 1994: 59)

Once the *Webster* ruling was actually announced, one task of the newscasters was to assess its legal impact. ABC's Tim O'Brien underscored that the ruling did not overturn *Roe* but was, nevertheless, "a major setback for abortion rights . . . [which] reinforced the right of all states to sharply regulate it." O'Brien suggested that the ruling's impact could be quite broad: "Most of the one and a half million abortions performed in the U.S. each year don't involve government aid, but today's ruling may open the door to new restrictions on them as well" (7/3/89). On CBS News's lead story Dan Rather introduced the "third of July sizzler here at the U.S. Supreme Court," which promised "to take some territory away from the landmark 1973 abortion ruling."

In today's ruling the U.S. Supreme Court made it easier for states to restrict a woman's right to an abortion. Now the justices stopped short of outright rolling back and reversing the landmark abortion ruling of 1973. But today's ruling here sets the stage for more decisions and debate on one of the most divisive and deeply felt social issues of our times.

Adding context to Rather's assertions, Rita Braver continued, "It was the antiabortion side which was gratified today. For while the Supreme Court stopped short of overturning the landmark *Roe v. Wade* decision giving women the right to abortion, the justices allowed states to severely restrict that right" (7/3/89).

Tom Brokaw's introduction of the ruling and its impact on NBC News cast *Webster* in a similar light:

The Supreme Court's abortion decision: it is complicated and it's not the last word. What now? . . . America's long, emotional involvement with abortion as a personal, moral, legal, and political issue is moving to new levels tonight. . . . Today's ruling is the most significant since *Roe v. Wade,* a decision sixteen years ago legalizing abortion. And while today's decision did not reverse that, it did return to the states more authority to determine who gets an abortion and under what circumstances. (7/3/89)

In assessing the legal impact of the *Webster* decision the newscasts walked a thin line. A great deal had been invested in covering the case, and the decision's announcement was met with extraordinary anticipation and attention. While stressing that the ruling was the most important abortion decision since *Roe,* newscasts were also forthcoming in noting that *Roe* had not been overturned. As Tom Brokaw asked on decision day, "What now?" In the wake of *Webster,* the answer given, at least on the evening news, was much the same as it had been in *Bakke. Webster,* like *Bakke,* was a "big" decision. Yet, also like *Bakke,* it had not produced the definitive landmark holding that could guide and control the future. Consequently, after decision day *Webster* would fade as the evening news cast its gaze forward for the next potential blockbuster case that could bring about the dramatic watershed that *Webster* failed to deliver. As with *Bakke* and affirmative action, coverage of the Court in the abortion arena had come full circle. This was even evident in the forward-looking commentary offered on decision day in *Webster.*

On ABC, for example, Tim O'Brien did not break stride: "Moments after today's ruling was announced, the Court said it would review three new abortion cases next term. Court scholars say these new cases are even more likely to doom *Roe v. Wade*" (7/3/89). On NBC, Carl Stern also highlighted the still present possibility that *Roe*'s days remained numbered:

Although the justices did not decide the issue today, it was clear that this Court may yet throw out *Roe v. Wade.* . . . The fact that the Court agreed today to hear . . . three [abortion] cases shows there is still concern [that] there is to be some balance between the rights of women and state efforts to limit abortion. . . . The key vote will be Justice

O'Connor's. Will she believe that the limitations on abortion in the Illinois law, the Minnesota law, and the Ohio law unduly burden the right of abortion mentioned in *Roe v. Wade,* or will she be convinced that the time has finally arrived to do away with *Roe v. Wade?* (7/3/89)

After decision day, speculation about *Roe* became even more direct. Indeed, the very day after *Webster* was decided CBS's Rita Braver opined, "But even with the current Court makeup, most Court watchers today are saying it's just a matter of when, not if, the broad right to abortion granted in the famous *Roe v. Wade* decision will fall" (7/4/89). On the eve of the next Court term, Braver reiterated this stance:

The new Supreme Court session begins as the last one ended with the focus on abortion. In the wake of their decision . . . giving states broader rights to regulate abortion the justices agreed to hear three more abortion cases this term. . . . It's the third case from Illinois that's considered most likely to further erode the right to abortion granted in the landmark *Roe v. Wade* decision. (9/30/89)

A few days later ABC News reported that Justice Stevens had withdrawn from the Illinois case, which involved a state law requiring abortion clinics to meet hospital standards of care for the performance of any and all abortions. In his report Tim O'Brien expansively discussed the potential implications of the case:

Justice John Paul Stevens has taken himself out of what is clearly the most explosive abortion case to reach the high court in years. . . . Some court scholars say that with Stevens now out of the picture, the increasingly conservative Rehnquist Court may be emboldened to overrule *Roe* completely. (10/2/89)

It is, of course, difficult to believe that "the most explosive abortion case . . . in years" was reaching the Court just months after *Webster.* Once again, however, newscasters' best laid predictions would come undone. Two weeks before the *Ragsdale* (Illinois) case was to be argued, a settlement was reached and the case was never heard by the Supreme Court. *Roe* again survived, and, indeed, its fundamental recognition of the existence of a right to choose to end a pregnancy still exists today.

ADDITIONAL PERSPECTIVES ON "GAME-DAY" COVERAGE: THE *BAKKE* CASE

All stories broadcast about unfolding Supreme Court litigation are not created equal, and we have already documented the extraordinary amount of

precious airtime and newscaster resources that were utilized across the networks in "game-day" coverage of both *Bakke* and *Webster*. In addition, we have
seen the widespread use of commentators and news analysts to underscore the
meaning and implications of these rulings. Clearly, network newscast resources are likely to be invested more heavily in decisional coverage than in
any other facet of Supreme Court case processing, and just as clearly, public
understanding of what the Supreme Court has done will be affected most by
the reporting of its actual decisions. Here, we offer additional focus on several facets of decision-day coverage of *Bakke* to gain added insights and understanding about how the case was reported.

While *Bakke* would, of course, dominate the network newscasts on June 23,
1978, the lead statements uttered by the news anchors would undoubtedly set
the tone for the analysis to follow and the context through which the viewing
public would digest the remainder of the broadcast. On ABC News, Sam Donaldson offered a well-balanced summary assessment of what the Court decided, although the first thing the viewer learned was that Bakke had won: "Allan Bakke won his reverse discrimination case today, but affirmative action
programs to help minority students won also." On CBS News, anchor Walter
Cronkite's lead assessment of the bifurcated *Bakke* holding suggested that the
case was of extraordinary importance, yet his message was somewhat less clear:

The Supreme Court today issued what may be its most important civil rights decision
since the 1954 school desegregation ruling. In the so-called reverse discrimination suit
of Allan Bakke, a white, the Court concluded that he had been denied admission to
medical school because of his race. But the Court also said, somewhat ambiguously,
that race may be considered in granting admission so long as there is not a rigid racial
quota system.

In the lead statement on NBC News, John Chancellor offered the most unbalanced assessment of what the Court had done, trumpeting Bakke's victory,
while making considerably less of the "victory" for the affirmative action concept. In the process, substantial oversimplification of the Court's decision can
be found:

The Supreme Court ruled today that Allan Bakke must be admitted to a school that
turned him down in a case of reverse discrimination. Bakke was not admitted to the
University of California Medical School at Davis because he is white. The place he
might have had was given to a minority applicant with lower test scores than he had.
The Court said that was wrong. But the Court also said that race can be a legal factor

in a school admissions program. The Court was deeply divided, five to four, and the various opinions ran to forty thousand words.

We have seen throughout *Bakke* coverage that the personage of Allan Bakke dominated the case, despite the fact that he refused to be interviewed and remained a very private person throughout the litigation process. It was, perhaps, the human element and human interest in the Bakke story that led to a primary focus on the outcome of the case for Allan Bakke on decision day. Such a focus was, indeed, understandable. Nevertheless, only on ABC News was the lead statement announcing Bakke's victory tempered by a clear and immediate recognition that his victory was solely a personal one and that affirmative action had won a victory as well. Regardless of what was to follow on the network newscasts, the dominant critical first impression received by most viewers was of a Bakke victory.

Earlier we noted that each network utilized several correspondents to "tell" the Bakke story on decision day and the contours of how that story was told did not differ greatly across the networks, although some differences existed in the content each network brought to each specific focus. Nevertheless, at the broadest level each network outlined the substance of the *Bakke* decision, analyzed the decision's meaning and its possible implications for related affirmative action contexts, dwelled on reaction to the decision among numerous actors and settings, and profiled Allan Bakke. ABC and NBC focused extensively on analysis of alternative affirmative action admissions programs, such as the Harvard Plan, that weighed so heavily in Justice Powell's controlling hybrid opinion. Alone among the networks, ABC's *Bakke* coverage included a commentary piece on the ruling.

It is important to underline that in presenting the Court's holding and Justice Powell's decisive position on decision day, the networks, for the most part, characterized the ruling accurately, albeit quite oversimplistically. All, for example, drew distinctions between the UC-Davis "quota" plan and Harvard-like programs that, in Powell's view, could be sustained. On other matters such as the thorny issue of what standards of review justices should utilize in the case, the decision's statutory or constitutional basis, and the characterization of "majority" and "dissenting" positions, the newscasts fared considerably less well.

Much of what the public could learn about *Bakke* would be based on its critical characterization by the networks' primary law correspondents who would be responsible for detailing the ruling at the outset of the respective newscasts. Performing the task on ABC News, Tim O'Brien started by noting that

[the] long-awaited *Bakke* decision . . . runs hundreds of pages, forty thousand words, and is subject to varying interpretations with the divisions in society over affirmative action reflected in the divisions among the justices themselves. The net result: a balancing act that will allow Allan Bakke into medical school, while leaving intact the principles of affirmative action.

O'Brien noted that four justices (Brennan, White, Marshall, and Blackmun) would uphold the California program in its entirety and deny admission to Bakke. The report included the only explicit attention to Justice Brennan's opinion for these four justices across all three networks, citing from Brennan's background discussion of the history of discrimination and underrepresentation of blacks in the medical profession. While this was not the linchpin of Brennan's analysis (which focused on the constitutional basis for the ruling and the appropriate standards of review), O'Brien's coverage of Brennan's grouping went well beyond that of his competitors. Indeed, on CBS and NBC News, Brennan's coalition was, less than accurately, simply labeled "the dissenters."

As was the case across all three newscasts, O'Brien did not focus explicit attention on the opinion authored by Justice Stevens for himself, Justices Stewart, Rehnquist, and Chief Justice Burger. O'Brien did note, however, that these jurists disagreed with the Brennan group and would reject the UC-Davis program as a violation of the 1964 Civil Rights Act, the wording of which regarding discrimination was quoted directly. Thus, while not placing emphasis on the constitutional basis for Brennan's opinion, O'Brien did underline that it was statutory construction that lay at the heart of Stevens's approach. O'Brien went on to note that "striking down the California program along those lines would have cast grave doubts on the validity of dozens of governmental finance programs involving over the years billions of dollars. But it was not to happen. Four justices out of nine is not a majority, and Stevens, Stewart, Rehnquist and Burger could not pick up the fifth vote."

This led to a central focus on the views of Justice Powell, whose bifurcated opinion resulted in the split ruling in the case: Bakke must be admitted, yet race could be used under some circumstances as a criterion in admissions. Of the Powell opinion Dreyfuss and Lawrence have suggested:

The gentleman from Virginia had written the ultimate political opinion. He had neutralized the anti-affirmative action forces by admitting Bakke and holding that quotas were illegal. And he had given his friends in the academic establishment what Mr. Cox had asked for: the freedom to continue to run their business the way they pleased. It was not clear that he had given minorities anything, but he had not shut the door on them entirely. It would be possible for them to claim victory and difficult to say they had been ignored. (1979: 212–123)

Powell's opinion stressed that rights were personal, racial distinctions were inherently suspect, and the UC-Davis admissions plan could not withstand "strict judicial scrutiny" with its fatal flaw of disregarding individual rights as guaranteed by the Fourteenth Amendment. The Harvard Plan was characterized by Powell as an admissions program that considered race as one variable among many in a single-tiered admissions process. Such a plan, unlike that from UC-Davis, did not rely on a quota system and might pass constitutional muster.

On ABC, O'Brien characterized Powell as "the swing justice . . . which means the only real holding of the Court is to be found in his opinion":

Justice Powell concluded that the specific program employed by the California medical school was unconstitutional because it excluded the participation of nonminorities. In the shortest but perhaps the most significant part of his opinion Powell writes that "the state has a substantial interest that legitimately may be served by a properly devised admissions program involving the competitive consideration of race and ethnic origin." The statement implied that the special admissions programs that give preferential treatment to minorities may be upheld so long as they do not preclude consideration of those that are not minorities.

On CBS News, Fred Graham began his deciphering of the decision by noting that the case was the Court's first look at "the emotional issue of reverse discrimination: whether affirmative action programs designed to benefit non-whites are illegal when they deny benefits to whites. In a complex decision the Supreme Court ruled five to four that some such affirmative action programs are illegal." By framing the case in terms of its outcome for Bakke, Graham was now able to characterize justices as being in the majority or in dissent, greatly oversimplifying the Court's division. Citing from the antidiscrimination language of the 1964 Civil Rights Act, Graham continued, "Under those provisions of the law a five-member majority of the Court, Warren Burger, Potter Stewart, John Paul Stevens, William Rehnquist, and Lewis Powell agreed that Bakke had been illegally denied admission because of his race and must be admitted to the Davis medical school," thereby obliterating the critical distinction between Powell's constitutional orientation and the statutory basis for his "majority" colleagues' views. Focusing his attention on "the dissenters," Graham noted that "they argued that racial quotas should be permissible as a way to make up for the years of discrimination that have frozen many nonwhites out of the medical profession."

Graham's focus on Powell was a less central one than O'Brien's. Graham did note, however, that Powell's opinion was the "prevailing one," which declared that

"preferring members of any one group for no other reason than race or ethnic origin is discrimination for its own sake," and thus any rigid racial quota that excludes all whites is unlawful. But Powell declared that some affirmative action plans are lawful, those that do not rule out all whites but give nonwhites an advantage to be considered along with other factors in selecting a well-balanced student body.

Thus, while Graham's analysis steered clear of the constitutional versus the statutory basis of the holding, muddied the nature of the Court's division, and ignored the issue of the status of racial classifications and the appropriate standard of judicial review, it did tap the likely legality of admissions programs structured along the Harvard model.

On NBC News, Carl Stern began his analysis by trying to place the decision in broader perspective:

What happened at the University of California may not end special admissions programs, but it will redefine the rules. Today's . . . decision said a university can take race into account as one element in a well-balanced admissions program, but the Court also said that the mere desire to help groups because of past injustices did not justify inflicting harm on Allan Bakke, who bore no responsibility for the past. . . . The case was heard more than eight months ago, and even after all this time there was no meeting of the minds of the justices.

Focusing on the Stevens coalition, Stern reported, they "said they didn't have to reach a constitutional question. They said that Congress in 1964 outlawed racial standards such as that which was used to exclude Bakke." Little attention was given to the views of the Brennan group, except to identify it as "the four dissenters." Stern offered the most succinct accounting of Justice Powell's role in the case, only noting that "the decisive fifth vote came from Justice Powell, who said the Constitution prohibited any playing of favorites on the basis of race," an extraordinarily parsimonious version of Powell's argument. Stern went on to add that

the Court singled out the procedures used at Harvard as a model for achieving student diversity without unfairness. It said Harvard's rules do not exclude applicants just because they're white or black. On other critical questions the Court rejected the idea of discrimination for good purposes, and it also implied that imposing numerical solutions might be acceptable where there was a specific finding of past discrimination.

Stepping back from the alternative network approaches to reporting the actual *Bakke* holding, it appears that what was done "best" by the newscasts was the drawing of a critical distinction (such as Powell had done) between affirmative action programs such as Harvard's (where overt racial quotas were not utilized and where admissions procedures focused on a single pool of applicants) and the program operative at UC-Davis (where places were "set aside" for minorities and separate admissions pools were established). Indeed, ABC and NBC even included feature byline stories on such "acceptable" programs as part of their decision–day coverage. George Strait's feature on ABC News even took note of the irony (as did Justice Blackmun's caustic *Bakke* opinion) that Harvard's "goal"-oriented program was allowable while Davis's results-oriented plan was not:

These "goals" may seem like thinly veiled quotas, but Harvard denies it and today the Court agreed. There are hundreds of other colleges with plans that are similar to Harvard's and, no matter how it seems, all, according to Justice Powell, are entitled to the presumption of "good faith." For all toe the now accepted legal line of making academic and individual qualities the criteria for admission. Race may be considered in the decision, but the decision cannot depend on it.

On other matters, network coverage of the decision did not fare as well. While the pivotal role of Justice Powell and the Court's bifurcated holding were underlined, only ABC's coverage by Tim O'Brien avoided characterizing the Brennan coalition as "the dissenters" and the Stevens group as "the majority." The important question of the statutory versus the constitutional basis for the Court's holding and the implications of this difference were either ignored or handled in sketchy fashion across the broadcasts. Other central questions focused on extensively by the numerous *Bakke* opinions included the constitutional status of racial classifications and the critical question of what standard of review the Court should utilize in examining them. While not "easy" issues to discuss, they can be explained and made intelligible to a lay public and, in a fundamental sense, are not simply arcane legal questions with little practical significance. Nevertheless, these concerns were not dealt with by decision-day broadcasts.

Further, while the depth of a viewer's comprehension of Justice Powell's compound holding would vary depending on which newscast one saw, it is quite clear that viewers' capacities to learn of the disparate positions of other Court members in *Bakke* would vary even more substantially, with the presentation of the richness and implications of alternative views not faring very well. None of the networks focused explicitly on Justice Stevens's opinion based on statutory construction of the "plain meaning" of Title VI of the 1964 Civil Rights Act. Attention to the Brennan opinion was aired only on ABC News and centered on his historical analysis of discrimination, not the primary thrust of his opinion, which focused on the constitutional basis for the ruling and the issue of appropriate standards of review.

Justice Marshall's opinion, of particular interest since it was penned by the Court's lone black member, outlined the historic plight of American blacks and alluded to the impact of the past on the contemporary status of all blacks. He concluded that group remedies were, consequently, a justifiable means to redress a history of group discrimination. The Marshall opinion was given some consideration on ABC and NBC, but not on CBS. ABC's Tim O'Brien cited from Marshall's opinion: "The Negro was dragged to this country in chains. . . . Bringing him into the mainstream of American life should be a state interest of the highest order." On NBC, David Brinkley cited from what he characterized as Marshall's "dissent" where the justice wrote, "he could not believe the Constitution prevented a state from trying to remedy the effect of centuries of discrimination. And he said, 'The dream of the American melting pot has not been realized for the Negro since, because of the color of his skin, he never made it into the pot.'"

Justice Blackmun's opinion, which noted that all kinds of preferential programs based on factors other than race (such as athletic prowess, residency, and alumni contributions) had a historic acceptance in American schooling, and which also demeaned the differences in the UC-Davis and Harvard plans, only received mention on NBC News. Curiously, Carl Stern's coverage seemed to miss the thrust of Blackmun's agitation with Powell and simply reported, "Blackmun's dissent was a weak one saying he regarded the California procedure as, perhaps, just barely constitutional." Justice White's separate opinion, which was procedural in nature, was, perhaps appropriately, ignored by all three networks.

ADDITIONAL PERSPECTIVES ON "GAME-DAY" COVERAGE: THE *WEBSTER* CASE

As was the case in *Bakke,* the opening statements by the newscast anchors on *Webster*'s decision day (7/3/89) served to frame the story and the lengthy coverage to follow. *Bakke* had offered two messages, with Allan Bakke's personal victory overshadowing clearly a victory for affirmative action per se. In *Webster,* attention in newscast openings was placed on the victory of the antiabortion movement and the upholding of Missouri's regulatory statute. It was also noted that, nevertheless, *Roe* had survived, albeit by the slimmest of margins. Anchor Barry Serafin's lead-in to ABC News's decision-day coverage was well balanced: "Today's long-awaited, last-minute ruling by the Supreme Court did not topple the landmark *Roe v. Wade* decision . . . but it did grant states broad new authority to limit the right to abortion. And the Court set the stage for further challenges." Dan Rather's introduction to CBS's newscast shed a similar light on the decision:

The ruling allows new state restrictions to take some territory away from the landmark 1973 abortion ruling. . . . In today's ruling the U.S. Supreme Court made it easier for states to restrict a woman's right to abortion. Now the justices stopped short of outright rolling back and reversing the landmark abortion ruling of 1973. But today's ruling here sets the stage for more decisions and debate on one of the most divisive and deeply felt social issues of our time.

On NBC News, Tom Brokaw opened the broadcast by noting that the Court's decision "is complicated and it is not the last word. . . . And while today's decision did not reverse [*Roe v. Wade*], it did return to the states more authority to determine who gets an abortion and under what circumstances."

As with *Bakke,* the networks traveled very similar terrain in the unfolding of *Webster* coverage on decision day. Each outlined the substantive holding of the decision, the validating of the Missouri statute at issue in the case, primarily through the reports of the network law correspondents. All the newscasts focused on reactions to the Court's ruling by spokespersons for both prochoice and antiabortion groups, and, similarly, each network examined the electoral and legislative battles that would now mushroom in the states with attendant efforts by these groups to control these contests.

Reaction to the decision was also assessed from the perspective of the Bush administration across all three newscasts. The Supreme Court story was transformed, in part, to a presidential one with a portrait drawn of a president who was happy with the decision but who, nevertheless, appeared less anxious to be identified as closely with the antiabortion activists as his predecessor, Ronald Reagan. As noted by ABC's Barry Serafin, "One of the pro-life movement's most vocal supporters did not react in person today. President Bush let someone else speak for him. . . . Yes, Sununu was quick to say, the president still supports a constitutional amendment to outlaw abortion. But he suggested today's decision, combined with those still to come from this Court, may make that unnecessary." ABC's Britt Hume added, "The Administration would, no doubt, prefer to see *Roe v. Wade* undone by the Supreme Court itself. That would get the issue out of Washington and into the state legislatures without the president first having to pitch a constitutional amendment through a Congress controlled by the other party."

On CBS, Wyatt Andrews took note that

President Bush welcomed today's decision but did not interrupt his vacation to say so himself. . . . Sununu insists that the president still supports a constitutional amendment banning abortion, but it's clear that Mr. Bush will not attack abortion with the same fervor he brought to the amendment to ban desecration of the flag. The flag issue last week drew the president's personal attention, even down to the drafting of the amendment. Today [visual shown of President Bush "recreating" on vacation]. . . . The White House claims Mr. Bush is not just reading the opinion polls, but yet the president's level of public commitment reflects what the polls say. Specifically, 70 percent public approval of Mr. Bush's flag amendment, but divided public opinion on abortion.

NBC's coverage of the presidential angle in the case was much less expansive, simply noting, "President Bush, who favored a constitutional amendment banning abortion, sent an aide to praise the decision." Additional facets of decision-day coverage on the networks included reports (on ABC and NBC) of the expected "real world" impact of the ruling on the Missouri abortion clinic (Reproductive Health Services) that had brought the litigation, a focus (on ABC and NBC) on several critical medical questions raised by the case regarding fetal viability, and a report (on CBS) on poll results gauging the public's stance on several abortion rights concerns.

Explicit attention to the actual Court ruling in *Webster* appeared to be considerably less central than it had been in reporting on *Bakke*. This may reflect, in part, a ruling that was somewhat more straightforward, albeit not quite as clear-cut as the newscasts made it seem. At least in *Webster*, unlike *Bakke*, there was a consistent holding (although not a majority opinion) that did not create one outcome for the litigant (Bakke) and another for the broader issue (affirmative action). Also present in *Webster* was a much greater potential to move the story away from the Court to its political implications for state legislative politics, electoral politics, and the ongoing battle of organized interests.

Five separate opinions emanated from the Court on *Webster*'s decision day. Delivering the Court's judgment (in an opinion joined only by Justices White and Kennedy), Chief Justice Rehnquist methodically discussed the rationales for the upholding of each facet of the Missouri abortion statute. While Rehnquist was highly critical of and rejected *Roe*'s trimester framework, and while he signaled that *Roe* might, in due course, be overturned, he nevertheless concluded in this instance that "this case . . . affords us no occasion to revisit the holding of *Roe* . . . and we leave it undisturbed." In separate concurrences Justice Scalia took the Court to task for not overturning *Roe*, while Justice O'Connor's concurrence made it clear that she was the stumbling block to that outcome. Dissents in the case were written by *Roe* author Harry Blackmun (joined by Justices Brennan and Marshall) and Justice Stevens. Stevens's dissent viewed the Missouri statute as an unconstitutional violation of the First Amendment's Establishment Clause (since its preamble's assertion that life begins at conception had no identifiable secular purpose), an approach not found in any other opinion. The outlier status of Stevens's dissent is underscored by its receiving no mention on any network newscast. In reporting the Court's decision, the networks placed different degrees of emphasis on the judicial divisiveness the case engendered. The nuances of the Court's division and the lack of a true majority opinion did not receive crisp or clear coverage on any newscast.

On ABC, Tim O'Brien eschewed any effort to present a voting breakdown of the justices. Rather, he offered direct quotations from Rehnquist's opinion upholding the various provisions of the Missouri law and concluded that the decision meant that states do not have to subsidize abortions or, in Rehnquist's words, "The Constitution confers no right to government aid." O'Brien pointed to Justice Blackmun who "dissented passionately," exclaiming, "I fear for the future. I fear for the liberty and equality of millions of women. I fear for the integrity of and public esteem for the Court." O'Brien took note that Justice Scalia "said the Court should have completely overruled *Roe*," while adding that Justices Kennedy, White, and Rehnquist "wanted to water it down, arguing that even in the first three months of pregnancy a woman's right to privacy must be balanced against the state's interest in protecting potential life." Turning to the pivotal justice for *Roe*'s survival O'Brien continued, "On that point Justice O'Connor refused to go along, saying modifying or over-ruling *Roe* was not necessary to decide the Missouri case." The report of the Court's actual ruling was parsimonious and, in avoiding any explicit discussion of voting divisions, avoided blatant error.

Such error is found in Rita Braver's decision coverage on CBS News where, after outlining the upholding of the specific provisions of the Missouri statute, she identified Justices White, O'Connor, Scalia, Kennedy, and Rehnquist as the Court's majority, while characterizing Rehnquist's opinion as the "major-ity opinion":

His majority opinion made clear that the Court still prohibits laws as severe as the one involved in the original *Roe v. Wade* case making all abortions criminal except when the mother's life was at stake. But he stated that today's decision would modify and narrow *Roe*.

Braver went on to note that "Justice Scalia, in fact, today said that *Roe v. Wade* should be overturned, and the other conservatives indicated that they're ready to do so if the right case comes along in the future," somewhat overstating Justice O'Connor's position. Of O'Connor, Braver noted that, "She was the swing vote in this case, and she did not seem to want to go as far as the other justices who are thinking about overturning *Roe v. Wade*. She indicated that there might be a case coming down the road where she would do it, but it would take longer to convince her that that's the right case." Turning to the dissenters, Braver took note that Justice Blackmun read his opinion aloud from the bench and she quoted his words: "For today, at least, the women of this nation still retain the liberty to control their destinies. But the signs are evident and very ominous, and a chill wind blows."

The least explicit attention to the actual case decision came in Carl Stern's coverage on NBC, which began with a presentation of the Court's "big rul-ing" outlining the explicit holdings on the Missouri law's provisions without any mention of Rehnquist's plurality authorship or identification of voting coalitions. Noting that while *Roe* did not fall in *Webster* it could be reversed in the future, Stern underscored that "if it does, it will be Sandra Day O'Con-nor's vote that makes the difference. At least four other justices seemed to fa-vor a ban on abortion. Justice O'Connor was unwilling to go that far today but indicated she is leaving open her options for next term when the Court will hear three other abortion cases." Turning to the dissenters Stern noted, "The man who wrote the *Roe* decision sixteen years ago, Harry Blackmun, said the signs are ominous, a cold wind blows. However, he added, for today at least, the law of abortion stands undisturbed."

Clearly, across all three networks on decision day in *Webster*, viewers learned that the Missouri regulations restricting abortion rights had been upheld and that *Roe*, while in jeopardy, had not been overturned. Coverage of the decision itself lacked richness and nuance. Interestingly, while considerable newscast attention had been placed on the Court's possible voting alignment in the case throughout its Supreme Court journey, an approach that is somewhat analogous to the dramatic horse-race presentation of American electoral contests, relatively little attention was paid to spelling out precisely the nature of voting alignments on *Webster*'s decision day. At the same time, extensive attention was paid to gauging the reaction to the ruling as well as its implications for the ongoing politics of abortion in America at both the state and federal levels. Such a political focus enabled network newscasts to present the ruling in a manner that placed it squarely in the context of a dramatic, mainstream, ongoing political story not unlike coverage of events in other controversial policy domains.

SUMMING UP

Our examination of television newscast coverage of *Bakke* and *Webster* began with the recognition that these were two very prominent litigation settings in which television was investing an unusual amount of resources. Clearly, television news had a clear understanding of the cases' potential importance, and our extensive analysis was warranted to underscore the nature of network news coverage of the Court when the networks were taking their best shot. Coverage of these two cases from their onset through the period following their resolution reveals many commonalities as well as distinct and important differences. Both the similarities and differences in coverage, however, can be understood from the perspective of how coverage of the Court can be presented to maximize or enhance the newsworthiness of the stories for the viewing public, while also framing the stories in ways that best enhance the ability of journalists to cover the least visible branch of government. Several observations can be made to underscore what we have found.

1. Both *Bakke* and *Webster* received extensive coverage with sixty stories broadcast on each case. *Bakke* stories were spread relatively evenly across all

three networks with some elements of pack journalism evidenced as stories tended to appear on multiple networks on given news days. Stories touching on the *Webster* case tended to be more broadly dispersed across newscasts reflecting the fact that the case represented one facet of an ongoing stream of events in an issue area with considerable history (unlike *Bakke*).

2. The majority of stories on *Bakke* and *Webster* were broadcast prior to their actual decisions, and more than a third of the stories on each case aired prior to oral argument. When decision day arrived in these cases (unlike, presumably, most other instances where decisions receive television coverage), they should not have been unknown events to the viewing public.

3. *Bakke* stories were relatively lengthy by television standards with a majority airing for more than a minute and a half, and one in five enjoying a relatively leisurely three-minute or longer duration. *Webster* stories did not fare quite as well on these metrics with the majority of them less than thirty seconds in length. Still, however, 40 percent of the *Webster* stories were longer than a minute and a half, and 15 percent ran for more than three minutes. On decision day, both *Bakke* and *Webster* received an extraordinary amount of network coverage ranging from eleven to sixteen and a half minutes of the broadcasts' news window. A clear majority of the time, stories on both cases included coverage by law correspondents and feature reporters beyond the news anchor.

4. The placement of *Bakke* and *Webster* stories in the nightly newscasts offers further evidence of the newsworthiness of these cases. *Bakke* was the lead story ten times (16.7%), and 60 percent of the *Bakke* stories were "up-front" pieces broadcast prior to a newscast's second commercial break. Here, *Webster* fared even better, serving as a lead story sixteen times (26.7%) and an up-front story nearly two-thirds (61.7%) of the time.

5. While all of the measures discussed above show that coverage of *Bakke* and *Webster* was extensive, it remains important to underscore that nearly half of the *Bakke* stories (45.0%) and nearly three out of four (73.3%) of the *Webster* stories could be characterized as somewhat sketchy in the sense that they lacked any specific content about the legal claims or the factual scenarios surrounding the cases.

6. Straight news stories were the most frequently utilized type of piece in *Bakke* coverage reflecting the fact that affirmative action was an emerging frontier issue and the case's processing was fraught with many newsworthy events. In contrast, *Webster* emerged in a much more well-developed issue do-

main. Consequently, a news/feature format dominated the case's coverage, and the litigation was continually cast in a broader setting.

7. Coverage of both cases emphasized that visual images are difficult for television to develop for Supreme Court stories with their processes dominated by legalisms far removed from everyday discourse, and cameras prohibited from capturing any drama that might transpire in the courtroom. The most dominant visual image in *Bakke* was a photograph or drawing of the Supreme Court building, which appeared in nearly 40 percent of the stories aired. A similarly sterile image appeared in more than half (53.3%) of the *Webster* stories.

8. Half of the *Bakke* stories included some predictive element in the comments of the network reporters, and nearly half (45.0%) included predictions made by news sources, interview subjects, or other interested parties. In the aggregate, predictions tended to be inflammatory or overexpansive in their forecasts, often comparing the importance of the case to *Brown v. Board of Education*. Even more graphically, three out of four (76.7%) *Webster* stories included predictive commentary by news reporters, and more than half of the stories (53.3%) incorporated predictions made by others. *Webster*'s potential importance was continually underscored by its relationship with *Roe*, and in nearly nine out of ten stories (87.0%) the possibility was raised that *Webster* would be the vehicle for *Roe*'s reversal. Commenting broadly on the phenomenon we have documented, Tom Brokaw has opined, "A problem in our business is that everyone wants to be a pundit in the last fifteen seconds of their piece" (in Fallows, 1996: 61). Clearly, a predictive focus can well serve a newscast's goal of making stories dramatic and interesting for viewers. Such a focus can, however, have important consequences. The point is made well by James Fallows:

As with medical doctors who applied leeches and trepanned skulls, the practitioners cannot be blamed for the limits of their profession. But we can ask why reporters spend so much time directing our attention toward what is not much more than guesswork on their part. It builds the impression that journalism is about spectacles and diversions – guessing what might or might not happen next month – rather than inquiries that might be useful. . . . Competing predictions add almost nothing to our ability to solve public problems or make sensible choices among complex alternatives. Yet this useless distraction has become a specialty of the political press. Predictions are easy to produce, they allow the reporters to act as if they possess special inside knowledge, and there is no consequence for being wrong. (1996: 32–33)

9. The benefits to newscasts of personalizing news events resulted in a central focus on Allan Bakke in *Bakke* coverage despite his refusal to publicly discuss the case or facilitate media coverage in any way. Bakke was identified in nearly nine out of ten (86.7%) stories, more than twice as often as UC-Davis, his faceless institutional opponent. *Webster,* unlike *Bakke,* did not have an individual litigant on whom case coverage could be anchored. Instead, interest-group leaders on both sides of the abortion controversy became major players in the case, and in five out of six stories (83.3%) some coverage was given to interest-group activities surrounding the case.

10. Television coverage of *Bakke* included substantial analysis of the political angle of the case and its relationship to the broader political process. This included, for example, substantial coverage of the Justice Department's efforts to fashion an amicus brief and the Congressional Black Caucus's attempts to influence the Carter administration in the defining of its position in the controversy. Similarly, *Webster* coverage included considerable attention to the role of the case in the Bush administration's political agenda, concentration on the case as a manifestation of the clash of well-organized interests on both sides of the abortion controversy, and attention to the implications of the case for ongoing legislative and electoral struggles in numerous state battlegrounds. All of these foci allowed correspondents covering the case to pursue the story through sources, interviews, and modes of analysis more common in political reporting outside of the Supreme Court venue. In effect, a legal story could be transformed into a story more suitable for television coverage. At the same time, however, a thorough vetting of the issues, both legal and policy-oriented, that could have been brought to public view, received lesser attention. Once again, Fallows amplifies the general point, noting that "a relentless emphasis on the cynical game of politics threatens public life itself by implying day after day that the political sphere is mainly an arena in which ambitious politicians struggle for dominance, rather than a structure in which citizens can deal with worrisome collective problems" (1996: 31).

11. The Court's members and the institution itself remained relatively invisible players in *Bakke* coverage. The affirmative action issue lacked a Supreme Court history (save for the moot case of Marco DeFunis), and a focus on the Court and its members would not serve to make the case more newsworthy. *Webster* arose in a markedly different setting. The history of abortion litigation resulted in justices having relatively well-known positions, and speculation about the implications of personnel changes on the Court allowed

newscasters to present the case in the context of the possibility that *Roe* might
be overturned.

12. Decision-day coverage of *Bakke* included discussion of Justice Powell's
prevailing opinion that could be characterized as "accurate," albeit quite oversimplistic. Coverage of the other opinions written in the case was quite limited.
In many respects, *Webster* was a less complex decision than *Bakke*. Coverage of
the actual decision itself, however, while on the mark in delivering the news that
Missouri's regulations of abortions were upheld, remained somewhat "breezy"
and sketchy with little attention to mapping out precisely the Court's division
and bones of contention. Clearly, attention to analyzing the legal questions and
their resolution (or lack thereof) was greater in *Bakke* than in *Webster* coverage.

13. Decision-day coverage of both cases could be characterized as taking a
"winner-loser" approach, particularly in the opening presentations of the news
anchors. In *Bakke,* the predominant message was that Allan Bakke, the individual litigant, had won his case while the more broadly important "victory"
for affirmative action per se was considerably less prominent in the framing of
the decision. In *Webster,* the decision was presented as a clear-cut victory for
the pro-life movement and, while viewers were told that *Roe* was not overturned, there was considerable speculation that its days were quite numbered.
In both case settings, such casting of the decisions could have resulted in mis-
perceptions about the rulings and their implications that were not met by
subsequent case outcomes in both the affirmative action and abortion arenas.

Importantly, in both the *Bakke* and *Webster* litigation settings, once the decisions were announced (and found to be less definitive than anticipated) the
networks showed no reluctance in moving on to and building up expectations
for the next "big case," television's new judicial spectacle. In starting the cycle anew, the newscasts demonstrated starkly television's difficulty in keeping
events in perspective. As noted by Fallows, "Kato Kaelin and a presidential
election are both interesting, but it is the election that will still matter ten years
from now. Part of the press's job is to keep things in proportion. TV's natural
tendency is to see the world in shards. It shows us one event with an air of ut-
most drama, then forgets about it and shows us the next" (1996: 53). This pattern is reiterated in the sports analogy drawn by Fallows:

Anyone who follows sports knows the disproportion between anticipation and aftermath. For the two weeks before the Super Bowl, it is built up as the most exciting show-
down in sportsdom . . . Then the game begins – and two hours after it's over, the TV

analysts are getting ready to talk about the next big event. . . . Public affairs writing
largely follows the same pattern. Weeks before an important Senate confirmation vote,
months before a congressional election, years before the presidential primaries begin,
the most influential figures in journalism spend their time predicting what is going to
happen. When the results come in, attention shifts almost immediately to what it all
means for the next tests of political strength. . . . The big difference between political
handicappers and those who set the point spread in sports is that in politics there is no
payoff day. For pundits, there is no financial penalty for being consistently wrong.
(1996: 169–170)

In the final analysis, detailed consideration of network news coverage of
Bakke and *Webster* highlighted some of the television medium's limitations,
as noted by Robinson and Levy:

[There are] barriers television faces in effectively transmitting news stories: too little
air time to tell most stories in sufficient depth; an easily distracted, often inattentive
audience; the lack of viewer control over the pace of story presentation; the absence of
clear separation between stories or story elements; inadequate historical perspectives
or causal explanations to make the story meaningful; frequent inconsistencies between
words and pictures; and the lack of redundancy to give content more than one perspective. (1986: 232)

Yet if such criticisms are taken to suggest that television news precludes substance in reporting, that clearly overstates the case. Coverage of *Bakke* and
Webster was substantial and, despite its warts, presented the fundamental outcomes of these two cases "accurately," albeit not with great sophistication,
nuance, or depth.

Doris Graber has noted that "if judged in terms of the information needs
of the ideal citizen in the ideal democracy," media coverage of the news, particularly that of television, is inadequate (1989: 105). According to Graber,

Television . . . provides little more than a headline service for news . . . which mirrors
the world like the curved mirrors at the county fair. Reality is reflected, but it seems
badly out of shape and proportion. Most of us, however, only faintly resemble the ideal
citizen, and most of us look to the media for entertainment rather than for enlighten-
ment. . . . By and large, American mass media serve the general public about as well as
that public wants to be served in practice rather than in theory. . . . Breadth of coverage is preferred over narrow depth. (1989: 105)

If coverage of *Bakke* and *Webster* serve as examples of the triumph of
breadth over depth, it also represents, of course, the "best" that network news

coverage of the Supreme Court has to offer. As much of our analysis through-out this volume underscores, coverage of the Court's work beyond the rari-fied air of the prominent litigation settings of cases such as *Bakke* and *Webster* may be a considerably different matter.

5

A Tale of Two Terms: The 1989 and 1994 Court Terms

"I don't think that television purports to tell you all that you need to know. It is not all the news that is fit to print. . . . [I]n television, all the news that fits, we air."

Carl Stern, former NBC news correspondent

The coverage of *Bakke* and *Webster* illustrates network performance when television news programs are taking their "best shot" at covering the Court's decisions. The careful examination of these two prominent cases has provided a detailed look into how the three major television network news programs reported the events leading up to the decisions in these cases, as well as the decisions themselves and their aftermath. Clearly, coverage of *Bakke* and *Webster* demonstrates that there are litigation settings that lead network news producers and reporters to invest substantial resources in covering the Court, despite much criticism to the contrary. Certainly, the evidence suggests that inattention is not a predetermined condition of the networks' relationship to the Court. Additionally, the analysis of *Bakke* and *Webster* has illuminated several structural and substantive components of television's coverage of the Court that may be important indicators of the nature of that coverage and, consequently, are suggestive of the public's opportunities to learn about the Court.

Armed, then, with the knowledge that television is limited in a number of ways that can potentially impact the nature of the coverage afforded the Court, but also with the knowledge that television is certainly capable of conveying important and useful information about the Court's activities, in this chapter we analyze network news coverage of two Court terms in their entirety, 1989–90 and 1994–95. By examining several hundred news stories that reported a multitude of Court-related activities, from case disposition to personnel changes, we have been able to paint a uniquely thorough picture of the overall coverage that the Supreme Court receives from the three major television networks. As a consequence, we are able to go well beyond our case studies of *Bakke* and *Webster* coverage to suggest that the attention and thoroughness that television reporters and editors have given to the Court's activities, in general, have not been constant during the course of any one term, or over time. Indeed, the evidence underscores enormous differences in the manner of reporting prominent cases such as *Bakke* and *Webster* when compared to the reporting of entire Court terms. More broadly and, perhaps much less obvious, there has been a distinct change from the reporting of the 1989 to the 1994 term, which underscores the diminishing interest in the Supreme Court by the network news explored in chapter 3.

THE 1989–90 AND 1994–95 TERMS
OF THE SUPREME COURT

The choice of these two terms for our analysis deserves some discussion. At the outset it should be noted that the 1989 term was the last full Supreme Court term for which a complete compilation of videotaped Court-related network news stories could be obtained from the Vanderbilt Television News Archive at the time that we began our research.[1] Clearly, the use of these videotaped news stories provides a much richer, complete, and accurate source of data than the utilization of the archive's written indices alone. Additionally, and as important, the 1989 term was one that allowed us the opportunity to view television news coverage of a period that, arguably, approximated judicial "normalcy."

Unlike the October 1988 term (which included not only *Webster*, but also the highly controversial ruling that overturned a Texas flag desecration statute, *Texas v. Johnson*), the 1989 term was not dominated by a single ruling or a single issue. True, abortion cases were still in the news as evidenced by both *Hodgson v. Minnesota* and *Ohio v. Akron Center for Reproductive Health*. These cases, however, dealt with state parental notification laws governing teenage women seeking abortions, not the sweeping state regulations at issue in *Webster* that many predicted would be the Court's vehicle for overturning *Roe v. Wade*. Similarly, the 1989 term also included another flag burning case, *U.S. v. Eichman*, which tested the constitutionality of the federal Flag Protection Act, passed in the wake of the earlier *Johnson* ruling. The previous term's case, however, seemed to have an "inoculation" effect, and public interest in

Eichman never reached the fevered pitch or stirred the political furor of the earlier litigation.

Analysts of the Court were quick to recognize the "generic" nature of the 1989 term. Linda Greenhouse, for example, observed in the *New York Times* that "assessments of the term from both ends of the political spectrum stressed that this was a period of incremental rather than dramatic change" (1990: E3). In a similar vein, Marcia Coyle of the *National Law Journal* noted that "adjectives describing the term just ended did not come easily to those usually most adept at analyzing the high Court. 'Cautious,' 'disappointing,' 'schizophrenic,' 'hard to pin down,' said court scholars. In the words of noted law professor A. E. Dick Howard, 'It was a term of transition which anticipates that which we will see more of'" (1990: S2).

This is not to suggest that the 1989–90 Supreme Court term lacked prominent or significant cases. Indeed, the end-of-term summaries published by the *Harvard Law Review* (1990), the *National Law Journal* (Coyle, 1990), and the *New York Times* (Greenhouse, 1990) together identified forty-four noteworthy or "leading" decisions (of the total 139 rulings with written opinions)[2] rendered by the Court during this term,[3] seven of which were categorized as leading cases by all three of these sources (see Table 5.1). They included *Missouri v. Jenkins,* which upheld the authority of federal judges to order local officials to raise monies to pay for desegregation efforts in the public schools, *Michigan State Police v. Sitz,* which upheld state sobriety checkpoints designed to catch drunk drivers, *Oregon Employment Division v. Smith,* which made it illegal to use peyote or other illegal drugs in religious ceremonies, and *Hodgson,* the abortion case previously mentioned. We will turn to a more detailed discussion of these and other cases later in this chapter.

Another factor lending additional interest to television news coverage of this particular Supreme Court term was the resignation of a prominent sitting justice, William Brennan, and the selection process that designated his replacement, David Souter. In a sense, the politics of judicial selection emerged as a coda to the Court's term. As underlined by Coyle, "All the drama and long-term implications of the 1989–90 Supreme Court term – difficult to see during the justices' eight-month session – exploded in a single event just three weeks after the term's end" (1990: S2). In some respects, however, the Souter nomination represented a relatively low-key appointment transaction. In the eyes of many analysts, conservatives already held a majority of seats on the Court, and, consequently, the Souter appointment, featuring a "stealth

Table 5.1. *Leading cases, 1989 term*

Atlantic Richfield v. USA Petroleum Co.	Austin v. Michigan Chamber of Commerce
FTC v. Superior Court Trial Lawyers Assoc.	Butterworth v. Smith
Cooter and Gell v. Hartmax Corp.	Board of Education of the Westside
Pavelic and LeFlore v. Marvel	Community Schools v. Mergens
Entertainment Group	Jimmy Swaggart Ministries v.
Peel v. Attorney Registration and	California Board of Equalization
Disciplinary Commission of Illinois	Milkovich v. Lorain Journal Co.
Metro Broadcasting v. FCC	Oregon Employment Division v. Smith[a]
Missouri v. Jenkins[a]	Osborne v. Ohio
Spallone v. U.S.[a]	Ohio v. Akron Center for Reproductive
Baltimore City Dept. of Social Services	Health
v. Bouknight	University of Pennsylvania v. EEOC
Blystone v. Pennsylvania	U.S. v. Eichman
Butler v. McKeller	Golden State Transit v. Los Angeles
Grady v. Corbin	NLRB v. Curtin Matheson Scientific Inc.
Holland v. Illinois	Pension Benefit Guaranty Corp.
Idaho v. Wright	v. LTV Corp.
James v. Illinois	Cruzan v. Dir., Missouri Dept. of
Maryland v. Buie	Health[a]
Maryland v. Craig	Hodgson v. Minnesota[a]
Michigan State Police v. Sitz[a]	Rutan v. Republican Party of Illinois[a]
Pennsylvania v. Muniz	Saffle v. Parks
McKesson v. Division of Alcoholic Beverages	Sullivan v. Zembley
and Tobacco	Office of Personnel Management
Sawyer v. Smith	v. Richmond
U.S. v. Verdugo-Uriquidez	Whitmore v. Arkansas
Wilder v. Virginia Hospital Association	Walton v. Arizona

[a] Leading cases identified by the *Harvard Law Review*, the *National Law Journal*, and the *New York Times* end-of-term summaries.

candidate," did not command the attention of the Scalia, Bork, and Kennedy nominations from recent years.

As for the 1994–95 term, this choice was made, in part, because it was the most recent completed Court term for which data on the network newscasts were available at the time of our writing. We wanted to include a relatively current term for the purposes of comparison and to check on the generalizability of our results from the earlier term. Due to the difficulty and expense of acquiring videotapes from the Vanderbilt Archive, we, as those before us, were left to use the archive's indices for the analysis of the 1994–95 term.[4]

In contrast to the 1989 term, 1994 was quite distinctive in several ways. For instance, this term did not feature abortion rulings, nor did it feature as historically significant a personnel change. The term, however, was arguably significant because "an energized conservative majority dramatically renovated doctrines affecting race relations, state and federal powers, and religious expression" (Coyle, 1995: C1). According to Linda Greenhouse, the Court's actions were "a gaudy show of zero-based jurisprudence," despite the presence of President Clinton's relatively new moderate appointees, Justices Ginsburg and Breyer, who found themselves on a Court that lacked a center and "was riven by competing visions of the Constitution and the country" (Greenhouse, 1995: 1). Especially noteworthy was an apparent shift among the justices in terms of activism. Whereas it has been a popular conception that liberals are more prone to overturn precedent and make policy from the bench (actions highly criticized by past and present conservatives both on and off the Court), the conservative bloc of Chief Justice Rehnquist and Justices Scalia, Thomas, Kennedy, and O'Connor was responsible for much of the activism during the 1994 term.[5] In contrast, the moderate-to-liberal Justices, including Ginsburg, Breyer, Souter, and Stevens, found themselves promoting restraint, adhering to prior rulings, and shying away from disputes considered inappropriate for the Court. Not only, then, were some major decisions made in 1994–1995, but some fairly dramatic behavioral shifts among the justices suggested future changes for the Court and its policy-making activities.

We used the same three publications noted previously to identify the leading cases of the 1994 Court term. Together, the *Review* (1995), the *Journal* (Coyle, 1995), and the *Times* (Greenhouse, 1995) classified thirty-four such noteworthy decisions from the term's eighty-six total rulings,[6] twelve of which were referenced by all three sources (see Table 5.2). Three of these involved racial discrimination. *Missouri v. Jenkins* revisited the issue of judicial authority in implementing desegregation plans by limiting that authority. *Miller v. Johnson* declared that congressional districts that are drawn largely on the basis of the racial composition of the districts are presumed unconstitutional until the state can show a compelling interest for doing so. Finally, *Adarand Constructors, Inc. v. Pena* required that the federal government's race-based affirmative action programs be subject to very strict scrutiny.

Also reported by all three networks were the Court's decisions limiting the

Table 5.2. *Leading cases, 1994 term*

U.S. v. Lopez[a]	*Adarand Constructors, Inc. v. Pena*[a]
U.S. v. X-Citement Video	*Miller v. Johnson*[a]
Arizona v. Evans[a]	*McIntyre v. Ohio Elections Commission*
Capitol Square Review Board v. Pinette[a]	*U.S. v. National Treasury Employees*
Florida Bar v. Went For It, Inc.[a]	*Union*
Rosenberger v. University of Virginia[a]	*Vernonia School District v. Acton*[a]
Plaut v. Spendthrift Farm	*Missouri v. Jenkins*[a]
U.S. v. Mezzanatto	*U.S. Term Limits v. Thornton*[a]
Schlup v. Delo[a]	*Rubin v. Coors Brewing Co.*
Oklahoma Tax Commission v. Jefferson	*New York State Conference of Blue*
Lines, Inc.	*Cross and Blue Shield Plans*
Babbitt v. Sweet Home	*v. Travelers Insurance Co.*
Commissioner v. Schleier	*City of Edmonds v. Oxford House, Inc.*
McKennon v. Nashville Banner	*Gustafson v. Alloyd Co.*
Publishing Co.	*Mastrobuono v. Shearson Lehman*
Wilson v. Arkansas	*Hutton, Inc.*
O'Neal v. McAninch	*Witte v. U.S.*
American Airlines v. Wolens	*Kyles v. Whitley*
NationsBank of North Carolina v. Variable	*Qualitex v. Jacobson Products*
Annuity Life Insurance Co.	*Hurley v. Irish-American Gay, Lesbian*
Sandin v. Conner[a]	*and Bisexual Group of Boston*

[a] Leading cases identified by the *Harvard Law Review*, the *National Law Journal*, and the *New York Times* end-of-term summaries.

power of government in the cases of *U.S. v. Lopez* and *U.S. Term Limits v. Thornton*. In the former, Chief Justice Rehnquist, writing for a five-to-four majority, invalidated the Gun-Free School Zones Act (1990), arguing that Congress had overstepped the boundaries of its power to regulate interstate commerce when it prohibited gun possession near schools. In so doing, "It was the first time in 60 years that the Court had invalidated a Federal law on the ground that Congress had exceeded its constitutional authority to regulate interstate commerce" (Greenhouse, 1995: 4). In contrast to *Lopez*'s limiting effects on the federal government's power, *U.S. Term Limits* marked a limitation on the power of state government, prohibiting states from imposing congressional term limits. Yet, the dissenters in this case (Thomas, joined by Rehnquist, Scalia, and O'Connor) argued that the federal government should govern only at "the sufferance of the sovereign states" (Greenhouse, 1995: 4).

An accommodationist view of religious expression was buttressed by the Court during the 1994 term. In two cases, *Rosenberger v. University of Virginia* and *Capitol Square Review Board v. Pinette,* the Court promoted the lowering of the "wall of separation" between church and state. Thus, in *Rosenberger* the Court held that the university had acted in a discriminatory manner when it refused to allow student activity funds to be used for the printing of a religious publication; in *Capitol Square,* the Court stated that the Ku Klux Klan could display a cross in a state park at the Ohio state capitol building.

In addition to these decisions, the Court issued several other rulings during the 1994 term that met with mixed commentary from various observers of the Court, and that will be the subject of greater discussion in the coming pages. As expected, considering the politically conservative tendencies of the Court during this term, liberals expressed grave concern about the future direction of the Court as a consequence of its decisions. While the threat of a counterrevolution to the Warren years had not come to fruition during the Burger and early Rehnquist years, Stephen Shapiro, the national legal director of the ACLU, indicated that the 1994 term "gives me pause" (quoted in Coyle, 1995: C1). On the other hand, conservatives like Clint Bolick of the Institute for Justice touted the 1994 term as "the finest in a generation," one that illustrated the justices' willingness to reduce the power of government at all levels in its effort to aggressively protect individuals from government's intrusion (in Coyle, 1995: C1).

While it is not likely that the conservative trends of this term will accelerate, given the reelection of Bill Clinton and his prospects for appointing additional justices, it is evident that the 1994 Court term was an important one. As such, it provides an attractive opportunity for us to compare two different Court terms, one generally deemed to be comparatively routine and the other seen as much more jurisprudentially exciting and potentially significant.

THE NATURE OF THE 1989 AND 1994 COURT COVERAGE

How Much Coverage?

The most fundamental question to be asked, and the starting point for our analysis of the nature of network news coverage of the Supreme Court, is how much coverage does the Court get? It is clear to anyone who watches the news on a regular basis that the networks' coverage of the Court is relatively less frequent than that of Congress and the White House, both of which are reported on a virtually daily basis. The absolute magnitude of the differences in the coverage afforded the three branches of our national government is starkly revealed in research reported by Doris Graber (1997).

Utilizing the index of the Vanderbilt Television News Archive, Graber found that between August 1994 and July 1995 an average of 107 stories per month were broadcast about the presidency, 24 stories per month focused on Congress, and only 5 stories per month centered on the Supreme Court across the three networks. (Note that Graber reports that the extent of congressional coverage would have virtually doubled if her measure had included pieces focusing on individual members of Congress.) Equally revealing, while more than fifty hours of newscast time were devoted to the presidency during the period studied, only about an hour and a half reported on the Court. Further, the average of eight minutes per month of broadcast time devoted to the Court by network newscasts in 1994–95 represented a precipitous decline from the twenty-six minutes per month average for a similarly defined period in 1990–91. In the earlier period studied, the Court received approximately 3.9 percent of the network newscast time devoted to the three branches of our national government; in 1994–95, that meager percentage fell even further to 2.4 percent (Graber, 1997: 270–272).

Throughout our analysis we have suggested many reasons for why there is such relatively infrequent and insubstantial attention to the Court on network newscasts. We have also explored the issue of the decline in the already spartan Court coverage brought about, in part, by changes in the broadcast news industry. Against this backdrop, Graber's findings remain quite sobering while also foreshadowing the thrust of the more extensive data reported in this chapter. Here, at the outset, we are particularly interested in how often the networks report the Court's activities, whether the three networks differ in the frequency of their coverage, and whether the frequency has changed over the course of time. This information is most generally important for reasons of democratic citizenship, which we have discussed in previous chapters. More specifically, though, it is important because it is one reflection of the degree to which the Court is considered newsworthy by the three major networks, and also because it suggests that viewers' choices of network may have implications for the amount and nature of the information they receive about the Court's activities.

The two Court terms in our analysis differ dramatically on both of these dimensions. Most obvious is the distinction in the total number of stories broadcast about the Court. During the 1989 term, the three networks collectively broadcast 245 Court-related stories. In dramatic contrast, 111 such stories were broadcast by the networks during the 1994 term.[7] Less obvious, but no less significant, are the differences among the networks in the frequency with which they cover the Court's activities. In their reporting of the 1989 term, ABC and NBC each broadcast seventy-five (30.6%) stories; CBS was more attentive, airing ninety-five such stories (38.8%), more than a quarter (26.7%) more than either of the other networks. This pattern reversed itself in 1994, when CBS aired the fewest stories (25, 22.5%) of all three networks. NBC paid the most attention to the Court, broadcasting forty-eight (43.2%) stories, while ABC aired thirty-eight (34.2%).

Overall, then, the total number of Court-related stories decreased on *each* of the three networks, while the proportion of stories aired by ABC and NBC increased. CBS's coverage of the Court declined most dramatically, at least in terms of the number of stories it broadcast during each term. The data preliminarily suggest, and rather disconcertingly so, that beyond receiving less information about the Court than it does about the other federal institutions, the American public has received even less of this information over the course of time. Moreover, the choice of network may, indeed, make a good deal of difference. Viewers of CBS, who were once "advantaged," appear to have become disadvantaged in terms of Court-related news. These findings are fully consistent with the trends in coverage of the Court discussed by the journalists we interviewed, both in an absolute sense and, in particular, with respect to CBS News. Recall, particularly, Pete Williams's concern that "there's only two of us that regularly hang out at the court, me and Tim. . . . CBS has a producer there now. But they don't listen to the arguments as much as we do so their coverage is declining," and Tim O'Brien's observation that "CBS does not appear to have any commitment at all."

What Is Covered?

The degree to which the Court is covered by the three networks and the extent to which that coverage has diminished over time are undoubtedly more complicated than is indicated simply by the number of stories reported. An examination of various elements of the Court's activities during each term reveals a more complete picture of network news coverage of the third branch of government.

The Court's activities, during any one session, can be distinguished, generally, by whether or not they are related to the Court's docket. It is readily apparent from the analysis of both of the Court terms we selected that the networks are overwhelmingly oriented toward the Court's current docket. Nearly three-quarters of the stories reported in 1989–90 (181, 74.0%) focused on the cases petitioned to and the policy outcomes of the decisions on the merits handed down during the term; focus on the Court's docket was even greater during the 1994 term (93, 83.8%). This clearly differs from the television reporting of other major political institutions, which often centers on the personalities of the officials, brewing scandals, institutional processes, relationships between institutions, and other personnel-focused, more sensational subject matters. Instead, this emphasis on the docket reflects the insulated nature of the Court, its distance from the rest of the political world, and the difficulty that reporters have in gaining access to the inner workings of Supreme Court processes and the relationships among its members, as portrayed in chapters 2 and 3.

This is not to say that all events outside of the Court's docket are considered unworthy of airtime. And, in fact, the imbalance between docket and other stories is not necessarily the preference of the reporters, some of whom would prefer to attend more closely, among other things, to the justices as people and politicians. For instance, Tim O'Brien has indicated,

We don't cover the Court personalities. I think we should. I believe all nine justices are honorable men and women. Certainly if we find . . . evidence to the contrary about any justice, I think the media would go after that justice as they would any politician, but by and large we don't cover the people – we cover what they do.

But, as the 1989 term clearly illustrates, changes in the Court's personnel sometimes attract quite a bit of news attention. The thirty-seven stories (15.1%) in our data set that dealt with the events surrounding Justice Brennan's resignation from the Court, which did not take place until after the Court's substantive work for the year had ended, are evidence of the highly publicized nature of some types of personnel-related activities. The networks were largely even in their coverage of the resignation, President Bush's nomination of David Souter, the prehearing, investigation phase of the process, and the confirmation hearings and vote of the Senate Judiciary Committee.

Additionally, six stories (2.4%) broadcast during the 1989 term focused on other events outside of the Court's docket. Four of these stories focused on Justice Marshall as he announced that he would begin to use the phrase "African-American" in his opinions, as he criticized Souter as Justice Brennan's replacement, and after he checked himself into the hospital after taking a fall. The remaining two stories focused on Chief Justice Rehnquist, who appealed to Congress to create additional federal judgeships to assist in the war against drugs, and who called for an overhaul of federal capital punishment laws in an effort to shorten the appeals process. CBS covered four of these stories, including both reports on Rehnquist, offering its attentive viewers a glimpse into the role of the Court vis-à-vis Congress.

The 1994 term also illustrates that some nondocket related events are considered newsworthy by television news producers. The successful confirmation of Justice Stephen Breyer, who took Justice Blackmun's seat on the Court at the end of the summer of 1994, received nearly as much network attention as the Brennan retirement/Souter appointment process did. Thirty-four stories were broadcast across all three networks from April 6, when Blackmun announced his retirement, to August 12, when Breyer was sworn in to office. Seven of these stories were included in our data set (which begins July 15), all involving the final stages of the appointment process. ABC and NBC reported on the Senate hearings, the Judiciary Committee's and the full Senate's vote to confirm, and Breyer's swearing-in ceremony. In contrast, but consistent with the network's declining attention to the Court over time, CBS reported only one of these seven stories, when the full Senate voted to confirm Breyer's nomination.

In addition to these appointment stories, there was another handful of personal stories about the justices (5, 4.5 %). Each of the networks reported the death of former Chief Justice Warren Burger in June 1995 by presenting retrospectives of his judicial legacy, and ABC and NBC reported Justice O'Connor's speech about her breast cancer surgery to the National Coalition of Cancer Survivors.

In the absence of any significant differences between the two terms in the frequency of personnel and other nondocket-related stories, the broadly diminished coverage in the later term is best understood in the context of the Court's docket, which has consistently shrunk over the past decade.[8] We have already demonstrated that network attention to the Court was dramatically diminished from the 1989 to the 1994 term, despite the latter term's relative importance. It may be reasonable to expect, then, that with fewer cases to decide and, therefore, fewer cases to report in 1994, the networks would have reported on more cases, or on the same number of cases more frequently than in the previous terms. However, this logic assumes that network attention to the Court is a constant and that producers designate the same amount of airtime to the Court from term to term, regardless of what the Court does. This is simply not the case. Rather, as our discussions with the network reporters have illustrated, if the Court does less, providing fewer opportunities for coverage, then the networks give it less attention. As Tim O'Brien (ABC) explained with regard to the Court's ever-smaller docket, "they [Justices] still take many very good cases, and they still deserve attention, but maybe not as much." Pete Williams's (NBC) thoughts were similar regarding both the number and the nature of the cases the Court is now hearing:

It is becoming harder and harder to put the Supreme Court on television. That is just all there is to it. Partly it is a reflection of the Court's work. . . . It's been widely noted, and I think it's true, that the Supreme Court seems to be spoiling less and less for fights. . . . There's no big area right now that the Supreme Court has jumped into . . . there is no big overarching unsettled question . . . [and] the caseload is getting smaller, so that just gives us fewer opportunities to get it on the air.

Thus, the nature of the Court's docket has implications for the coverage by the network news programs. The networks do not allocate a standard amount of airtime for the reporting of the Court each session. Rather, and independent of the seeming significance of cases heard by the Court from term to term, it appears that the size of the docket is one factor in determining the amount of airtime the Court receives. Our data indicate clearly that, beyond reporting fewer stories about the Court during the 1994 term, and despite the relatively considerable attention to the Court's docket relative to its personnel, the network coverage of the Court's docket was limited in a variety of ways.

As we have mentioned previously, the justices handed down 139 decisions on the merits during the October 1989 Court term and 86 such decisions during the 1994 term. Our three legal sources collectively identified forty-four leading or significant cases during the 1989 term, including seven that all three agreed were particularly important (refer to Table 5.1); these same sources recognized thirty-four leading cases during the 1994 term, twelve of which they all considered especially noteworthy (refer to Table 5.2). Television reporters, particularly those who have been on the Court beat for some time, are aware of which cases are likely to be those that will be the most legally significant and, more important, those that will be the most conducive to television coverage and interesting to television audiences. Thus, it is not surprising that our data show that the bulk of the cases on which the networks reported are those that are considered leading cases by the legal experts.

Tables 5.3 and 5.4 present the cases for which the Court made decisions on the merits and that received coverage on at least one of the networks. Several points are readily apparent. One is that for both terms, only a small proportion of the total number of cases ruled on each term were reported by any one of the networks. In 1989, 32 cases of the total 139 (23.0%) were reported on some network newscast;[9] in 1994, only 15 cases of the total 86 (17.4%) were reported on a newscast. Not only were fewer than half as many case decisions reported on in 1994, but the data also illustrate that an even smaller proportion of them were covered during this later term. So, despite the fact that the bulk of network news stories about the Court focus on the docket, they focus on a very small part of the docket (fewer than a quarter in each term of our analysis). It is obvious, then, that as the docket has shrunk, so has network attention to the docket, and therefore, to the Court more generally.

Tables 5.3 and 5.4 also illustrate that the vast majority of the rulings that are reported by the networks are those that have been identified as leading cases. In 1989, twenty-two of the thirty-two rulings reported were leading cases (69.8%), while in 1994, all fifteen of the rulings reported were leading cases. This is not to say, however, that *all* of the leading cases were considered newsworthy by the networks. Recalling Tables 5.1 and 5.2, in 1989, half of the leading cases were reported (22 of 44, 50.0%) and in 1994 less than half were covered (15 of 34, 44.1%). Additionally, while the 1989 term is characterized by coverage of all cases deemed noteworthy by all three of our legal sources (7 of 7, 100%), ten of the 1994 term's twelve such cases were covered (82.3%).[10] Finally, all three networks reported the rulings in six of the seven noteworthy cases in 1989; the exception was CBS's exclusive coverage of *Spallone v. U.S.* In contrast, in 1994, rulings in only six of the ten noteworthy cases covered by the networks were reported by all three; *Schlup v. Delo* and *Florida Bar v. Went For It, Inc.* were reported by ABC only, and *Adarand* and *Missouri v. Jenkins* were reported by ABC and NBC.

Thus, it appears that when the Court has a larger docket, the networks cover more of the docket. And, while the set of cases they report includes a smaller

Table 5.3. *Cases reported by the three networks by docket stage, 1989 term*

Case	Leading	Stage	ABC	CBS	NBC
Metro Broadcasting v. FCC	L	Argument		x	
		Decision	x	x	
Missouri v. Jenkins	L*	Argument	x		x
		Decision	x	x	x
Alabama v. White		Decision	x		x
Holland v. Illinois	L	Decision		x	x
Idaho v. Wright	L	Decision	x		
		Other[a]	x		
Illinois v. Perkins		Decision	x		
Maryland v. Buie	L	Decision	x	x	x
		Other[b]			x
Maryland v. Craig	L	Certiorari		x	
		Decision	x	x	x
		Other	xx		
Cruzan v. Dir., Missouri Dept. of Health	L*	Argument	x	x	x
		Decision	x	x	x
		Other	xx	x	x
Hodgson v. Minnesota	L*	Certiorari	x	x	x
		Argument	x	x	x
		Decision	x	x	x
		Other	xx	xx	xxx
Michigan State Police v. Sitz	L*	Certiorari	x	x	x
		Argument		x	x
		Decision	x	x	x
		Other	x		
Minnesota v. Olson		Decision		x	
Pennsylvania v. Muniz	L	Decision	x	x	
U.S. v. Verdugo–Uriquidez	L	Decision	x	x	x
		Other			x
Washington v. Harper		Decision	x	x	
General Motors v. U.S.		Decision		x	
Perpich v. Department of Defense		Certiorari		x	
		Argument			x
		Decision	x	x	x
Austin v. Michigan Chamber of Commerce	L	Decision		x	
Board of Education of the Westside Community Schools v. Mergens	L	Argument	x	x	
		Decision	x	x	x

Table 5.3. *(cont.)*

Case	Leading	Stage	Network		
			ABC	CBS	NBC
Jimmy Swaggart Ministries v. California Board of Equalization	L	Decision	x	x	
Milkovich v. Lorain Journal Co.	L	Decision		x	
Oregon Employment Division v. Smith	L*	Argument		x	
		Decision	x	x	x
Osborne v. Ohio	L	Argument			x
		Decision	x	x	x
University of Pennsylvania v. EEOC		Decision		x	
California v. American Stores		Decision	x	x	
Rutan v. Republican Party of Illinois	L*	Argument		x	
		Decision	x	x	x
U.S. v. Eichman	L	Certiorari	x	x	x
		Argument	x	x	x
		Decision	x	x	x
		Other	xx	xxxx	xx
Pension Benefit Guaranty Corp. v. LTV Corp.	L	Decision	x	x	x
FW/PBS v. Dallas		Decision	x		x
Spallone v. U.S.	L*	Argument		x	
		Decision		x	
Baltimore City Department of Social Services v. Bouknight	L	Certiorari		x	
		Argument		x	
		Decision	x	x	
Horton v. California		Decision		x	

Notes: L = leading case by one of three legal sources; L* = leading case by all three legal sources; x = single story.
a This story by ABC also included mention of *Craig*, as noted in the appropriate column of this table.
b This story by NBC also included mention of *Verdugo-Uriquidez*, as noted in the appropriate column of this table.

proportion of leading cases, they also report on some of the nonleading cases of the term; during the 1989 term, ten "routine" rulings were covered by at least one of the networks. In contrast, our data indicated that when the Court has a smaller docket, the networks expend less resources on the institution and cover fewer cases. Furthermore, at least in the instance of the 1994 term, the attention is paid exclusively to the term's leading cases, with no coverage whatsoever of the remainder of the Court's docket.

It is also evident from Tables 5.3 and 5.4 that the networks differed in their coverage of the merits decisions in these cases. CBS had by far and away the most complete coverage of this stage during the 1989 term, reporting on twenty-one of the twenty-two leading cases reported; the only case that it did not report at this final stage of the decision-making process was *Idaho v. Wright* (in which the Court ruled that a child abuse defendant's civil rights were violated when an alleged victim's courtroom testimony was replaced by that of a doctor after an interview with the child). In contrast, ABC reported on nineteen and NBC reported on fourteen leading cases at this stage during this Court term. Furthermore, CBS covered all of the "top" seven cases (L* in Table 5.3) at the merits stage, while both ABC and NBC failed to report the ruling in *Spallone v. U.S.* CBS also had the most extensive coverage of "routine" rulings receiving airtime (7 of 10, 70.0%), with ABC and NBC offering less complete coverage (5 and 3 rulings, respectively).

Coverage of the 1994 term was dramatically different. In contrast to 1989, CBS exhibited the most meager record of reporting merits decisions, reporting only eight of the fifteen rulings covered during this term, and only six of the ten "top" cases (L* in Table 5.4). More specifically, CBS failed to report the rulings in some of the term's most significant cases: *Adarand, Jenkins,* and *Capitol Square.* ABC had the most complete coverage of the Court's rulings during 1994, reporting on thirteen of the rulings covered and all ten of the most noteworthy cases; NBC reported on eleven and eight cases, respectively.

Also clearly documented by the data is the fact that the plurality of cases that are reported on the news receive their coverage at the merits stage (refer, again, to Tables 5.3 and 5.4). In 1989, sixty-nine of the docket-related stories (38.1%) examined the Court's decisions on the merits, and in 1994, thirty-three (35.5%) focused on merits decisions. This is not surprising, considering that the ultimate ruling in a case establishes judicial policy and is likely to be of greatest interest to the public, fitting the outcome-oriented focus of much television reporting. Yet, attention to the certiorari stage and oral arguments is also important to the extent that it educates viewers about the complexity of the process as well as provides greater legal context for the eventual ruling. The argument stage is particularly conducive to television coverage since the dates of the arguments, unlike the dates of certiorari decisions and final rulings, are known to reporters, who can then plan to report

Table 5.4. *Cases reported by the three networks, by docket stage, 1994 term*

Case	Leading	Stage	Network ABC	CBS	NBC
U.S. v. X-Citement Video	L	Decision			x
American Airlines v. Wolens	L	Argument	x		x
		Decision			x
Schlup v. Delo	L*	Decision	x		
U.S. v. Lopez	L*	Decision	x	x	x
		Other		x	
Wilson v. Arkansas	L	Certiorari	x		
		Argument	x		x
		Decision	x		
U.S. Term Limits v. Thornton	L*	Argument	x	x	x
		Decision	x	x	x
		Other			xx
Adarand Constructors, Inc. v. Pena	L*	Argument	x		
		Decision	x		x
		Other		x	
Missouri v. Jenkins	L*	Argument			x
		Decision	x		x
		Other			x
Hurley v. Irish-American Gay, Lesbian and Bisexual Group of Boston	L	Decision	x	x	x
		Other[a]	x		
Florida Bar v. Went For It, Inc.	L*	Decision	x		
Vernonia School District v. Acton	L*	Certiorari	x		
		Argument	x		x
		Decision	x	x	x
		Other	x		
Rosenberger v. University of Virginia	L*	Certiorari		x	
		Decision	x	x	x
		Other[b]	x	x	x
Capitol Square Review Board v. Pinette	L*	Decision	x	x	x
		Other	x		
Miller v. Johnson	L*	Certiorari	x		
		Decision	x	x	x
		Other	xx		x
Babbitt v. Sweet Home	L	Argument	x	x	x
		Decision	x	x	x
		Other	x		

Notes: L = leading case by one of three legal sources; L* = leading case by all three legal sources; x = single story them. Recall Fred Graham's explanation, "You know when it's coming . . . so that . . . permits you to lay out your thinking a lot better than on the day of the decision." Additionally, arguments often present conflict that has the potential to make exciting copy for the broadcast.[11]

Table 5.3 illustrates that in only two of the thirty-two cases reported during 1989 were the three major stages of the decision process covered by all three networks (*Hodgson* and *Eichman*), and only one other case was covered at these stages by one or more of the networks (*Sitz* by CBS and NBC). Understandably, oral arguments were covered more often than the granting of certiorari; in twelve of the thirty-two cases, argument was reported, and in five the granting of cert was noted.[12] With one exception (*Perpich v. Department of Defense,* which allowed the federal government to order state National Guard troops to participate in peacetime exercises abroad, despite objections by a governor), leading cases tended to be covered at more decision points than the nonleading cases of the term; in fact, nonleading cases were covered *only* at the decisions on the merits stage. And, again, CBS covered more cases at both the oral argument and certiorari stages than the other two networks during the 1989 term.

Apparent from Table 5.4, and consistent with our findings thus far, coverage of the multiple stages of the decision process diminished in 1994. Only two cases (*Wilson v. Arkansas* and *Vernonia School District v. Acton*) were reported at all three stages, both only by ABC. In fact, ABC had the best record overall, reporting at the cert stage for three cases and the argument stage for six cases; CBS, again, had the least coverage overall during this later term, reporting the cert decision for only one case, *Rosenberger,* and argument for only *Babbitt v. Sweet Home* and *U.S. Term Limits.* Despite this distinction between networks, though, the most important characteristic of the 1994 term drawn from the data is the relative paucity of coverage by all three networks.

One final point about the extent of network coverage of the Court's docket warrants attention before we consider *how* the networks covered Court-related activities. As we discuss in greater detail in chapter 6, the choice of the

Notes to Table 5.4 *(cont.)*
[a] This story by ABC also included mention of *Capitol Square, Acton, Babbitt,* and *Miller,* as noted in the appropriate columns of this table.
[b] This story by NBC also included mention of *Miller* and *Adarand,* as noted in the appropriate columns of this table.

Court *not* to hear a case is a significant element of the Court's authority, one that is made for thousands of cases petitioned to the Court every term. It would be unreasonable to expect that the networks would report on more than a fraction of these certiorari denials, and, as our data show, they do so in only a very small proportion of cases. During the 1989 term, the Court denied certiorari in eighteen different cases that were reported in twenty-nine stories. These cases included subjects such as the settlement made with regard to those who suffered from the use of the Dalkon Shield, an Iowa law that made it mandatory to wear a seatbelt, military regulations that prohibited acknowledged homosexuals from serving in the armed services, the use of federal racketeering laws to sue trespassers at abortion clinics, and bans on blocking access to abortion clinics by members of the interest group Operation Rescue.

In the 1994 term fifteen stories were broadcast covering ten different certiorari denials, once again demonstrating a decline in coverage in the more recent term. These cases included subjects such as wrongful birth suits, limitations on the rights of pro–life demonstrators to approach doctors who perform abortions and to access abortion clinics, and the reversal by state governments of affirmative action plans.

THE NATURE OF NETWORK COVERAGE
OF THE COURT: STRUCTURAL INDICATORS

The story of the networks' coverage of the Court is undoubtedly more complicated than the frequency and substantive focus of the coverage alone suggest. We have shown that reporting on the Court is relatively infrequent and that it emphasizes particular and limited aspects of the Court's activities, as well as only a small proportion of the cases heard by the Court. What we have not yet demonstrated is *how* the networks cover what they do report. As our examination of coverage of the *Bakke* and *Webster* cases indicated, there are other characteristics of the networks' broadcasts of Court-related activities that indicate the degree to which they convey information about the third branch of government. In other words, there are indicators of the nature, or the quality, of the networks' coverage that can be broadly categorized as structural (characteristics related to the format of the stories) or substantive (characteristics related to the subject matter of the stories). In light of the signifi-

Table 5.5. *Comparison of the structural indicators of the nature of network coverage of the Supreme Court (percentages in parentheses)*

	1989 Court term	1994 Court term
Number of stories	245	111
Story length		
Shorter than or thirty seconds	125 (51.0)	43 (38.7)
Longer than two minutes	68 (27.8)	40 (36.0)
Placement		
Lead story	37 (15.1)	13 (11.7)
Before the first break	87 (35.5)	59 (53.2)[a]
Before the second break	167 (68.2)	
Reporters		
Anchor only	100 (40.8)	49 (44.1)
Anchor and correspondent	145 (59.2)	62 (55.9)
Story format		
News only	99 (40.4)	51 (45.9)
News plus feature	145 (59.2)	55 (49.5)

Note: Unit of analysis is Court-related story; percentages will not necessarily equal 100% because some categories are not included.

[a] Number of stories broadcast during the first ten minutes of the program.

cance of knowledge for democratic citizenship that we have previously discussed, these factors are particularly important for the evaluation of the networks' coverage of the Court.

We begin with an examination of the former and find that for both terms the networks' coverage of the Court is limited in a number of ways. Generally, the data continue to illustrate that the opportunities for television viewers to learn about the Court are somewhat restricted, and that the networks have treated the Court as less newsworthy over time. Overall, it is impossible to escape the conclusion that the coverage of the Court's activities during the 1994 term was much less substantial than the 1989 term (see Table 5.5).

One of the structural variables we examined was the length of the individual stories.[13] It has been noted that longer stories may be better able than shorter ones to provide the viewer with the detail often necessary for a good understanding of the subject matter (Robinson and Levy, 1986). The time spent to report an event may be especially important for Court-related events because of the often complicated nature of the law and judicial processes as well as the lack of public understanding and sophistication about the Court.

We found, and not surprisingly considering what we know about the commercial constraints of network news programs and the brevity of the evening newscasts, that a substantial proportion of the Court-related stories were quite short (see Table 5.5). This was clear in 1989, when more than half of the stories reported across the networks were thirty seconds or shorter and only slightly more than a quarter were longer than two minutes. Included among the shortest stories were thirty-four reports, by at least one of the networks, covering the decisions on the merits of most of the leading cases of the term. For example, reports of the rulings in *Jenkins* (ABC), *Maryland v. Craig* (CBS, NBC), *Maryland v. Buie* (ABC, CBS, NBC), *Smith* (CBS, NBC), *Rutan v. Republican Party of Illinois* (CBS), *Jimmy Swaggart Ministries v. California Board of Equalization* (ABC), and *Metro Broadcasting v. FCC* (ABC, CBS) were all thirty seconds or shorter. In contrast, and not surprisingly given the potential drama and the ease of scheduling, reports about oral arguments were never shorter than thirty seconds. In fact, many of these stories were longer than two minutes, including those about arguments in *Jenkins* (ABC, CBS), *Cruzan v. Director, Missouri Department of Health* (ABC, CBS), *Eichman* (ABC, CBS, NBC), and *Hodgson* (CBS, NBC).

There were, however, a few reports on the Court's rulings during the 1989 term that were among the longest stories of the term; they were decisions in leading cases that dealt with particularly sensitive social issues such as abortion (*Hodgson,* 4 minutes), religion (*Swaggart,* 4.5 minutes), and the right to die (*Cruzan,* 5 minutes). Interestingly, the lengthiest stories of this term were seven pieces about Justice Brennan's retirement and his replacement, Justice Souter (each more than 6 minutes). Of particular note, five of these had as their primary emphasis one or the other justice's view on abortion, arguably the most highly charged social and political issue of the term and one on which personnel changes might have a substantial impact.

The 1994 term provides an even bleaker picture in terms of the length of the networks' reports about the Court. While the networks aired a smaller proportion of short stories and a greater proportion of longer stories in this term than they did in 1989, the figures do not overcome the striking difference between the terms in the number of stories in each of these categories.

More specifically, among the longest stories of the term were two reports by ABC on the rulings in *Adarand* and *Miller* (both longer than four minutes). Like the 1989 term, however, reports about the rulings in the Court's leading cases were often less than thirty seconds long; these included stories about the decisions on the merits in *Jenkins* (NBC), *Lopez* (NBC), *Rosenberger* (NBC, CBS), *Hurley v. Irish-American Gay, Lesbian and Bisexual Group of Boston* (NBC, ABC), and *Capitol Square* (NBC, CBS). And, unlike the 1989 term, there were also a few reports on oral arguments that were among the shortest of the 1994 term. Furthermore, and as we have noted previously, the seven reports about the replacement of Justice Blackmun by Justice Breyer were all less than thirty seconds long; this was in sharp contrast to coverage of the Brennan resignation and Souter appointment in 1990 and the three stories about the death of former Chief Justice Burger and his legacy, all three of which were between two and three minutes long. The change in focus and the overall and prominent decline on this dimension of the quality of the networks' coverage of the Court are clear. As Carl Stern lamented about his Court-reporting days, "Where television falls down is that there is so little time available for the report that it has to be truncated beyond belief. . . . When I was doing pieces, I generally had something in the range of six sentences to convey what the Court did. Most cases can't really be done justice in six sentences."

Another factor we examined in our evaluation of the coverage afforded the Court was the placement of the stories within the half-hour newscasts. As noted by Herbert Gans, "The news program is structured like a newspaper. The day's most important story is the lead, and the first two sections are generally devoted to the other important hard news of the day" (1979: 3). In addition, story placement has been linked to comprehension of the news, as "initial stories are generally better remembered" (Robinson and Levy, 1986: 180). As Table 5.5 shows, viewers of the network news programs during the 1989 term were presented with a higher proportion and nearly three times as many of these lead stories than they were in 1994. The two terms were also distinguishable in terms of the subjects that were provided this prime position in the program. During 1989, fifteen of the thirty-seven leading stories were about Brennan's resignation and Souter's appointment, while in 1994 not one of the stories about Blackmun's resignation and Breyer's appointment had this desirable place; instead, these stories were most commonly broadcast in the middle of the program. Additionally, and even with this greater emphasis on the Court's personnel changes, the 1989 term is characterized by a greater number of docket-related stories in this up-front position (20) than the 1994 term (12). Once again, the data clearly indicate that the Court was treated as a less important source of news for the three networks in the later term.

Furthermore, the networks reported more than a third of their Court-related stories prior to the newscast's first commercial break, and more than two-thirds prior to the second break during the 1989 term. In contrast, considerably fewer, albeit a greater proportion of, stories were broadcast in the first segment of the programs during 1994.[14] These figures suggest even more clearly than story length alone that viewers of these network news programs had a greater chance of exposure to and, presumably, comprehension of the Court and what it had done during the 1989 term than they did in 1994; in addition, the data indicate once again that the networks saw the Supreme Court as a more important source of news during the earlier term.

Two other structural factors that may be illustrative of the nature of the networks' news coverage of the Court are the number and type of reporters involved in presenting the story, and the format of the stories themselves. Every story involves the network anchor who reports from the television studio. Frequently, he or she is assisted by one or more field correspondents, who generally report the news from a location outside of the studio. For Court-related stories, the field correspondent is usually the network's primary law correspondent, who tends to be more knowledgeable about the Court and the law than other reporters. From even a superficial examination of news broadcasts, it is evident that stories reported only by the anchor provide many fewer visuals (either still photos or live footage) and contain much less detail and discussion about the Court's actions. Both of these factors may have some impact on how likely the story is to draw attention from viewers and on how much information they are able to glean from the report.

Additionally, and relatedly, we examined the format of each story to determine whether it was a straight news report (a presentation of the facts involving the occurrence of a newsworthy event), a feature story (an elaboration on a subject matter going beyond the simple reporting of the event's occurrence), a story combining elements of both, or a commentary piece. The news reports tend to be reported by the anchor, while features and feature-plus-news stories tend to be covered by the anchor and one or more correspondents. The former tend to be relatively short and the latter relatively longer, which may have implications for communication of subtle and complex information.

As Table 5.5 presents, more than half of the stories reported by the networks during the 1989 term were of the news/feature variety, and an equal proportion utilized network correspondents, evidence of an effort to go beyond the straight reporting of facts in presenting Supreme Court news and activities. It is also true, however, that only ten of the one hundred stories that were reported by the anchor alone and only eight of the ninety-nine news-only stories were related to the Court's loss of Brennan and its gain of Souter; in contrast, the bulk of these stories were docket-related and included the reports of the decision on the merits of many of the leading cases of the term (including *Jenkins, Smith, Buie, Swaggart, Craig,* and *Rutan*).

During the 1994 term, on the other hand, significantly fewer stories were reported by correspondents and in the news/feature format. The personnel stories of this term, including the change from Blackmun to Breyer, were largely news reports; similarly, and like the 1989 term, many of the term's significant rulings were reported only by the anchor in a news-only format (including *Jenkins, Capitol Square, Lopez, Hurley, Rosenberger,* and *Babbitt*).

In the final analysis, the data demonstrate that the three network news programs do not routinely provide for their viewers news reports about the Court that are structured in such a way as to increase attention to and promote the comprehension of information about the Court. Furthermore, it is very clear from this examination of structural variables that the 1994 term showed a dramatic decline in the focus on the Court by the networks. Thus, the nature of the networks' treatment of the Court as a less significant and competitive source of news reflects the continually shrinking Court docket as well as the triumph of "infotainment" as primary criteria motivating network news broadcasts.

THE NATURE OF NETWORK COVERAGE
OF THE COURT: SUBSTANTIVE INDICATORS

The nature, or quality, of the networks' coverage of the Court can also be measured by its substantive characteristics. There is a multitude of information that may be communicated by the televised news stories that would likely increase the general understanding and knowledge that viewers have about the Court and its activities. As the following discussion reveals, the transmission of this information by the three networks has been quite limited. This is particularly true for the 1994 term, for which we might have expected to see an increase in substantive information from 1989 given the networks' virtually exclusive focus on the 1994 docket, particularly on the leading cases of that term. Rather, and as we have seen repeatedly to this point, neither term is characterized by very thorough, substantial coverage of the Court, and 1994 evidences a dramatic decline in this regard.

Perhaps the most obvious substantive information that might be included in a news story about the Court is the names of the justices. This information is readily available to reporters, and including it in the news reports might, at the very least, make the names of the justices more commonly known, contributing to the development of a more informed citizenry. Our data indicate, however, that the justices are mentioned by name infrequently, even when nondocket-related stories are included. During the 1989 term, Justices Brennan and Souter were noted most often (in 31, 12.7% and 33, 13.5% of the stories, respectively),[15] while Justice White emerged as the least frequently mentioned jurist (11, 4.5%). Interestingly, the networks showed no propensity toward identifying the Court by its Chief Justice, as is commonly done by scholars; reference to William Rehnquist was made in only sixteen (6.5%) of the stories broadcast during the 1989 term.

Network attention to the justices during the 1994 term appears to be even less frequent, especially considering the particular attention paid to the Court's docket during this term.[16] The most often noted justice was the newest member of the Court, Stephen Breyer (12, 11.5%), followed closely by Chief Justice Rehnquist (10, 9.7%).[17] Justice Ginsburg was mentioned the least frequently, in only one story (1%), but Justices Souter and Thomas followed her closely, each being mentioned in only two stories. As previously noted, considering that this information is accessible, not to mention particularly meaningful in the context of the Court's docket activity, its absence from the vast majority of reports about the Court is quite striking.

Other pieces of information important to the understanding of the Court's decision making have been communicated in varying degrees to television news audiences in stories related to the Court's docket (see Table 5.6). The data from both Court terms indicate that the networks have, with some frequency, presented some facts about the cases that are petitioned to the Court, including mentioning the parties in the cases as well as other groups and individuals interested in the outcomes of the cases. Case facts are essential for even a rudimentary understanding of the legal disputes and issues that are at

Table 5.6. *Comparison of the substantive indicators of the nature of network coverage of the Supreme Court (percentages in parentheses)*

	1989 Court term	1994 Court term
Case facts		
yes	106 (61.6)	77 (92.8)
no	66 (38.4)	6 (7.2)
Litigants noted		
none	78 (45.3)	21 (25.6)
one	38 (22.1)	36 (43.9)
two	56 (32.6)	25 (30.5)
Interested groups noted		
yes	87 (48.6)	48 (51.6)
no	92 (51.4)	45 (48.4)
Interested groups quoted		
yes	84 (46.9)	48 (51.6)
no	95 (53.1)	45 (48.4)
Case vote		
yes	45 (54.2)	2 (5.9)
no	38 (45.8)	32 (94.1)
Ideological division		
yes	5 (6.3)	0 (0.0)
no	75 (93.8)	33 (100.0)
Division of justices		
yes	10 (12.7)	0 (0.0)
no	69 (87.3)	33 (100.0)
Concurrence writer identified		
yes	2 (2.5)	2 (6.1)
no	79 (97.5)	31 (93.9)
Concurrence opinion quoted		
yes	1 (1.3)	2 (6.1)
no	79 (98.8)	31 (93.9)
Dissenting writer identified		
yes	25 (32.5)	10 (30.3)
no	52 (67.5)	23 (69.7)
Dissenting opinion quoted		
yes	23 (29.5)	11 (32.4)
no	55 (70.5)	23 (67.6)

Table 5.6. *(cont.)*

	1989 Court term	1994 Court term
Majority opinion writer identified		
yes	30 (36.6)	18 (54.5)
no	52 (63.4)	15 (45.5)
Majority opinion quoted		
yes	29 (35.4)	18 (54.5)
no	53 (64.6)	15 (45.5)
Case history		
yes	33 (19.2)	5 (6.4)
no	139 (80.8)	73 (93.6)
Amicus brief filed		
yes	5 (2.9)	0 (0.0)
no	167 (97.1)	33 (100.0)

Note: Unit of analysis is Court–related story. Total number of stories in each cell represents those docket–related stories for which each variable was applicable.

the basis of the Court's cases, and it is instructive to note that television news programs often include such information. During the 1989 term, nearly two-thirds of the stories reported about the cases addressed by the Court included some consideration of case facts; however, those stories that did not mention facts included reports of the rulings in several of the noteworthy cases of the term, including *Sitz, Smith, Hodgson, Craig, Metro Broadcasting,* and *Swaggart.* In 1994, nearly all of the stories about the Court's docket addressed the facts behind the cases; three notable exceptions were ABC's report of the rulings in *Schlup* and *Wilson,* and NBC's report of the ruling in *Lopez.* This is one of several substantive variables for which the 1994 term appears to surpass the 1989 term in terms of information provided. However, the high proportion of stories in which case facts were presented in 1994 is, at least in part, a function of the networks' exclusive focus on the Court's leading cases during that term.

The identification of the litigants involved in the cases was relatively common during both terms. At least one of the litigants was noted in a majority of stories in 1989 (54.7%) and in nearly three of four stories in 1994 (74.4%). The names and issue positions of interested individuals and groups were often noted as well, illustrative of the networks' efforts to look to group spokespersons, concerned individuals, and acknowledged "experts" for additional perspectives on the Court and its work. Among these individuals and groups were Kate Michelman of the National Abortion Rights Action League (NARAL), William Webster, then-Attorney General of Missouri, Kenneth Starr, then-Solicitor General of the United States, Molly Yard of the National Organization for Women, Susan Smith of the National Right to Life Committee, Paul Jacobs of U.S. Term Limits, Inc., representatives from the NAACP, ACLU, Mothers Against Drunk Driving (MADD), various elected officials from state and national government, and professors from universities across the country.

To the extent that the networks pay attention to facts, litigants, and interested parties, this focus is not terribly surprising as it facilitates the telling of a story, the human element that is an often necessary facet of network newscasts. These pieces of information contribute drama and, at times, sensationalism to the stories, both of which are likely to attract viewer interest and consequently an audience for the newscast. As noted by Tim O'Brien, "We can really grab the viewer's attention with the actual person who wins or loses, or both." Indeed, it *is* surprising that the case facts, litigants, and interested parties are not *more often* noted in news stories in light of their propensity to personalize and increase interest in the Court's activities. As Pete Williams noted, in comparing broadcast and print news, "it's sometimes easier for us in television to let you see the person who brought the case or let you see someone who is affected by the case."

Interestingly, particularly given the attention paid to case facts, the networks do a less thorough job of presenting other, easily attainable information related to the Court's docket (see Table 5.6). Most noteworthy is the relatively infrequent reporting of the case vote in stories about the Court's decisions on the merits or their implications. In 1989, the vote was reported in slightly more than half of these stories and dramatically plummeted to almost never in 1994. Additionally, the votes of individual justices and the ideological division among them were given short shrift by the networks, particularly in 1994 when there was absolutely no mention in any of the stories of either of these pieces of information, both of which provide potentially important information about judicial policy making.

Given this tendency, it is not surprising that justices who wrote concurring and dissenting opinions were rarely identified, although it is interesting to note the variation between terms and between the two types of opinions. Clearly, information about dissenting opinions was reported much more frequently in both 1989 and 1994. This tendency to focus on dissents appears to be, in part, a function of the appeal of the drama of disagreement and conflict for television audiences. Nor is it surprising that the author of the majority opinion is the most cited and quoted in news stories during both Court terms, although the ease by which this information is available makes the degree to which this information is *not* provided in the news somewhat noteworthy. Thus, it appears that the preparation by Pete Williams for his stories on the Court is fairly typical: "I just start with the majority opinion and read right through it, all the concurrings right through until the last word of the dissent . . . [and to reach as many people as possible] you try to say who wrote the majority opinion and you try to say who wrote the dissent."

Perhaps slightly more inaccessible, but no less important to viewers' ultimate understanding of the Court's actions, are the case history and the positions of various interest groups. A case's litigation history offers a context for the Supreme Court's involvement in the case, suggests how the dispute might be resolved, and, often, can hold a key to understanding what the bones of contention are in pending Court litigation. Moreover, reference to lower court decisions helps to develop a better public understanding of the Supreme Court's role in our political system. Cases do not arrive on the Court's doorstep on a clean slate, and portraits of the Court's work that suggest otherwise are incomplete and may seriously misrepresent it to the public. This important information is, however, infrequently presented in television news stories. During the 1989 term, reference to litigation history occurred in only one of five stories (19.2%); during the 1994 term, case history was reported much less frequently, in only five stories (6.4%).

Finally, the formal action of interested groups and individuals vis-à-vis the Court's docket has received short shrift in the televised news broadcasts. The submission of amicus briefs, the important and not infrequent input to the Court by interested parties often requesting that the Court take a particular stand in a case, has gone virtually unnoticed by the networks, which reported such activity in only 2.9 percent of the case-related stories during the 1989 term and did not report on it at all during the 1994 term.

CONCLUDING THOUGHTS

We began this chapter with the recognition, based on our analysis of the network coverage of the *Bakke* and *Webster* cases, that the three television networks do, at times, provide extensive coverage of particularly noteworthy cases. Acknowledging that all cases are not created equal and that television and the Court are limited in a number of ways that make reporting on the Court difficult, we have sought to determine how the Court is reported over the course of two entire terms. Our analysis of the 1989 and 1994 Court terms reveals quite clearly that television network news coverage of the Court is somewhat unbalanced in its focus on the Court. For example, emphasis is placed on the Court's docket work, to the relative exclusion of any other Court-related activities and the justices themselves; the exception to this, as both terms illustrate, is the resignation and appointment of justices, which attracts relatively substantial coverage when it occurs. More specifically, the networks invest most of their resources in covering the terms' leading cases, which make up less than half of the Court's docket in any single term.

The coverage of these cases, despite their apparent importance, is limited both structurally and substantively. The news stories are often short, not well placed in the broadcast, reported by the anchor only and in a news-only format, all of which indicate that the Court is a relatively uninteresting and/or unimportant source of news to television networks. Additionally, the news stories infrequently include important, and in many instances easily attainable, substantive information about the Court's docket activities; while many stories in our analysis included references to case facts, the litigants, and interested individuals and groups, most stories lacked references to the justices, the case vote, the ideological division in a case, the case history, and the amicus briefs filed.

Beyond and, we think, even more significant than this characterization of coverage during both the 1989 and 1994 terms is the dramatic decline in the extent and nature of the coverage between these two terms. It is truly striking that during a term described as noteworthy by legal experts, as 1994 was, the network coverage would diminish to the extent that it did from a term that was described as not particularly significant by these same legal experts, as 1989 was.

The primary explanation for this decline is, as we have discussed, the triumph of "infotainment" in the broadcast news industry, aided and abetted by the Court's shrinking docket. As the number of cases decided each term has decreased, so has network television attention to the Court. Network producers clearly do not allocate a particular amount of time and other resources to reporting on the Court each term. Rather, it appears that as the Court makes fewer rulings, the networks broadcast fewer news reports on the Court. And, as we have noted throughout, the Supreme Court is not a subject matter that often meets the standards for newsworthiness in the commercially driven broadcast news industry.

6

"The Supreme Court Decided Today . . ." – or Did It?

"Every time Dan Rather says 'The Supreme Court today upheld . . .' I want to smack him. . . . He has got to know better. He's been around too long."
Toni House, Public Information Officer, U.S. Supreme Court

Throughout our narrative we have documented at many junctures that the Supreme Court is a uniquely invisible institution in the eyes of the American public both in a relative as well as in an absolute sense. As Gregory Caldeira notes, numerous studies have demonstrated that "there is only a shallow reservoir of knowledge about . . . the Court in the mass public. . . . Few . . . fulfill the most minimal prerequisites of the role of a knowledgeable and competent citizen vis-à-vis the Court" (1986: 1211). At any given moment if the average American were queried about any decisions the Court had rendered in its current or past term, the questioner would likely come up largely empty. Considerable research documents "that many Americans little recognize or little remember the Court's rulings. On open-ended questions that probe for specific likes or dislikes about Court rulings, only about half (or fewer) . . . can offer an opinion on even the most prominent Supreme Court decisions" (Marshall, 1989: 143). The lack of public information about the Court extends beyond its decisions, per se, to a similar lack of familiarity with the justices who comprise the Court. Thus, in one study, fewer than 10 percent of the public could name the Chief Justice of the United States while, somewhat ironically, more than a quarter of the populace could recognize the name of Judge Wapner of the *People's Court* television fame (Morin, 1989).

Lack of information is just one facet of the problematic relationship between the Court and the American public. *Mis*information about what the Court has done may, in some respects, be even more consequential for a

189

public whose beliefs and actions may be structured by its conception of existing public policies that have been brought about by judicial decisions. Here,
too, data exist to underscore the potential for a misinformed public as well as
an uninformed one. Perhaps the most telling examples emerge from a dated
Wisconsin study that tested respondents' recognition of whether the Court
had recently rendered a decision in eight controversies, half of which the
Court had actually decided and half of which it had not. A *majority* of the actual decisions and non-decisions were correctly identified by only 15 percent
of the respondents. Only 2 percent could identify correctly all of the controversies the Court had decided as well as all of those it had not. Six times as
many people (12%) got all eight test items wrong as got all of the test items
right (Dolbeare, 1967: 194–212).

Given the centrality of the media and, in particular, television news to what
the public "knows" about the Court, one does not have to look very far to find
a source for at least some of the erroneous beliefs people hold about the institution and its behavior. Indeed, we have already documented that network reporters have, at times, gone on the air and delivered reports that they, themselves, did not believe reflected accurately what the Court had done. Such
instances generally followed in the wake of negotiations between the reporter
and the newscast's producers and editors, who were, at times, responding to
different imperatives from those facing the journalist.

If there is one area where the propensity for misreporting the Court's actions is most pronounced, that area would almost certainly be the media's relatively infrequent forays into reporting on the Court's docketing decisions
and, in particular, its decision to *not* hear a case, the denial of certiorari. Indeed, when asked what television news did least well in its coverage of the
Court, Supreme Court Public Information Officer Toni House bemoaned,
"The cavalier attitude that they have about when we deny cert . . . which mis-
leads people into thinking that we are ruling on things. . . . I mean every time
Dan Rather says, 'The Supreme Court today upheld . . .' I want to smack him.
I pleaded with Fred Graham and Rita Braver to stop him. He has got to know
better. He's been around too long."

Linda Greenhouse agrees that this is a particularly problematic area in
press coverage of the Court, noting, "Every time I think I have seen it all when
it comes to denials of certiorari, I find a new example" (1996a: 1545). Greenhouse's own employer – America's "paper of record," the *New York Times* –
is not blameless in this regard. Indeed, Greenhouse admits, "Any time I err

on the side of self-righteousness on this subject, I am likely to be betrayed by my own copy desk" (1996a: 1546).

The pronounced tendency of the media to misreport certiorari decisions has not gone unnoticed by the justices themselves. Indeed, Justice Ginsburg, for one, has written:

Still too often, in my view, the press overstates the significance of an order denying review. Headlines, particularly, may be as misleading as they are eye-catching. For example, when we declined to review a decision of the Illinois Supreme Court in what has come to be known as the "Baby Richard" case, one headline read: "Controversial Illinois Adoption Rule Upheld: Without Comment, Supreme Court Affirms Biological Father's Right to 'Baby Richard.'" And when we declined to hear a constitutional challenge to a curfew for minors in Dallas, Texas, a headline reported: "High Court Appears to Uphold Curfews." (1995: 2123)

Justice Ginsburg's general concerns were manifested further when she took the extremely unusual step of issuing a short, striking concurring opinion (joined by Justice Souter) in a certiorari denial in the 1995–96 term in a case that had received considerable media attention when decided by the lower federal courts. Seemingly fearful of what the consumers of the Court's action would glean from media coverage, the justices underscored their belief that the fundamental substantive issues raised by the case were not, in any sense, resolved by the certiorari denial.

The case, *Texas v. Hopwood* (1996), centered on an affirmative action program at the University of Texas Law School aimed at increasing black and Hispanic enrollment. The Texas program that was in place when the lawsuit was initiated utilized separate admissions pools and committees for evaluating white and nonwhite applicants while also holding them to different minimum threshold scores on standardized exams for consideration of their candidacies. That program was clearly at odds with the Supreme Court's landmark 1978 ruling in the *Bakke* case, and it was invalidated by a federal District Court in 1994. When the Fifth Circuit Court of Appeals upheld the lower court ruling, it took the added and unusual step of noting that *Bakke*, which allowed race to be taken into account in some fashion in admissions decisions (albeit not in the manner that UC-Davis was pursuing in *Bakke* and, by extension, not in the way the University of Texas was attempting in *Hopwood*), was no longer an accurate reflection of the state of equal protection law. In effect, in the Fifth Circuit's view, *Bakke* had been overruled. An appeal of its *Hopwood* decision to the Supreme Court would present the Court with a case that leveled a frontal attack on the *Bakke* precedent.

As oftentimes occurs when the Supreme Court chooses not to hear a controversial case raising critical public policy questions, it can avoid doing so through procedural means or by offering a procedural rationale. Indeed, there is considerable irony in the recognition that the very *Bakke* precedent under attack by the Fifth Circuit in *Hopwood* had been "delayed" four years by the Supreme Court's finding of mootness in an earlier affirmative action case, *DeFunis v. Odegaard* (1974).

A similar theme would now serve Justice Ginsburg in her concurrence with the certiorari denial in *Hopwood*. After the District Court's *Hopwood* ruling, the university altered its affirmative action program and dismantled its "two-track" admissions approach, the fatal flaw in UC-Davis's program invalidated by the earlier *Bakke* majority. The "new" affirmative action plan in place at Texas differed significantly from that contested in the initial litigation and appealed to the Fifth Circuit. In effect, the affirmative action program considered by the Fifth Circuit was no longer in existence at nor was it being defended by the university. In appealing the circuit court's decision, the university was really contesting the language of its opinion and not presenting a live controversy necessary for Supreme Court review. Thus, as Justices Ginsburg and Souter reminded their readers in *Hopwood*:

Whether it is constitutional for a public college or graduate school to use race or national origin as a factor in its admissions process is an issue of great national importance. The petition before us, however, does not challenge the lower courts' judgements that the particular admissions procedure used by the University of Texas Law School in 1992 was unconstitutional. Acknowledging that the 1992 admissions program "has long since been discontinued and will not be reinstated," . . . the petitioners do not defend that program in this Court. . . . Instead, petitioners challenge the rationale relied on by the Court of Appeals. "This Court," however, "reviews judgements, not opinions." *Chevron U.S.A., Inc. v. Natural Resources Defense Council, Inc.* (1984). . . . Accordingly, we must await a final judgement on a program genuinely in controversy before addressing the important question raised in this petition.

Commenting on this unusual opinion, Linda Greenhouse opined that "Justice Ginsburg appeared to be . . . advising the public not to interpret the Court's refusal to hear the case as an endorsement of the Fifth Circuit's analysis" (1996b: A1).

In the absence of videotapes of the network newscasts' coverage of the certiorari denial in *Hopwood*, it is difficult to assess to what degree the Court's action was actually misreported, although we were informed by a local newscaster in Columbus, Ohio, that the Court had "signaled its displeasure" with *Bakke*. Further, a transcript of the *News Hour with Jim Lehrer* broadcast by PBS on July 1, 1996, does reveal the newscaster making reference to the "Supreme Court's affirmative action decision" as well as to "a seven-to-two vote" that "let stand an appeals court ruling." More generally, returning to the randomly chosen "average" American alluded to earlier, if we were lucky enough to draw an unusually "knowledgeable" individual, it is a safe bet that *Hopwood* would be among the "decisions" he or she was likely to "remember" from the 1995–96 term and, more than likely, he or she would "get it wrong." Our inference flows, in part, from extensive analysis of network newscast presentations of certiorari decisions made during the 1989–90 Supreme Court term. Before turning to that analysis, however, additional consideration should be given to the issue of just what a certiorari denial "means" or "does not mean" as a matter of substantive law.

ON THE MEANING OF CERTIORARI DENIALS

Developing examples of mischaracterizations of Court actions such as certiorari decisions would not be significant if the media were not the major source of public information about the Court or if, indeed, decisions on certiorari were generally tantamount to definitive decisions on the merits with widespread precedential value. The dominance of the media, however, particularly television, in informing people of the Court's work has been well documented. Katsh (1980: 31) has noted that most people claim to receive *all* of their information from television, while Iyengar and Kinder have argued, "As television has moved to the center of American life, TV news has become Americans' single most important source of information about political affairs" (1987: 112). Clearly, as Marshall notes and we have stressed throughout, "Public awareness of Supreme Court decisions depends heavily on the quality of coverage provided by the mass media" (1989: 142).

Answering the question of whether the Court's decision to *not* hear a case has substantive meaning is somewhat more difficult, and, indeed, persuasive arguments have been made on both sides of the question. In a technical and legal sense, of course, all that a certiorari denial means is that the Supreme

Court, utilizing its appellate discretion, has refused to hear a case, thereby leaving a lower court decision and its immediate holding undisturbed. This formal view of certiorari denial suggests that the Court, in not hearing the case, has not given any indication whatsoever of where it stands on the merits of the lower court judgment or on the issues involved. Consequently, the lower court decision carries no broad legal precedential or policy significance.

Many justices and commentators have consistently and aggressively insisted that this minimalist perspective on the meaning of decisions not to decide is, indeed, an accurate one. Felix Frankfurter argued the position most frequently and in greatest detail. At the most general level, Frankfurter noted that "a denial no wise implies agreement" with a lower court decision. Rather, "It simply means that fewer than four members of the Court deemed it desirable to review a decision of the lower court as a matter 'of sound judicial discretion'" (*State v. Baltimore Radio Show* [1950]). In a 1950 dissent in *Darr v. Burford,* Frankfurter expounded on what a denial of review could, indeed, actually signify:

It seemed . . . to at least six members . . . that the issue was either not ripe enough or too moribund for adjudication; that the question had better wait for the perspective of time or that time would bury the question or, for one reason or another, it was desirable to wait and see; or that the constitutional issue was entangled with nonconstitutional issues that raised doubt whether the constitutional issue could be effectively isolated; or for various other reasons not related to the merits.

On yet another occasion Frankfurter opined simply that denial "means only that, for one reason or another, which is seldom disclosed, and not infrequently for conflicting reasons, which may have nothing to do with the merits and certainly may have nothing to do with any view of the merits taken by a majority of the Court, there were not four members of the Court who thought the case should be heard" (*Brown v. Allen* [1953]).

Frankfurter's voice is not an isolated one on this issue. Also writing in the *Brown* case, Justice Robert Jackson asserted that "denial of certiorari . . . creates no precedent and approves no statement of principle entitled to weight in any other case." Further, several more contemporary jurists have echoed this stance. Thus, according to Thurgood Marshall, "Reliance on denial of certiorari for any proposition impairs the vitality of the discretion we exercise in controlling the cases we hear" (*U.S. v. Kras* [1973]). According to Justice Stevens, "an order denying a petition for a writ of certiorari is not a ruling on the merits of any question presented by the petition" (*Hambasch v. U.S.* [1989]). More recently Justice Stevens has added, "On occasion it is appropriate to restate the settled proposition that this Court's denial of certiorari does not constitute a ruling on the merits" (*Barber v. Tennessee* [1995]). William Rehnquist, the current Chief Justice, has also pointed to the alternative interpretations a certiorari denial may suggest, all of which fall well short of a merits decision: "Some members of the Court may feel that a case is wrongly decided, but lacking in general importance; others may feel that it is of general importance, but rightly decided; for either reason, a vote to deny certiorari is logically dictated" (*Huch v. U.S.* [1978]). Stating the matter succinctly, Justice Ginsburg concluded that "reasons why a petition fails to attract the four votes needed to grant certiorari vary from the technical to the prudential" (1995: 2123).

Documenting such juridical prudence, David O'Brien has pointed out that "liberal members of the Burger and Rehnquist Courts have dissented from the denial of a large number of cases dealing with obscenity and capital punishment," cases that they would surely lose on the merits and "that illustrate the difficulties of determining the meaning of a denial of certiorari." In view of the statements of several justices coupled with such illustrations it is easy to conclude that "because denials are usually not explained, there may be no way of knowing how a majority views the merits of particular cases" (O'Brien, 1990: 238–239).

Nevertheless, many analysts and jurists continue to dispute this minimalist interpretation of certiorari denials, often taking as their starting point additional words in Justice Jackson's *Brown v. Allen* (1953) concurrence: "Some say denial means nothing, others say it means nothing much. Realistically, the first position is untenable and the second is unintelligible. . . . The fatal sentence that in real life writes finis to many causes cannot in legal theory be a complete blank."

As Wasby and others have noted, cases accepted for review are not decided randomly but, rather, are reversed approximately two-thirds of the time suggesting, conversely, to some, that certiorari denial generally equates with affirmance (1988: 212–216). Clearly, lawyers and even some justices themselves have been known to cite certiorari denials and to draw inferences from them. David Neubauer takes note that "some infer consideration of the merits when the Court consistently leaves undisturbed lower court decisions seemingly at variance with past Court rulings" (1991: 382). According to Earl Warren,

"Denials can and do have a significant impact on the ordering of constitutional and legal priorities. Many potential and important developments in the law have been frustrated, at least temporarily, by a denial of certiorari" (quoted by Wasby, 1988: 213). Further, utilizing logic some might find faulty, Peter Linzer argues, "If a denial of certiorari were a purely discretionary act, largely or totally unconcerned with the merits of a particular case, it would be anomalous for justices to note their dissents" (1979: 1255). (Surely, however, it can be argued that even if denial were substantively *meaningless*, a justice seeking a substantively *meaningful* decision might find cause to dissent from the Court's refusal to hear a case!)

Clearly, there is no obvious or absolute answer to the question of what a certiorari denial means substantively. According to Henry Abraham (1993: 179), "No matter which of these . . . contrasting views may be 'correct,' the effect in the eyes of the disappointed petitioner is necessarily the same: at least for the present, he or she has lost." Offering a broader view, Sheldon Goldman and Thomas Jahnige (1985: 188) summarize the considered arguments:

> At the most, a denial of certiorari may represent an approval of lower court decision-making; at the least, it is a nondecision, that is, a decision not to do anything. Because they involve the Court neither in new policy departures nor in the overt responsibility for existing policy, such nondecisions are generally perceived as not being politically salient.

Abraham is certainly correct in noting that, in the immediate case at hand, certiorari denial means that the petitioner has "lost." This does not, however, necessitate or, indeed, necessarily suggest a "loss" from a broader judicial policy-making perspective. Returning to our (and, indeed, Justice Ginsburg's) discussion of the *Hopwood* case, it would be difficult (and certainly premature) to characterize the Court's refusal to grant certiorari as the death knell for *Bakke* or as definitive in any fashion. Many of the considerations outlined by Justice Frankfurter and others could easily have been applicable in this case at this time, and, we would posit, the issues avoided here will, in due course, be revisited on the merits by the Court in the foreseeable future.

Assessing the potential substantive implications of the Court's certiorari denial in *Hopwood* is, of course, purely speculative at the time of this writing. A much more graphic example of television news mistakenly portraying a certiorari denial as a substantive holding on the merits and drawing erroneous

policy implications from it can be found in our data set. For now let us simply note that several network news stories during the Court's October 1989
term focused on "legal defeats" for Operation Rescue, an activist antiabortion
group continually portrayed as being stifled in its efforts to blockade abortion
clinics. In several instances, as will be seen, the Court was characterized as deciding against Operation Rescue when, in truth, the Court's only "actions"
were its refusals to hear the cases. When Operation Rescue raised a similar
claim in a case that was ultimately resolved by the Court in a subsequent term,
the antiabortion group won on the merits as the Court refused to apply a dated
civil rights law in the present circumstances to block Operation Rescue's actions (*Bray, et al. v. Alexandria Women's Health Clinic, et al.* [1993]).

TELEVISION COVERAGE OF CERTIORARI
DECISIONS IN THE 1989–90 TERM

Our research on television coverage of the Supreme Court by network newscasts reported in this book has, as its primary focus, those television news stories that cover, in some way, the Court's handling of its docket. As teachers of
constitutional law and judicial politics, we have, at times, encountered students who were misinformed about docketing decisions that had been made
by the Court, and each of us could recall clearly several instances in which we,
ourselves, had been misled initially about the Court's actions by the manner
in which they were reported on the network news. Our sensitivity to this
issue notwithstanding, we still found that when we first coded the docket-
related stories for this book we classified several pieces as merits decisions and
were subsequently unable to match them with any decisions actually rendered
by the Court during the term. Through exacting detective work in the pages
of the *U.S. Reports* and, in some instances, calls to the Court's Public Information Office, we were ultimately able to pair what were, at times, expansive
newscast presentations of what the Court had "done" with certiorari denials
from the term. Our own coding errors when first viewing these news stories,
coupled with our less systematic realization of significant misreporting of
docketing decisions by television news, led to the analysis reported in this
chapter. We have isolated for analysis all network newscast stories from the
Court's October 1989 term that were, in fact, focused on docketing decisions,
whether or not they were characterized in that fashion by the newscast. In the

analysis that follows we will assess both the nature and the magnitude of television's propensity to misreport the Court's certiorari decisions.

Forty-two stories about the Court's docketing decisions were broadcast across the three network news programs during the 1989–90 term. The stories were coded along a number of variables tapping the technical facets of the news coverage including, for example, story length and placement. In addition, a number of variables gauging the substantive content of the stories were coded as well. These included, for example, whether litigants in a case were identified or quoted, whether interest group activities were noted, whether the case issue was identified, whether the history and facts of the case were presented, and whether the federal government's position in the case issue was noted. This information provided preliminary evidence about the nature and scope of the coverage of the Court's docketing decisions.

In addition, and most important for this analysis, the stories were coded according to the Court's actual action in the case at hand (whether it granted or denied certiorari); how the network portrayed the Court's action (whether certiorari was granted or denied or whether the case was treated as a decision on the merits); whether the network projected any policy motivation, direction, or implications from the Court's action; and how definitive the Court's action actually was. This information was crucial in assessing the nature of the networks' coverage of the Court's docketing decisions during the term examined here. Our analysis demonstrated that while the networks' reporting of grants of certiorari was, for the most part, accurate, reporting of the Court's denials of certiorari was considerably more problematic.

Of the forty-two stories on docketing decisions broadcast by the three networks on their evening news programs, thirteen (31.0%) covered the Court's granting of certiorari (see Table 6.1). Nine of these stories (69.2%) reported on three different cases involving important, controversial issues. These cases centered on flag burning (*U.S. v. Eichman*), discrimination against women of childbearing age in work involving hazardous chemicals (*International Union v. Johnson Control*), and abortion counseling (*Rust v. Sullivan*). Each of these certiorari grants was reported by each of the networks, with only *Eichman* actually decided on the merits in the October 1989 term. The remaining four stories focused on four other grants, each reported by only one of the three networks. They involved issues of mandatory life sentencing without the possibility of parole for those in possession of specified amounts of cocaine (*Harmelin v. Michigan*), a search-and-seizure case involving the establishment of road blocks

Table 6.1. *Network newscast presentation of docketing decisions, 1989 term (percentages in parentheses)*

	Supreme Court docketing decision	
	Certiorari grant	Certiorari denial
Number of stories	13	29
Number of cases	7	18
Presented as cert grant	13 (100)	0
Presented as cert denial	0	7 (24.1)
Presented ambiguously	0	8 (27.6)
Presented as merits decision	0	14 (48.3)
Presented "accurately"	13 (100)	7 (24.1)

to catch drunk drivers (*Michigan State Police v. Sitz*), a federalism question centering on state control of the deployment of national guard troops (*Perpich v. Department of Defense*), and a trial procedure question of whether an alleged child abuser has the right to face his or her accuser (*Maryland v. Craig*).

Obviously, these cases represent only a small proportion of those that were actually granted certiorari during the 1989–90 term. Such sparse coverage is not at all surprising, however, as stories on the Court's docketing decisions, particularly the granting of certiorari as distinct from a controversial denial, will generally be less newsworthy and television friendly than a report on a dramatic (and predictably scheduled) oral argument or an emotionally laden and divisive Supreme Court ruling. Television reporters covering the Court today do not have the Court as their sole assignment and, consequently, do not have sufficient time to invest in studying the Court's docketing decisions, which would be necessary to flesh out more than the occasional and seemingly compelling certiorari story, particularly in a setting where such a story would face substantial barriers to getting on the air. As noted by NBC's Pete Williams, "It just depends on how big the case is. I mean the term limits case we covered every step of the way. We covered it when they granted cert, we covered it when it was argued, we covered it when it was decided." Generally, however, the television Court reporter lacks the luxury of paying much attention to the Court's docketing choices. Williams continued:

What would I do differently if I covered the Court full-time? I would be one of those reporters who, when the cert list comes out, I say "Ah ha, well, they've taken the *Schwartz v. Farn* case, so that's a great thing." I'm not one of those guys. That's just not a very productive expenditure of my time. . . . There's already a high homework-to-getting-on-the-air ratio for the Supreme Court, and that would just make it a lot higher.

If a case granted certiorari warrants network coverage, such attention can and is generally given in the subsequent stages of its Supreme Court journey at the time of oral argument and/or when there is an announcement of a decision on the merits.

As one would expect, the stories that did address certiorari grants received very little airtime or prominence in the network newscasts. Ten of the stories were thirty seconds or less, and twelve were presented after the newscast's first commercial break. Only two stories, both about the abortion counseling case, included considerable substantive information such as the identification of the litigants or interested groups, the case facts, and the case history. Nearly half of the stories (6) offered absolutely no such substantive information, with the remainder including bits and pieces of information. Thus, despite the importance of many of the issues that were the subject of these cases, stories covering their certiorari grants were not very substantial.

Nevertheless, and of primary importance to this analysis, all thirteen of these certiorari grant stories reported accurately the Court's decision to review the case at issue. Language such as the Court agreed to "decide," "take up," "take on," make "a quick ruling," "review," "hear arguments," and "consider" made the action in the Court's decision to grant certiorari quite clear. The same, however, is far from true for the stories covering the Court's denials of certiorari, the focus of the remainder of this analysis.

Twenty-nine of the forty-two stories (69.0%) focusing on the Court's docketing decisions concerned the decision to deny certiorari.[1] These stories reported on eighteen different cases, quite commensurate with Bradley Canon's finding that during the seventeen terms of the Burger Court an average of 14.5 cases denied certiorari were reported on each year by television newscasts (1995: 5). The certiorari denial stories fell broadly into four issue areas: equal protection, privacy, abortion, and the First Amendment. The greatest number of stories (10, 34.5%) were about abortion-related cases, despite the fact that these cases constituted only four of the eighteen. These four cases concerned Operation Rescue blockades and demonstrations in Atlanta and New

York (*Hirsch v. City of Atlanta* and *Terry v. New York State NOW*), the use of racketeering laws to sue antichoice groups (*McMonagle v. Northeast Women's Center, Inc.*), and the legitimacy of tax exemptions for the Roman Catholic Church when it has engaged in antichoice lobbying (*Abortion Rights Mobilization, Inc. v. U.S. Catholic Conference*).

Cases involving the issue of equal protection, including gender discrimination in a Maryland country club (*Burning Tree Club, Inc. v. Maryland*), the rights of homosexuals in the armed services (*Ben-Shalom v. P.W. Stone*), school programs for handicapped children (*Rochester, New Hampshire School District v. Timothy W.*), and an affirmative action suit by Gulf Oil employees (*Bernard v. Gulf Oil Corporation*), were the focus of six stories. Five stories centered on privacy concerns, including three cases about random drug testing (*Bell v. Thornburgh; National Federation of Federal Employees, et al. v. Cheney;* and *American Federation of Government Employees, AFL-CIO, et al. v. Skinner*), one about seat belt laws (*Clark v. Iowa*), and another about cordless phones (*Tyler v. Berodt*). The First Amendment was the focus of two cases that were covered in three stories, two about school dances in a public high school (*Clayton v. Place*) and the other about the sinking of the Greenpeace ship, *Rainbow Warrior* (*Knight v. CIA*). Finally, three other cases were the focus of five stories, three about a case that proposed the reevaluation of the trust fund established for the victims of the Dalkon Shield, a faulty birth control device (*Menard-Sanford v. A. H. Robins Company, Inc.*), one about a case involving disputed water rights in Wyoming (*Shoshone Tribe v. Wyoming*), and one about a case questioning the immunity from liability for caseworkers involved in the placement of children in foster-care homes (*Babcock, By and Through Babcock v. Tyler*).

Thus, the eighteen certiorari denials reported on involved some of the most contentious political issues of the day, particularly as they related to the abortion, equal protection, and privacy domains. This is not surprising since such issues allowed for interesting television stories and were likely to be attractive to the most television viewers. Nevertheless, it must be underscored that these eighteen certiorari denials constituted a minute proportion (substantially less than 1 percent) of the total number of denials made by the Court during its 1989–90 term ($n = 4,705$) and, by no means, could they be considered broadly representative of all matters the Court chose not to hear. Thus, not surprisingly, viewers were exposed to very select types of cases that were denied certiorari, and they were exposed to only a very few of them.

As was the case in the stories covering the granting of certiorari, almost all of the certiorari denial stories were quite short and not prominently placed in the broadcast. Twenty-five of the twenty-nine stories (86.2%) were thirty seconds or less in length, and twenty-two (75.9%) were aired after the newscasts' first commercial break. Distinguishing the certiorari denial stories from those on certiorari grants, however, every denial story, with only four exceptions, included at least one piece of substantive information. Most denial stories (23, 79.3%) included some case facts, and nearly half of the stories (13, 44.8%) identified at least one of the litigants in the case. Only eight stories, however, noted the case's history, the existence of any governmental position was mentioned on only three occasions (all in stories about homosexuals in the armed services), and the attorneys in the case were never identified. For the most part, only the five stories about the Operation Rescue cases presented a substantial amount of substantive information.[2] Overall, the coverage of the Court's denials of certiorari was quite thin, thereby compounding the problem of misreporting examined below.

Coverage of certiorari denials was divided relatively evenly across the three television networks. NBC aired the most stories about certiorari denials (12, 41.4%), CBS aired nine (31.0%), and ABC reported eight. NBC (as assessed below) reported the greatest proportion of its stories accurately (4, 33.3%), but it also tied CBS in reporting the greatest number of its stories inaccurately (8). CBS reported only one story accurately, while ABC reported only two correctly and six with demonstrable error. These differences among networks are, admittedly, based on a small number of observations, and it is not our intention to gauge which did a "better" job of covering the Court's denials of certiorari. Rather, in the final analysis, in those rare instances where certiorari denials were reported, none of the networks did a very thorough or accurate job in presenting a picture of what the Court had actually done.

Indeed, inaccuracy in the newscasts' characterization of the Court's action is clearly the most important deficiency of these stories. In contrast to the stories about grants of certiorari, most of the stories about certiorari denials (22, 75.9%) were coded as fundamentally inaccurate or, at best, misleading or ambiguous in reporting what the Court had done. In nearly half of the certiorari denial stories (14, 48.3%), the Court's actions were blatantly misreported as decisions on the merits rather than as denials of certiorari. In eight additional stories (27.6%), the terminology used was sufficiently ambiguous to cause the viewer considerable difficulty in determining whether a merits decision had been made or cert had been denied. (In our own coding of these instances, it was only after extensive investigation that we could determine that the cases that were the subject of these "ambiguous" reports were, indeed, denials of certiorari.) Only seven of the twenty-nine stories about denials of certiorari (24.1%) were reported clearly and accurately as Supreme Court decisions not to hear a case!

The actual language in the stories best serves to illustrate the manner in which the Court's actions were characterized by the three networks during their evening news programs. It is quite apparent from a number of stories that there are instances in which the Court's decision to deny certiorari is reported correctly. For example, Peter Jennings of ABC News did a serviceable job in describing the Court's action in a case involving the effort to use federal racketeering laws to sue antichoice demonstrators: "The Court *refused to get involved* in a Philadelphia case where federal racketeering laws were used to sue more than two dozen demonstrators for damages after they had broken into an abortion clinic" (10/10/89). The phrase "refused to get involved," while far from crisp, is a reasonable representation of the Court's denial of certiorari in this case. Even more clear is Jennings's discussion of the Court's docketing decision in the Dalkon Shield case: "In Washington, the Supreme Court today removed the last major roadblock facing a $2.5 billion settlement for women injured by the Dalkon Shield. . . . The Court *refused to hear* a challenge to the settlement which sets up a trust fund to be shared by thousands of the victims" (11/6/89).

Similar language was used by Tom Brokaw of NBC News when he reported that "the Court *refused to hear* [the petitioner's] arguments" in a case involving mandatory seat belt laws in Iowa (12/11/89). In this instance, as well as others, "refused to hear" is exactly what the Court did when it denied certiorari. Another phrase, "refused to review appeals," was used by Dan Rather of CBS News on February 26, 1990, to explain accurately the Court's decision not to hear the case involving homosexuals in the armed services. Clearly, there are instances in which the three networks and their reporters can and do report correctly the Court's denials of certiorari as such.

There are, however, many more examples of inaccuracy and misreporting by the networks. As noted above, twenty-two stories (75.9%) were, to a greater or lesser degree, erroneous in their portrayal of the Court's action, fourteen, we would argue, quite blatantly, and in eight other instances somewhat more ambiguously. In each instance, the impression that viewers were likely to gain was that the Court had made a decision on the merits in the cases rather than denied them certiorari.

Ambiguous Language

Ambiguous language such as "refused to overturn" was used in a number of stories including one about the ban on homosexuals in the military. As ABC's Jennings stated, "In Washington, the Supreme Court has *refused to overturn* the regulation that forbid acknowledged homosexuals from being members of the armed forces," language suggesting that the case had been heard by the Court and that an existing policy had been left in place (2/26/90). Brokaw used similar terminology in NBC's story on the same case (2/26/90).

In a story about the Dalkon Shield settlement, CBS's Dan Rather reported that "the U.S. Supreme Court *turned down* the last major challenge and cleared the way today for a $2.5 billion dollar settlement for women injured by the Dalkon Shield birth control device" (11/6/89). The Court's action in a random drug testing case was also misreported when Rather stated:

The U.S. Supreme Court today *gave qualified approval* for random drug testing among government workers in sensitive jobs. The Supreme Court *turned down appeals* from Justice Department employees and civilian army counselors. (1/22/90)

In this instance, imprecise characterization of the Court's action is linked with the assertion of a substantive direction in the Court's holding, thereby compounding the problem.

In reporting this same case quite similarly, NBC's Brokaw stated that, "mandatory drug laws *got another vote of confidence* today from the Supreme Court. Without comment, the Court *rejected challenges* to two testing programs for Justice Department employees with top security clearance and for the Army's civilian drug counselors" (1/22/90). Finally, when reporting on a petition by a pro-choice group to take away the tax-exempt status of the Roman Catholic Church, Rather stated, "Justices, without comment, *killed a lawsuit* by an abortion rights group" (4/30/90).

These examples illustrate some of the language which we conservatively (and, we feel, generously) characterized as ambiguous or misleading for this analysis, that was used in many of the stories about the Court's decisions to deny certiorari. While phrases such as "turned down," "refused to overturn," "rejected challenges," and "killed a lawsuit" may have appeared to professionally trained ears as indirect or imprecise ways of describing certiorari denials, such a characterization would not likely be drawn by an average television newscast consumer. It is much more likely that the typical viewer of the evening's news would interpret this language to mean that the Court had heard a case and rendered a substantive judgment. (Even we, as noted previously, had difficulty determining from such news stories what type of action the Court had taken and several errors were made in our initial coding.) In the most positive light, then, the networks failed to portray clearly and accurately the Court's action in these stories.

Blatant Error

Most important, the largest proportion of stories about the Court's denials of certiorari could not be deemed ambiguous at all. Rather, they were clearly wrong. The most frequently used word to characterize the Court's action in such stories was *upheld*. In reporting on the Court's decision to deny certiorari to the petition challenging a ban on dances in public schools, Brokaw reported that "the Court *upheld* a ban on dances in the public schools of Purdy, Missouri, where many people are Southern Baptists who believe that dancing is sinful and satanic" (4/16/90). On April 30, Brokaw stated in a story about one of the cases of random drug testing that "the Court *upheld* random drug testing of thousands of air traffic controllers and other Transportation Department employees in safety-related jobs." The clear implication of these and other stories was that the Court had made a decision on the merits of the cases rather than denying them certiorari.

Other reports included the equally misleading and erroneous words *ruled* or *ruling*, stating clearly that a decision had been made. Bob Schieffer of CBS News, when reporting on a case regarding special education programs in public schools for handicapped children, stated that "in effect, today's *ruling* means that these schools must keep trying to find programs that will help these children" (11/27/89). Similarly, when explaining the Court's action in the aforementioned case involving dances in public schools, Brokaw reported, "The U.S. Supreme Court *ruled* today on an issue that most youngsters in this country say is a fundamental right: the school dance" (4/16/90).

Somewhat different, yet similarly misguided, language was used in other stories. When reporting on the case of the sinking of Greenpeace's *Rainbow Warrior*, Rather stated, "The Supreme Court today *refused to force* the U.S.

Central Intelligence Agency to release documents on the 1985 sinking of the *Rainbow Warrior*" (2/26/90). Jennings, in ABC's coverage of the public school dances case, reported that "the Supreme Court has *left in place* a law that bans a high school in . . . Missouri from holding school dances" (4/16/90). And in the case involving the attempt to revoke the Roman Catholic Church's tax-exempt status, Jennings reported, "The Court . . . *rejected an effort* to strip the Catholic Church of its tax-exempt status" (4/30/90).

Another variant of the misreporting of a certiorari denial came in a setting where the Court's inaction was linked to its definitive ruling in a prominent case (*Baltimore City Department of Social Services v. Bouknight*) that was part of our leading case sample for 1989–90. The *Bouknight* case was covered at all three decision stages by CBS News. When the merits ruling in *Bouknight* was reported in a lengthy (about two and a half minutes) piece on decision day, Dan Rather described another "related" Supreme Court action (*Babcock, By and Through Babcock v. Tyler*) at the end of the piece: "In another child abuse case today, the Supreme Court let stand a ruling that public social workers may not be sued when children suffer abuse in Court-approved foster homes" (2/20/90). *Babcock* was, however, simply a certiorari denial, and, we should add, the *Bouknight* case itself was a Fifth Amendment self-incrimination ruling where the legal issue did not deal with the issue of child abuse per se.

Each of these examples illustrates the extent to which network newscasts can be misleading in their reporting of the Court's actions. Television viewers were very likely to believe that the Court had made decisions on the merits in each case when, in fact, the justices had actually denied certiorari in each of these cases except, of course, *Bouknight*.

Perhaps the most blatant misreporting of certiorari denials during the 1989–90 term occurred in the stories about the demonstrations and protest activities of the antiabortion group Operation Rescue. On May 14, 1990, both ABC and CBS reported on the Court's refusal to hear the group's assertion that blocking access to abortion clinics in Atlanta, Georgia, was protected by the First Amendment's guarantee of free speech. Ted Koppel of ABC introduced the story by reporting that "before the Supreme Court *a defeat today* for the antiabortion group Operation Rescue. The Court *said* that a claim of free speech does not give them the right to block access to abortion clinics in Atlanta, Georgia."

Bettina Gregory followed up on this story by stating, "Today, the Supreme Court *said* those restrictions [on Operation Rescue blockades instituted in

Atlanta] did not violate freedom of speech because these protestors had a history of unlawful conduct." She continued, "Today's *action* affects Operation Rescue in Atlanta."

CBS's coverage of this case was, perhaps, even more misleading. Schieffer reported:

The Supreme Court split five to four today and *upheld* a ban on antiabortion demonstrators who tried to block entrances to Atlanta abortion clinics. The Court *rejected the demonstrators' arguments* that they were just exercising free speech.

Beyond using the words *upheld* and *rejected . . . arguments,* all of which imply that the Court made a substantive decision, Schieffer's report included the outcome of a vote taken by the justices. By reporting the vote, it appeared (even to us) that the justices had made a decision on the merits. After extensive but unsuccessful searching for such a decision, we found evidence indicating that the vote was actually taken to determine whether an application by Operation Rescue for a stay should be granted. By a vote of five to four, the application was denied (see n. 1 for this chapter)

If this was not confusing enough, a week later (5/21/90) each of the three networks aired stories about Operation Rescue's activities in New York. In this instance the presentation of the litigation setting, which was, indeed, a certiorari denial, was quite problematic. Further, the stories included erroneous references to the earlier Atlanta case, treating it as if a merits decision had been made. For instance, Jennings reported:

There has been a second *legal defeat* at the Supreme Court for the antiabortion group Operation Rescue. The justices today *agreed with lower courts,* which ruled the Operation Rescue pickets may not block access to abortion clinics in New York. Last week the Court made a similar *ruling* for clinics in Atlanta.

CBS's explanation of the Court's action went even farther down an erroneous road. The opening visual headline for the evening's newscast was, "The Supreme Court *Bans* Abortion Clinic Blockades" – not the best of beginnings! Dan Rather introduced the story by reporting:

The U.S. Supreme Court *approved* new limits today on protests by antiabortion groups. The justices *upheld* a permanent ban on demonstrators who physically try to block entrances to abortion clinics. Today's *ruling* was on a case from New York.

In an expansive follow-up report, Rita Braver repeated the problematic reference to the Atlanta case stating that "last week the Court voted five to four to allow a temporary ban against Operation Rescue to stand in Atlanta. But today's action is considered even more significant because it involves a permanent ban and can have an impact on similar cases now under way in other states."

Elaborating on the seeming implications of the "case," Braver opined, "The Supreme Court action is bad news for Operation Rescue. . . . Abortion rights activists call it a victory for them." Confirmatory interviews were then conducted with spokespersons for the Legal Defense Fund of NOW and the Feminist Women's Health Centers.

For NBC, Tom Brokaw reported that "today, the U.S. Supreme Court *upheld* the ban on [blocking entrances to abortion clinics] by Operation Rescue in the New York City area. Last week, the Court *let stand* a similar ban against the group in Atlanta."

These five stories about two abortion-related cases sharply illustrate the extent to which the network news programs may misreport the activities of the Court. Both cases were, at some level, denied review by the Supreme Court, yet the stories that aired about them gave the distinct impression that the Court had made a decision on the merits in each case. This impression was further substantiated for the Atlanta case by subsequent references in the stories about the New York case. Moreover, in addition to mischaracterizing certiorari denials as merits decisions, these examples also demonstrate that network newscasts may unjustifiably draw broad policy implications from the Court's certiorari action. Anyone viewing these stories (as well as the other seventeen that we have characterized as reported ambiguously, at best, or as merits decisions at worst), regardless of which channel they were watching and how knowledgeable they were about the Court, would have likely misperceived the nature of the action the Court had taken and its public policy implications.

Despite the relative frequency of misreporting documented in our data, it might be argued that for some cases a denial of certiorari is, indeed, tantamount to a decision on the merits. As noted previously, that is surely the case for the actual litigants involved. More broadly, however, there are likely to be instances where a case's policy issues are resolved definitively by a certiorari denial. When, for example, the issue before the Court is a very narrow one and quite fact intensive, as in the Wyoming water rights dispute mentioned earlier, certiorari denial clearly ends the matter for all intents and purposes and may serve the same function as a merits ruling. In such a setting, misreporting the certiorari denial as a merits decision seems to be a less egregious media error.

It is not our intention to enter the debate outlined earlier regarding the meaning of certiorari denials. Indeed, it is clear that in some instances it makes good sense to talk in terms of the broad substantive implications of the Court's refusal to hear a case, while in other instances it does not. With this in mind, the certiorari denial news stories were coded for whether the Court's docketing action definitively resolved the underlying policy issue raised by the case. In only four of the twenty-two certiorari denial stories deemed inaccurate (18.2%) could the Court's refusal to hear a case be deemed definitive in nature. Three of the eighteen certiorari denial cases were the focus of these stories: the case of the Dalkon Shield settlement, the sinking of the *Rainbow Warrior,* and the water rights case from Wyoming. In these instances, the networks' misreporting of the Court's action may not have been very consequential since the denial of certiorari in these three cases amounted, as a practical matter, to the resolution of the issue involved.

This leaves, however, an overwhelming majority (18, 82%) of inaccurate stories about the fifteen other cases for which the Court's certiorari denial was not definitive in nature. Faulty reporting here is especially problematic since the issues involved in these cases were very controversial and would likely arise again in subsequent litigation before the Court.

Reporting such certiorari denials as if the Court had made substantive decisions on the merits was clearly avoidable. As several examples we have presented make clear, the networks are indeed capable of reporting certiorari denials accurately. Thus, despite its relative frequency on television evening news programs, it appears that there was and is little reason for misreporting the Court's docketing decisions. The consequences of such misreporting can best be seen in instances where the Court ultimately makes a merits ruling inconsistent with earlier reporting of a certiorari denial on the issue involved. A striking example of such an occurrence emerged when the Court resolved the substantive issues in the Operation Rescue cases in our data set *in favor* of the antiabortion group (*Bray, et al. v. Alexandria Women's Health Clinic, et al.* [1993]) in a subsequent term.

SUMMING UP

The picture that emerges of network news coverage of Supreme Court docketing decisions is not a very happy one. Understandably, coverage of such decisions is quite limited. In our 1989–90 data set the granting of certiorari in seven cases received coverage on at least one network newscast, and in three of those instances (cases dealing with abortion, flag burning, and gender discrimination) all the network newscasts reported the Court's decision to hear the case. These stories illustrated that when certiorari grants are covered, they deal with prominent and much anticipated cases brought before the Court. Importantly, in all instances when a certiorari grant was reported, the networks got the story fundamentally "right." In each instance the Court decided to hear a case and it was reported as such. Interestingly, policy implications were never projected from the Court's granting of certiorari.

Reporting in network newscast stories covering certiorari denials, however, was considerably more problematic. Twenty-nine stories were broadcast on certiorari denials in eighteen different cases. Broadly, the issues raised by the cases denied review and receiving newscast attention fell almost exclusively in the legal domains of abortion, privacy rights, the First Amendment, and equal protection. Focus on such emotional and controversial areas is, of course, not surprising. Four instances of certiorari denials were prominent enough to receive attention across all three network newscasts. These included denials in a case contesting a product-liability settlement involving the Dalkon Shield, a case dealing with the rights of homosexuals in the Armed Services, a case dealing with efforts to remove the Catholic Church's tax-exempt status because of its antiabortion activities, and a case dealing with the efforts of Operation Rescue to blockade abortion clinics.

Most striking in our findings is the fact that of the twenty-nine stories focusing on certiorari denials, only seven (24.1%) accurately and unambiguously characterized the Court's refusal to hear the case. In the plurality of stories covering certiorari denials (14, 48.3%) the Court's inaction was presented as if it were a decision on the merits! Coupled with the eight stories coded conservatively as "ambiguous" in their presentation of what the Court had done, essentially three out of four of the certiorari denial stories (22, 75.9%) misrepresented the Court's action. Importantly, in only four (18.2%) of these instances could the Court's certiorari denial be characterized as "definitive" in any sense. Moreover, there were a number of stories in which the network newscast included a projection of broad policy implications from the Court's "action."

The data clearly underscore that coverage of the Court's docketing decisions by the network newscasts is cursory at best. By no means do we wish to suggest, however, that the Court's docketing decisions warrant more substantial coverage than they now receive. Rather, it is our contention that coverage, when given, can be more accurate than that we have analyzed. Indeed, we have seen a range of reporting from that of the Operation Rescue certiorari denial, which was characterized as a decision on the merits across all three networks (a "merits" characterization that the Court "reversed" when the issue was actually resolved on the merits in the *Bray* case alluded to above), to a certiorari denial in a case dealing with the Catholic Church's tax-exempt status, where one network correctly presented the case as a denial, a second network characterized the denial ambiguously, and a third newscast presented the denial as a merits holding by the Court!

Viewed in the context of several examples of accurate reporting of the Court's docketing decisions, even certiorari denials, it is puzzling why the newscasts do not present docketing decisions more accurately more of the time. Given our earlier discussions of the commercial imperatives of network newscasts, the cynical observer may suggest that a central focus on accuracy often diminishes the drama associated with a story lacking a definitive resolution, thereby hampering a broadcast's commercial appeal. Certainly, as we have seen, certiorari stories are generally terse presentations delivered by news anchors without the benefit of elaboration by the network's Supreme Court correspondent, perhaps a recipe for inaccuracy in reporting. When questioned about the greatest difficulty that television journalists faced in covering the Court, Supreme Court Press Officer Toni House asserted, "The major problem [for] the journalist covering the Court is for him to get it right" (quoted in C-SPAN, 1996). This admonition carries great weight when reporters (and news anchors) make the decision to cover a docketing decision of the Court. First, "get it right." Having done so, the reporter remains free to analyze, speculate about, and draw implications from a docketing decision that, in the first instance, has been presented accurately.[3]

The thrust of our analysis in this chapter is clearly substantive, not theoretical. We have proceeded from the premise that media coverage of the Court has consequences for the information that the citizenry possesses about what the Court has done. We have demonstrated that the mass public may often be constrained in its knowledge by faulty presentations or misrepresentations of the Court's behavior. Clearly, such misinformation can misdirect individual decision-making and behavior in directions not contemplated by or gleaned justifiably from the Court's decision *not* to decide.

7

Which Decisions are Reported?
It's the Issue, Stupid!

"They're more driven to stories that will produce ratings, and, therefore, they may be evaluating stories not on the basis of their importance, but how they'll play – whether it meets sort of a bar-stool test, whether people will fall off their bar-stools when they see the story coming on television."

Carl Stern, former NBC news correspondent

The data we have presented throughout this volume make very clear that the networks' primary interest in the Court is focused on its docket and the decisions that are handed down each term. Further, as chapter 5 has illustrated, the Court's rulings in the terms' leading cases were the primary focal point of network news coverage. It was equally clear, though, that only a small proportion of cases, even of these leading cases, were reported during each of the terms in our analysis. The question remains, then, what influences the choice of which cases to cover? There have been others before us who have examined this question empirically, and their work is discussed briefly below. This research, while noteworthy, has been infrequent and limited in a number of ways. We then turn to our own analysis of the factors related to the coverage by the three networks of the cases that were granted certiorari and eventually decided on their merits with full opinions during the 1989 term. Our effort builds on and attempts to overcome many of the limitations in the previous research and has enabled us to understand more precisely how the choice of which cases to report is made by network news personnel.

PREVIOUS RESEARCH

Over the past several years there have been three studies that speak directly to the question of which factors influence the choice of which Supreme Court

212

cases to report. One examined the coverage afforded the Court's rulings by television, newspapers, and news magazines during the 1986 term (O'Callaghan and Dukes, 1992), another examined just newspaper coverage of decisions in the 1985 and 1986 terms (Gates and Vermeer, 1992), and the third study focused exclusively, as we do, on television coverage of the Court's rulings (Greco–Larson and Tramont, 1993). Together, these studies provide a foundation for our research, but all three yield very different results and are weakened significantly by limitations that we have sought to overcome in our analysis.

Jerome O'Callaghan and James Dukes's (1992) analysis was modest, focusing on the issue in each case as the primary explanatory variable in the reporters' choices of cases to report. The authors defined the issues in their study utilizing the categories employed in the *National Law Journal*'s annual summary of decisions: civil rights, criminal law, economic, First Amendment, and other issues. Their data indicated that civil rights cases were afforded the greatest attention (indeed, grossly disproportionate attention in light of their proportion on the Court's docket) by all three forms of media, not surprising considering the appeal of such issues to most audiences. More specifically, they found that the newspapers gave somewhat greater attention to economic issues than the other news sources, reflecting, perhaps, a recognition that they served a more educated and politically sophisticated audience; this seems particularly plausible considering the elite nature of the papers analyzed (the *New York Times*, the *Los Angeles Times*, and the *Chicago Tribune*). The networks gave less coverage to economic issues than newspapers, but more than the news magazines, which focused almost exclusively on civil rights cases. This suggests the possibility that the news magazines aimed their coverage at the least sophisticated following of all three mediums.

Melissa Gates and Jan Vermeer's (1992) more ambitious multivariate analysis of newspaper coverage of the Court was based on their assumption that reporters, in their effort to make efficient use of their time and other resources, would use cues to make choices about which cases to cover. The authors posited that cues would fall into two general categories, case importance and conflict in the decision. They operationalized conflict as (1) whether the Court overturned the most immediate lower court decision, and (2) whether there was unanimity in the case (as measured by the number of opinions written). Case significance was operationalized by (1) the seniority of the justice writing the majority opinion, (2) participation by the U.S. government as an amicus in the case, (3) participation by the United States as a direct party to the litigation, and (4) the length of time between oral argument and a merits decision. Several additional variables were also included, such as the number of decisions announced on the same day, whether the case had been petitioned from a federal or state court, and the issue involved in the case.

Their data, collected from four newspapers, revealed that conflict in a case (measured by the total number of opinions written) served as a primary cue to reporters that they should report the decision. Other important cues were the number of cases decided on the same day and the case issue.

Stephanie Greco–Larson and Tramont's (1993) study is, perhaps, the most relevant to ours since they examined network news coverage of the Court's decisions. Like Gates and Vermeer, these authors used a cue-driven theory to guide their analysis of the length and placement of news stories broadcast about decisions made during the 1989 calendar year. Their model included many of the variables included in Gates and Vermeer's study, in addition to several others including (1) the number of dissents written, (2) the page length of the case, and (3) whether Chief Justice Rehnquist wrote the majority opinion. Additionally, (4) the involvement of a famous or "quirky" person or incident, (5) the involvement of sex, (6) interest groups and/or the U.S. government, (7) whether the majority opinion was written by Justices Marshall or O'Connor, (8) whether the case was a class action suit, and (9) the case issue (First Amendment, race discrimination, abortion, and criminal rights) were included. Finally, the model included as independent variables indicators of the legal importance of a decision, measured by (10) the number of law review articles that cited the case in the two years following the decision, and (11) the number of federal court opinions that cited the decision in the subsequent two years.

Interestingly, and in contrast to the other studies, Greco–Larson and Tramont's analysis revealed that the amount of television coverage decisions received (measured by the length of the stories) was almost completely attributable to the "legal importance" variables. While the placement of the news stories in the newscast was in part predicted by other variables in the model, their analysis clearly emphasized the legal community's attention to the case as a cue for network television reporters.

Our analysis of television coverage of the Court's decisions is informed in part by this research, but it also represents our effort to avoid several limitations of these studies. For example, Greco–Larson and Tramont's use of data from a calendar year means that their analysis is based on cases from two distinct Court terms. Since Court terms may differ in a number of respects, including personnel and docket, this is somewhat problematic and unnecessary, particularly since data from discrete terms are certainly available. Additionally, their model appears to be underspecified as their choice of variables is not as theoretically driven as it might be. This is particularly evident in the power of the legal importance variables in their model, which would appear to be important on their face, but are also post hoc and may reflect rather than cause media attention. Other variables, such as whether Marshall or O'Connor authored the opinion or whether the case was a class action suit, seem to lack any theoretical basis for inclusion in their model.

Another potential problem we have identified can be found in O'Callaghan and Dukes's use of the *National Law Journal*'s summary of decisions. Our own work has convinced us that the *Journal's* classifications are frequently based on an inaccurate identification of the fundamental legal conflict in the cases. For example, for the 1989 term, the *Journal* categorized *Missouri v. Jenkins* as a civil rights case because the substantive issue in the case was the racial segregation of public schools. However, as noted in chapter 5, the conflict before the Court, and on which the ruling was made, was whether a federal judge had the power to order local officials to raise taxes to pay for desegregating the schools. The issue at hand, then, was the limits of judicial authority, not desegregation.

Similarly, the *Journal* categorized *Peel v. Attorney Registration and Disciplinary Commission of Illinois* under the rubric Attorneys when in fact the case involved a question about commercial speech implicating the First Amendment's application to legal advertising. Because of these and other examples, we believe that focus on the *Journal's* issue areas calls O'Callaghan and Dukes's analysis into question.

These difficulties are exacerbated by collapsing the many *Journal* issue categories into the four that they do (Gates and Vermeer's analysis is also limited in this way). For example, their Economic Issues category subsumes decisions categorized by the *Journal* as Federalism or Labor and Employment, both of which are clearly not necessarily economics cases.

Finally, Gates and Vermeer's analysis contains some limitations in the operationalization of key variables. For instance, conflict on the Court is measured by the total number of opinions written in a decision. The authors do not, however, examine the actual case vote. In their analysis, then, a case decided five to four may, depending on the number of opinions written, be seen as less conflictual than a unanimous decision accompanied by several concurring opinions. Additionally, attention to the senior justices' authorship of opinions and the length of time between oral argument and the decision on the merits are lacking a theoretical basis for their inclusion in the model.

DATA AND VARIABLES

Our analysis of the networks' choice to cover particular Court rulings is based on data collected about the 128 decisions on the merits handed down with full opinions during the 1989 Court term.[1] The networks' news stories on the cases reported during the term were the source of our dependent variable; the independent variables in our model were measured from analysis of the case summaries reported in the *U.S. Reports.*

Dependent Variable

Our purpose in this analysis is to understand why some rulings are reported and others are not. To that end, our dependent variable is simply the number of network newscasts that reported on a particular Supreme Court decision. The variable ranges from no coverage (coded zero) to coverage by all three networks (coded 3). We believe that this measure of coverage is more meaningful and precise than that used by Greco-Larson and Tramont, for example, whose dependent variables were the length and placement of the news stories. The fundamental question, we feel, particularly given the nature of the coverage of the Court our data have revealed, is whether or not a decision is reported *at all.*

Independent Variables

The independent variables in our model include measures that are case specific and/or institutionally determined (such as amicus participation, governmental involvement, and case vote), as well as those that tap media constraints and notions of newsworthiness (such as the number of cases decided on a particular day and the issue area of the case). The full model included the following variables.

Decision Date. It is an empirical reality that a disproportionate number of Supreme Court decisions are announced and concentrated at the end of the Court's term, and that decisions are announced more sporadically and unpredictably throughout the remainder of the Court's annual session. Additionally, and as chapters 2 and 3 indicated, reporters and news producers are well aware that the rulings announced at the end of the term are most likely to contain a disproportionate number of the term's most important ones. Consequently, television news is likely to pay greater attention to the Court's actions at the end of the term than at any other time during the session. In other words, television coverage of decisions handed down in June (coded 1) is more likely than when decisions are handed down during the other eight months of the term (coded zero).

Number of Cases Announced on the Same Decision Day. As we know, airtime on a network newscast is a very scarce resource and the news' content represents a far cry from the *New York Times*'s adage, "All the news that's fit to print." Not only does news about the Court always compete with the rest of the day's news events, but on a particularly busy Court decision day, cases compete with each other as well. This variable simply measures the number of decisions handed down on the same day, varying from one to nine decisions. The expectation is, of course, that as the number of cases announced on the same day increases, the likelihood that any one of them will be reported will decrease.

Lower Court. Cases arrive at the Supreme Court's doorstep from lower federal courts as well as from state supreme courts. These courts vary along a number of dimensions, including the populations that they serve and, we think, in the perceived policy importance of cases that they hear. Thus, there may be a link between the court that was the most immediate source of the case and the likelihood that the Supreme Court decision would be reported. To test the possibility of this link, we determined the lower court source of the case and created a dummy variable, assigning a 1 if the case had come to the Court from the D.C. Circuit Court of Appeals, the Second Circuit (which includes New York), the Ninth Circuit (which includes California), the Supreme Court of New York, or the Supreme Court of California, and a zero for any other lower court.

Action of Supreme Court vis-à-vis Lower Court. Conflict is often a signal to television personnel of a newsworthy event. In the context of the Court, conflict may be manifested in a variety of ways, including the stand that the Court takes in relation to the lower court's ruling. We make the argument that Supreme Court affirmances of lower court decisions are perceived as less newsworthy and, consequently, are less likely to be reported. In contrast, reversals of lower court rulings are more likely to receive coverage, while "mixed" Supreme Court holdings are likely to fall between reversals and affirmances in terms of their newsworthiness along this conflict dimension.

Supreme Court Case Vote. Another, perhaps more obvious, manifestation of conflict in Court decisions is the final vote in the decision, as it reflects the degree to which there is disagreement among the justices. We expect that greater division, as it is reflected in the final vote, is likely to result in greater attention by the network newscasts. We measured this conflict with a five-point scale, ranging from a unanimous vote (coded zero) to a highly divided vote (5–4, 4–3, coded 4). In between these extremes are the possibility of a highly cohesive (8-1, 7-1, 6-1, or 5-1 coded 1), a moderately cohesive (7-2, 6-2, or 5-2, coded 2), and a moderately divided (6-3, 5-3, or 4-2, coded 3) vote. In three instances, the Court's holding in a case resulted from a mixed vote by the justices on separate issues; as a result, the vote in these three cases was coded as not ascertainable, and the cases were eliminated from our analysis. This left 125 cases in our analysis.

U.S. Government Involvement in a Case. It has become commonplace in judicial politics research to take note of the "most favored status" of the federal government in federal court processes. In particular, analysts have taken note of the government's successful contribution to shaping the Court's docket as well as its propensity to win cases on the merits at the Court. We expect that the government's involvement in a case will be a signal to reporters covering the Court that the case represents a potentially important instance of litigation, with a greater level of governmental involvement increasing the likelihood of coverage. Our measure of the government's involvement ranges from no involvement in the case (coded as zero) to being a direct party in the litigation (coded as 3). In between these two possibilities, the government may have filed an amicus brief (coded 1) or may have fallen just short of being a direct party by filing an amicus brief and participating in oral argument (coded 2).

Total Number of Amicus Briefs Filed in a Case. The examination of interest group activity in the judicial process has been the subject of a long and continuing tradition of scholarship. In recent years, the focus on groups has gone beyond studying *their* behavior in pressing for policy change through the courts to include consideration of how the participation of groups affect the behavior of others in ongoing judicial processes (see, for example, Caldiera and Wright, 1988). The most common form of interest group participation in the courts is the filing of amicus briefs and, certainly, as groups represent the interests of particular subsets of the American population, amicus filings in a case may alert reporters to the potential policy significance and/or the potential impact of a case. Our expectation, then, is that cases that attract a greater number of amicus briefs will have a greater chance of being reported on the network newscasts. We measured the number of briefs filed in a case by intervals of five, with zero indicating no briefs, 1 indicating up to five briefs filed, 2 indicating up to ten briefs, and so on. If there were more than twenty-five briefs filed in a case, it was coded as 6.

Issue Area of Case. Given the commercial dictates of television news and concerns about audience appeal, interesting visuals, conflict, and drama, the subject matter of litigation has often been regarded as a potentially important factor in the choice of which decisions to report. As our consideration of previous research has illustrated, however, operationalizing and measuring issue areas have been problematic enterprises. One primary difficulty has been the categorization of issues, for which others have relied on the *National Law Journal*'s end-of-term summary. We have found this summary lacking, for reasons previously stated, and have instead defined issue areas on the basis of a full reading of each case's syllabus reported in the *U.S. Reports.* Doing so has allowed us to be sensitive to differences among issues while, at the same time, limiting the number of categories utilized for meaningful data analysis. Our coding resulted in categorizing cases as First Amendment, criminal justice, other rights and liberties, judicial power, federalism, economic (including taxation, commerce, antitrust and bankruptcy cases), and other (including, but not limited to, civil procedure, federal programs, labor and employment, attorney-related) cases. We included these issue areas as dummy variables in our model, with each case coded as 1 if it involved the issue and zero if it did not.

RESULTS

As Table 7.1 illustrates, nearly three-quarters of the Court's 1989 decisions on the merits were not reported by any one of the three networks. Interestingly,

Table 7.1. *Decisional coverage, 1989 term*
(percentages in parentheses)

Amount of coverage	Number of decisions
No coverage	95 (74.2)
One network	9 (7.0)
Two networks	9 (7.0)
Three networks	15 (11.7)
Totals	128 (100.0)

of the decisions that did receive airtime on some network, the plurality (45.5%) were covered by all three networks and the vast majority (72.7%) were covered by at least two networks. At the same time, however, some independence can be seen in the networks' choices with nearly three out of ten decisions reported (27.1%) airing on only one newscast. The following discussion suggests several factors that were related to these choices during the 1989 term.

Several interesting relationships emerge from an examination of the bivariate correlation matrix presented in Table 7.2. First, the choice to report a case is clearly associated with a number of variables that are included in our analysis. As we expected, the correlation between the number of amicus briefs filed in a case was significantly related to that case being covered ($r = .428, p < .01$), as were the case vote ($r = .190, p < .05$), the decision date ($r = .246, p < .01$), and three issue areas, First Amendment ($r = .316, p < .01$), other rights and liberties ($r = .182, p < .01$), and economic issues ($r = -.167, p < .05$). All of the relationships were in the predicted direction. A greater number of briefs filed was associated with network coverage of a case, as was a case ruled on in June, greater internal conflict (in the form of a divided vote among the justices), and cases involving First Amendment and other rights and liberties issues. On the other hand, the negative coefficient for cases involving economic issues suggests that the networks chose not to report rulings that involved this type of issue, as we expected.

It is also interesting to point out that several of our variables were not significantly related to whether or not a case was reported by the networks. Apparently, the involvement of the U.S. government had very little relationship

Table 7.2. *Correlation matrix of decisional coverage and independent variables, 1989 term (coefficients are Pearson's r)*

	TV coverage	Action cf. lower court	No. of briefs	Decision date	First Amendment issue	Criminal justice issue	Other rights issue	Judicial authority issue	Federalism issue	Economic issue	U.S. gov't	Case vote[a]	Lower court source	No. of cases on same day
TV coverage	1.00													
Action cf. lower court	-.008	1.00												
No. of briefs	.428**	-.114	1.00											
Decision date	.246**	.023	.405**	1.00										
First Amendment issue	.316**	.003	.096	.088	1.00									
Criminal justice issue	.083	.032	-.158*	.002	-.219**	1.00								
Other rights issue	.182*	-.040	.360**	.066	-.112	-.184*	1.00							
Judicial authority issue	-.015	-.033	-.068	-.123	-.094	-.155*	-.079	1.00						
Federalism issue	-.073	.023	.010	-.031	-.106	-.175*	-.089	-.075	1.00					
Economic issue	-.167*	-.074	-.034	-.047	-.143	-.235**	-.120	-.101	-.114	1.00				
U.S. gov't	-.109	.044	-.061	.036	-.110	-.112	-.071	.024	-.065	.172*	1.00			
Case vote[a]	.190*	.086	.107	.091	.064	.302**	.055	-.101	-.172*	-.218**	-.157*	1.00		
Lower court source	-.086	-.065	.040	-.046	-.063	-.040	-.086	.030	-.002	.203*	.016	-.052	1.00	
No. of cases on same day	-.019	-.063	.069	.488**	.045	.165*	-.033	-.042	-.057	.007	.007	.084	.029	1.00

* $p < .05$, 1-tailed; ** $p < .01$, 1-tailed; $n = 128$.
[a] $n = 125$.

to whether the networks reported a case; and, indeed, the negative correlation coefficient suggests that cases with less involvement by the government were associated with greater network attention. Similarly, and surprisingly, the number of decisions handed down on the same day was not related to the choice made by networks.

While bivariate statistics provide a starting point from which to understand the relationship between our independent variables and television coverage of the Court's rulings, they are limited because they do not consider the independent effect of multiple factors on the dependent variable. To get a more complete understanding of why the networks chose to report the Court decisions that they did, we conducted a multivariate, ordinary least squares analysis. The results are presented in Table 7.3.

The analysis revealed that, when controlling for other factors, the internal conflict (case vote) was not significantly related to the likelihood of network coverage of Court decisions. Additionally, the predictive strength of cases that did not involve issues related to the First Amendment, criminal justice, or other civil liberties was not great in the multivariate model. Similarly, the involvement of the government, the Court's action vis-à-vis the lower court, and the lower court source of the case were not important factors in the decision to report.

Several important variables that we expected to influence this decision did, in fact, do so. It is quite clear that the greater number of amicus briefs filed in a case increased the likelihood that the case would be reported by at least one of the networks. Also, and quite interestingly, the date of the decision and the number of cases decided on the same day were predictors of decisional coverage in 1989. Based on the correlation matrix in Table 7.2, which indicated that the number of cases handed down on the same day was not significantly correlated with decisional coverage but was correlated to the date of the decision ($r = .488$, $p < .01$), we might have removed from our model the number of decisions made on the same day. Since the two variables are substantively distinct, however, including both was appropriate. The multivariate analysis suggests, even when both variables were included in the model, that the networks were, indeed, more likely to report a case when it was the only one or one of only a few handed down on the same day. Similarly, the networks were more likely to report a case when it was ruled on in June, as opposed to other times during the term.

The data are also quite clear about the significant influence of the case is-

Table 7.3. *Multivariate ordinary least squares analysis of decisional coverage by network TV, 1989 term (estimates unstandardized; standard error of estimates in parentheses)*

Variables	B
No. of cases on decision day	$-.085$**
	(.040)
U.S. government involvement	.013
	(.063)
Lower court source	$-.071$
	(.197)
Action vis-à-vis lower court	$-.012$
	(.082)
No. of amicus briefs	.316****
	(.094)
Case vote	.034
	(.051)
Decision date	.392*
	(.216)
First Amendment issue	1.221****
	(.277)
Criminal justice issue	.659***
	(.227)
Other rights and liberties issue	.602*
	(.326)
Judicial authority issue	.204
	(.363)
Federalism issue	.177
	(.319)
Economic issue	.082
	(.267)
$n = 126$	$R^2 = .371$
	Adj. $R^2 = .297$

* $p < .10$; ** $p < .05$; *** $p < .01$; **** $p < .001$.

sue in the choice by the networks of which cases to report. Two types of issues, First Amendment and criminal justice issues, are those that are most likely to attract the attention of network newscasts and these issues clearly influence the choice about which decisions to report.

DISCUSSION

Conflict within and outside the Supreme Court was included in our model as a cue for reporters for essentially two reasons. First, we believed that conflict among the justices in a case, and conflict between courts, would be potentially interesting to those judicial and other political actors concerned with the function of precedent and the balance of power between courts. Second, and particularly important from the perspective of television, conflict tends to be dramatic and can make for interesting viewing; it gives onlookers the opportunity to take sides in the debate and to participate, albeit indirectly, in the event. We expected, then, that Court decisions that involved conflict, in one form or another, would be more likely to be reported on network news programs than those in which conflict did not exist.

The results presented above indicate that both forms of conflict were not compelling factors in the choice of which decisions to report during the 1989 term. One explanation of the apparent lack of interest in conflict, both within and between courts, may be related to the absence of public knowledge about the Court. With very little information about what the Court does or how justices reach their decisions, viewers may see conflict within the Court as neither important nor exciting. It may be that a five-to-four or six-to-three decision does not mean very much to the average viewer and, consequently, such conflict may not make a decision newsworthy. Similarly, with viewers having little public information about the processes by which cases get to the Court and what it means for the Court to overrule a lower court's decision, this type of conflict is likely to be seen by reporters as not particularly newsworthy. Finally, and related, conflict with regard to the Court is not made easily visual; considering the significance of visual information for television, the inability for the networks to capitalize on this aspect in their medium may dissuade them from relying on conflict as a primary cue for whether to report a decision or not. And, indeed, as chapter 5 indicated, the case vote and the case history were only reported infrequently in the stories broadcast by the networks.

The absence of any relationship between the federal government's involvement in a case and decisional coverage is somewhat surprising. If average viewers lack knowledge and are unconcerned about the Court's activities, they are likely to be at least *more* aware of and interested in the current administration and its activities. When the administration files an amicus curiae brief, it has gone public with its concern about the outcome of the case; certainly, when the government's attorneys argue the cause, federal interest in the outcome is even more evident; and, as a direct party to the case, the extent of the federal government's interest is quite clear. Nevertheless, while the American public may be interested in the government's position on important political and social issues, and such information is potentially newsworthy, the data indicate that the government's position, as communicated in the ways that we have measured, does not act as a cue for reporters when they are making choices about which cases to report.

One possible explanation for this is that, with limited resources, reporters are affected most by factors that have a direct and immediate bearing on their time constraints and provide readily available information. For example, the number of decisions announced on the same day and the date of the decision appear to be important predictors of decisional coverage. As we expected, decisions are more likely to be reported when there is only one or very few announced on the same day, making it easier for reporters to develop stories and get airtime for them. Similarly, the data indicate that it is true, or at least it was in 1989, that decisions announced in June are treated as more newsworthy. This is so despite the difficulties that reporters have when too many decisions are announced on the same day, an occurrence that happens most often at the end of the term.

Our data also indicate that the number of amicus briefs filed in a case, including but not exclusively those submitted by the government, acts as a significant cue for reporters. As we have noted previously, the recent research on interest groups and the Court has emphasized the role that these briefs have played in the justices' decisions to grant or deny certiorari, concluding that these briefs are often an indicator of a case's societal and political significance (Caldeira and Wright, 1988). In addition, the past decades have seen a renewed interest in the role of groups utilizing the judicial process to pursue their policy ends.

It appears, then, that the political importance of interest groups is not lost on the networks when choosing cases to cover. Group spokespersons are a primary and frequent source of information and commentary about Court decisions, as our data presented in previous chapters have demonstrated. Additionally, the activities of interest groups, including demonstrations and press conferences, can make for interesting and, at times, dramatic television. Thus, the utilization of amicus briefs as a cue for reporters is not surprising.

Finally, it is not at all surprising to find that the issue involved in a case is a primary factor in the choice to report the decision handed down in that case. While the American public may be relatively uninterested and uninformed about the Court and its activities, it is not lacking interest in many of the substantive issues with which the Court ultimately deals and about which it fashions policy. In addition, the medium of television is more amenable to presenting some issues than others; those that arouse controversy or emotion, for instance, are likely to be covered more often than those that do not.

Thus, during the 1989 term, cases about First Amendment issues or criminal justice issues were those that were the most likely to receive network television attention. Additionally, cases involving other rights and liberties also served as cues to reporters looking for newsworthy stories to broadcast on the evening news. In contrast, cases involving debates about judicial power, federalism, economic issues, and other miscellaneous issues were considered less newsworthy by the networks and, consequently, were less likely to attain decisional coverage.

A closer look at the actual decisions made in each of our issue categories makes the choice to report them even more obvious (see Table 7.4). Among the First Amendment decisions receiving airtime were those about the right to burn the flag (*U.S. v. Eichman*), pornography (*FW/PBS v. Dallas* and *Osborne v. Ohio*), religious freedom (*Oregon Employment Division v. Smith*), political patronage (*Rutan v. Republican Party of Illinois*), and the separation of church and state (*Jimmy Swaggart Ministries v. California Board of Equalization* and *Board of Education of the Westside Community Schools v. Mergens*). A total of twenty-two stories were broadcast across all three networks about these ten cases, with five of the cases broadcast on each of the three networks.

The criminal justice cases included several search and seizure decisions (*Alabama v. White, Michigan State Police v. Sitz, U.S. v. Verdugo-Uriquidez, Maryland v. Buie, Minnesota v. Olson,* and *Horton v. California*). The other decisions in this category that were reported, with one exception (*Holland v. Illinois,* a Sixth Amendment case), were about rights guaranteed by the Fifth Amendment. A total of twenty-four stories were broadcast across the networks on these twelve cases.

Finally, our other rights and liberties category included three important and controversial decisions about the right to die (*Cruzan v. Director, Missouri*

Table 7.4. *Cases reported by the networks in various issue categories, 1989 term*

Issue area/cases	Number of stories reported
First Amendment	Criminal justice
U.S. v. Eichman (3)	*Alabama v. White* (2)
FW/PBS v. Dallas (2)	*Michigan State Police v. Sitz* (3)
Osborne v. Ohio (3)	*U.S. v. Verdugo-Uriquidez* (3)
Oregon Employment Division v. Smith (3)	*Maryland v. Buie* (3)
Rutan v. Republican Party of Illinois (3)	*Minnesota v. Olson* (1)
Board of Education of the Westside Com-	*Horton v. California* (0)
munity Schools of Mergens (3)	*Holland v. Illinois* (2)
University of Pennsylvania v. EEOC (1)	*Baltimore City Dept. of Social Services*
Austin v. Michigan Chamber of	*v. Bouknight* (2)
Commerce (1)	*Maryland v. Craig* (3)
Milkovich v. Lorain Journal Co. (1)	*Pennsylvania v. Muniz* (2)
Jimmy Swaggart Ministries v. California	*Idaho v. Wright* (1)
Board of Equalization (2)	*Illinois v. Perkins* (1)
Other rights and liberties	Judicial power
Cruzan v. Dir., Missouri Department	*Spallone v. U.S.* (1)
of Health (3)	*Missouri v. Jenkins* (3)
Metro Broadcasting v. FCC (2)	Economics
Washington v. Harper (2)	*California v. American Stores* (2)
Hodgson v. Minnesota/Ohio v. Akron	
Center for Reproductive Health (3)	Miscellaneous Other
Federalism	*General Motors v. U.S.* (1)
Perpich v. Department of Defense (3)	*Pension Benefit Guaranty Corp v. LTV*
	Corp. (3)

Department of Health) and abortion rights (*Hodgson v. Minnesota* and *Ohio v. Akron Center for Reproductive Health*). It is interesting to note the disproportionate coverage received by these cases and that all were reported by all three networks.

In contrast, among the two categories of cases that received the least amount of television coverage were miscellaneous other decisions and economic decisions. These cases included an environmental case (*General Motors v. U.S.*) and a case involving a federal program (*Pension Benefit Guaranty Corp. v. LTV Corp.*). Only one economic decision was reported, *California v. American Stores*, an antitrust case.

The decisions in the first three categories are clearly those that were potentially more interesting, stimulating, controversial, and sexy to viewers, and that made for the potentially "best" television coverage of the term. Far fewer of these types of cases fall into the latter categories. Thus, it is not at all surprising that First Amendment, criminal justice, and other rights and liberties decisions were reported with greater frequency than others, and we would expect this to be the case in any Court term.

CONCLUDING REMARKS

Unraveling the mystery of which Supreme Court case decisions are reported and which are not on the television news is a vexing, albeit not intractable, problem. Clearly, careful attention must be given to measurement concerns, the derivation of variables, and their theoretically driven justification.

Our analysis is suggestive of the overriding importance of the subject area of Supreme Court cases coupled with interest group amicus participation in those cases for understanding which Supreme Court decisions receive coveted network news time. Clearly, the myriad of issues housed under the rubric of civil rights and liberties is more telegenic than the considerably less emotional, divisive, and personalized facets of the Court's docket that make up the bulk of its publicly "invisible" workload. In addition, substantial interest group activity cues reporters that a case of potentially widespread public policy importance with interested publics "out there" has been decided and warrants coverage consideration. In this sense, our findings about the importance of amicus filings for understanding which case decisions receive television coverage resonate well with collateral work in other areas of judicial politics research that has focused our gaze on the importance and implications of group activity in the judicial process.

The relationships that we have uncovered are, we believe, substantively as well as statistically significant. The seemingly low amount of variance explained by our model is, in our view, more robust than suggested by the numbers alone. At bottom, we believe that the Court is and will remain a relative "side show" on the network newscasts and that, to a certain extent, coverage of Supreme Court decisions will always represent, except for the truly rare "landmark" rulings, a residual of scarce broadcast time left over from the day's more pressing and more television-friendly events. In this sense, we believe that no model of decisional coverage by television newscasts can completely explain the variance in coverage simply because many of the most important variables are not readily identifiable or easily measured. As Tim O'Brien admitted, he was often forced to concede that newscast producers had "bigger fish to fry" than some cases he was seeking to get in the lineup. In this sense, the ability of a Supreme Court case decision to enjoy scarce airtime may depend at least as much on events emanating from the Oval Office, Capitol Hill, international "hot spots" and crises of the moment, and "sensational events" both home and abroad as it does on the variables explored in our analysis.

8

Television News and the Supreme Court: All the News That's Fit to Air?

"Television . . . provides little more than a headline service for news . . . which mirrors the world like the curved mirrors at the county fair. Reality is reflected, but it seems badly out of shape and proportion."

Doris Graber, *Mass Media and American Politics*

"I think the network television coverage of the Supreme Court has atrophied to the point that it's not informing the public very much about what's going on."

Fred Graham, former Supreme Court reporter for CBS News

"*Of course* the news media can contribute to a more democratic society. The job of the press is to help produce a more informed electorate. A more informed citizenry will create a better and fuller democracy."

Michael Schudson, *The Power of the News*

Our inquiry began with the recognition that a democratic polity presupposes meaningful linkages between governmental institutions, the political elites who staff such institutions, and the mass public that is governed by these institutions. In the American context such linkages are most readily seen, perhaps, in the systematic operation of free and open elections that, the theory goes, make the institutions and the elites who govern through them "accountable" to the mass public. One key ingredient in this recipe for the democratic brew, of course, is the recognition that a free flow of meaningful information is critical for the mass public if their efforts at assessing governmental behavior and assuring accountability have any hope of being the product of informed and reasoned judgments. As Michael Delli Carpini and Scott Keeter underscore, "The more citizens are . . . informed about the issues of the day, the behavior of political leaders, and rules under which they operate, the better off they are, the better off *we* are. . . . Ultimately, democracy rests on the backs of its citizens" (1996:61).

The ingredients in the recipe that constitutes the democratic ideal are spelled out by Michael Schudson:

Suppose that citizens are rational, interested in public affairs, and have access to effective participation in politics. Classical democratic theory takes this for granted. Classical thinking about journalism also takes this for granted and then assumes that the job of the news media is to help citizens achieve what political scientist Robert Dahl calls an "adequate understanding" of political issues. Helping citizens toward "adequate understanding" has long been and still should be a leading aim of the news media. (1983: 13)

When the ingredients in Schudson's recipe blend as they should, societal gains will follow. As Schudson argues elsewhere, "Of course the news media can contribute to a more democratic society. The job of the press is to help produce a more informed electorate. A more informed citizenry will create a better and fuller democracy" (1995: 204).

The correspondence of reality to this democratic ideal regarding the relationship between the government and the governed will be most problematic in institutional settings such as the Supreme Court, where direct electoral accountability does not exist and where informational flows are the weakest. Clearly, the federal judiciary is the most invisible branch of our national government and the branch about which the public is most ill-informed. The implications of this context for the lack of reporting on the Court and for misreporting on the Court are underscored by the observations of Linda Greenhouse:

Given such widespread ignorance, and in light of the Court's role as an important participant in the ongoing dialogue among American citizens and the various branches and levels of government, journalistic miscues about what the Court is saying and where it is going can have a distorting effect on the entire enterprise. (1996a: 1539)

We have argued throughout that the most critical conduit for information about courts generally and, in particular, the Supreme Court, is television news. Indeed, the Court as an institution has an unusually limited public presence save for the manner in which it is portrayed on the evening newscasts and, to truly account for the low informational base the public displays regarding the Court and its work, we must first understand how the Court is presented to the public on television. That effort has been the primary thrust of this volume. Understanding the nature of the linkage between the Court and the public that television news provides is particularly critical since the

Court, lacking the power of the purse and sword must, perforce, rely in part on a willing public to follow its policy dictates. As Richard Davis has observed, "Without the legitimacy bestowed by the public, the Court's effort to resolve . . . issues would be futile. The Court's ability to affect public policy would be weakened" (1994: 146).

Our inquiry into network television newscast coverage of the Court began with the exploration of the world of the journalist, particularly the television reporter, covering the institution. We relied a great deal on extended interviews with television journalists, past and present, who covered and continue to cover the Court beat. We found, not surprisingly, that the Court itself is the source of many obstacles that stand in the way of "better" Supreme Court reporting, while the nature of the journalistic profession and, in particular, the broadcast news industry, is far from blameless.

The working reality of the Supreme Court beat starts with the recognition that covering the Court is different in kind from covering other governmental institutions for a number of reasons. Perhaps first and foremost, the Court straddles the worlds of law and policy with the consequence that judicial "politics" has a very different flavor from that practiced in the executive and legislative realms. The Court is much less open and accessible to and more insulated from the press than other governmental settings. Clearly, the Court is less interested, because of its insularity, in what the media has to say about it and, by extension, to what the public knows and learns about it.

Partly as a consequence of the nature of the Court itself, the substantive focal point of the Supreme Court beat is different from that of other institutional coverage as well. Reporters, by and large, do not cover the Court's personalities and its processes of decision. Rather, it is largely the Court's output, its decisions, and, particularly, those rendered with written opinions that serve as grist for the media mill. In reporting those decisions, reporters are "soloists" to a greater degree than they are in other institutional settings in their efforts to make sense of what it all means, however complex and nondefinitive a ruling may appear to be. While the Court does have an active and extremely helpful Public Information Office, the office serves primarily as a conduit for publicly available information, not a "source" for journalists. The Public Information Office does not attempt in any way to place a "spin" on Supreme Court news. In this context, the relatively small Supreme Court press corps emerges as a close-knit group of colleagues. They share information and perspectives widely on a beat where group interests and their spokespersons, and not the decision makers themselves, serve as the primary actors attempting to manipulate the media interpreters of the Court's activities.

While a good deal of our analysis relates generally to the manner in which the Court is reported, our primary focus was on television coverage of the Court. Clearly, television does bring some unique strengths to its coverage of the institution. Primary among them is its ability to place a human face on a case and to portray the human drama and consequences that often lie behind the complex legal issues brought to the Court for resolution. Just as clearly, however, there is much about the Supreme Court beat that makes it particularly inhospitable for television coverage, especially within the constraints of the networks' nightly newscasts.

Perhaps the most obvious problem faced by television journalism in covering the Court is the inability to bring its cameras and microphones into the Courtroom for coverage of oral argumentation and the announcement of decisions. While this liability is a real one and receives considerable press and public attention, it is important to recognize that there are a number of other factors that also create vexing problems for television coverage of the Court.

These include, for example, relative paucity of "action" at the Court for long periods of time, coupled with its propensity for backloading announcements of important decisions at the very end of its yearly term and, often, on the same crowded decision days. While some cases do offer television interesting stories to tell, just as often they involve complex legalisms and technical issues that are not conducive to broadcast news coverage. The problem is particularly acute given the limited news window enjoyed by network newscasts, which necessitates that Supreme Court decisions often have to be reported in time frames well under half a minute long. Further, the Court itself has taken on an increasingly shrinking docket in recent years. This, combined with its seeming reluctance to issue pathbreaking "landmark" rulings, has resulted in newscast producers pulling in the reins on the resources they expend in covering the Court, while also diminishing their expectations about its importance as a source for television news stories. Clearly, reporters who cover the Court on television news today generally cover more widely defined beats than they did years ago, and they find it more difficult to get Supreme Court cases on the air than once was the case.

The current state of television news coverage of the Court reflects, in part, a coming together of the difficulties the beat creates for journalists, with important changes in the broadcast news industry that surfaced in the mid-1980s with the emergence of "infotainment" as the dominant mode of newscast coverage. Our interviews underscored the perception that, all too often, news values have been trumped by production values in the business. The judgments of editors and producers, including their substantive interpretations of events they were not, necessarily, qualified to assess, often supplanted the professional judgments of senior Court journalists. We were struck by the candid admissions of two extremely well-respected journalists that, as network correspondents, they occasionally went on the air and reported on the Court in a manner that was not, in their view, factually correct or, alternatively, in a fashion that they viewed as incomprehensible.

Our examination of television coverage of the Court has benefited immeasurably from the observations and perceptions of the journalists who gave freely of their time and their perspectives. The richness of their observations is impossible to quantify. The major thrust of our analysis, however, was empirical in its orientation, and several complementary efforts were taken in our study to portray, systematically, the manner in which the Court is covered by television news.

We began at the microlevel with a detailed examination of newscast coverage of two unusually prominent and potentially landmark case settings in the controversial and emotionally laden areas of affirmative action (the *Bakke* case) and abortion (the *Webster* case). Both case decisions were widely anticipated, and both litigation settings were marked by record-breaking interest by organized groups in the Court's decision as evidenced by historic levels of amicus participation.

While neither *Bakke* nor *Webster* turned out to be the definitive rulings widely expected, both demonstrated that, at times, television expends considerable resources in covering the Court. The stories reported multiple facets and decision points in each of these cases, including many prior to the cases' oral arguments and before the decisions were rendered in each case. *Bakke* and *Webster* served as a lead story on newscasts with relative frequency, and an extraordinary amount of airtime was devoted to each of these cases on decision day.

In both case settings, the networks seized on those facets of the case that best enabled them to turn coverage from the Court itself to those focal points considered much more television friendly and "newsworthy" for network newscasts. In *Bakke,* that meant a focus on Allan Bakke himself as well as on the internal struggles within the Carter administration as it arrived at a heavily negotiated affirmative action policy position. *Webster*'s case setting, while somewhat different, also resulted in television turning away from the Court itself. In this instance the primary story became the underlying group struggle that the case reflected in American society, coupled with considerable analysis of the political implications of the litigation, particularly for state legislative processes and ongoing electoral battles. The modes chosen to present these cases allowed television news to transform ostensibly legal stories into more comfortably reported political and human dramas, thereby allowing journalists to utilize sources, attempt to obtain dramatic footage, and, more generally, report the cases in a manner that much resembled other politically oriented journalism.

Despite the resources spent on reporting *Bakke* and *Webster*, television news coverage of these two cases still fell somewhat short on several substantive dimensions. Reporting of both cases was visually bland with respect to the focus on the Court and substantively thin in many respects, such as the relative infrequency with which both case facts and case history were presented to establish a context for coverage. "Spin doctoring" the news occurred with regularity in both case settings through the observations of the newscasters themselves as well as through the utilization of sources. Often, prognostications would inflate the likely impact and importance of the cases while accentuating the emotionally laden aspects of the cases' content. When the cases didn't "deliver" what was expected of them, newscasters came full circle and began to place their eggs in the basket of the next "great" case that they could see clearly on the horizon.

Coverage of decision day in these two widely reported case settings was ostensibly "accurate" but still substantively thin, accentuating a winner/loser approach that clearly outdistanced attention to decisional detail. Thus, in *Bakke* coverage, the personal victory for Allan Bakke weighed more heavily than the focus on the meaning of the case for the broader affirmative action issue; in *Webster*, the victory for the pro-life forces in the Court's upholding of Missouri's strict regulation of abortion clearly overshadowed the coverage of the survival of *Roe v. Wade*. In the final analysis, the networks took their best shot in these two case settings, resulting in coverage that was comparatively substantial and, for the most part, accurate. It offered, however, little sophistication, nuance, or depth.

Our macrolevel study of television coverage of two full Supreme Court terms (the October 1989 and October 1994 terms) underscored that coverage of cases such as *Bakke* and *Webster* represented television coverage at its best, with general coverage of the Court considerably more lacking in breadth and depth. Our analysis confirmed that most coverage of the Court is focused on docket-related activities. In the 1989 Court term coverage of some facet of fewer than one in four Supreme Court cases was aired on some newscast at some time. In the 1994 term such coverage fell to less than one in five cases drawn from a considerably smaller docket. Indeed, partly as a reflection of that docket change, fewer than half as many stories were broadcast about the Court in the 1994 term when compared to 1989!

While "leading" cases received, as they should, the lion's share of television interest and coverage (indeed, coverage of the 1994 term focused exclusively on such leading cases), importantly, there is not wide-ranging coverage even in this rarified case subset. Thus, in the 1989 term, some coverage was given to half of the cases operationalized as leading cases, while in the 1994 term fewer than half of such cases were covered in any way. More generally and, in our view, most importantly, several of our indicators gauging the substantive content of television coverage (in both leading and routine case settings) further substantiated the message gleaned from our interviews. Television newscast coverage of the Court diminished from the earlier to the later Court term that we studied, and the decline in coverage of the Supreme Court was dramatic.

As generally problematic as television's coverage of the Court appears, it was also evident that some facets of the coverage offered are patently more blameworthy than others. Few would dispute the notion that misinforming the public is a greater sin than not informing them, and our analysis revealed that in television's relatively infrequent focus on the Court's docketing behavior – the decisions to hear or decline to hear cases – inaccuracy in reporting was a relatively common happenstance.

Interestingly, while newscasts portrayed accurately the Court's decisions to hear cases in their understandably infrequent forays into covering the granting of certiorari, reporting on certiorari denials was much more problematic and replete with error. Indeed, such decisions to not hear a case were routinely reported as decisions on the merits upholding the rulings of the courts below. Such misreporting has clear and important implications for the state of citizen knowledge about judicial policy and, indeed, can have a direct link to errant behaviors that can be traced to inaccurate public perceptions of the state of the law. This problem is exacerbated in the majority of circumstances where our analysis revealed that the certiorari denial being misreported was not, in any sense, a definitive resolution of the underlying issue. In short, more than two out of three stories covering the Court's docketing decisions covered certiorari denials, and in more than three out of four of these stories television news "got it wrong" through ambiguous or blatantly erroneous mischaracterization.

The final facet of our empirical analyses was an effort to explain the relative importance of several case characteristics for the networks' choices to devote scarce airtime to covering Supreme Court decisions. Variables tapping the nature of a case and its level of conflict were utilized in the multivariate statistical analysis. As we expected, our results underscored the critical importance of the case's underlying issues, more specifically whether it involved the First Amendment, criminal justice, or other rights and liberties concerns, for explicating television's decision to cover a case decision. In addition, we found that while group involvement in a case as an amicus does not, necessarily, lead to airtime for the group in eventual coverage of the case, it does appear to serve as a cue for reporters suggestive of the policy importance of and public interest in the Court's resolution of the litigation. Thus, as group participation as amici in Supreme Court litigation increased, so did the likelihood that the case's decision would be reported on a network newscast.

The intent of our analysis was not, in any sense, to develop a case for the indictment of network television newscast coverage of the Court. Nor do we mean to suggest that in linking television news to public knowledge about the Court that the evening newscasts are the sole television venue providing the public with its information about the institution and its work. As Pete Williams pointed out, "remember, television is a big critter":

If you watch COURT TV and watch Fred Graham's weekly preview and if you watch CNN's thing, . . . and if you watch an occasional *Nightline* story about the Court [the *Today Show* and our competition], then you're going to have a pretty good idea of the bare bones of the Supreme Court. . . . So, you know, television is a big thing.

Granting Williams his point, the evening newscasts remain, nevertheless, the primary vehicle through which most of the public, most of the time, will obtain its information about what the Court has done.

While indicting network newscast coverage of the Court was not our goal, uncovering the nature of that coverage was. Further, one of the guiding premises of our study was the suggestion that what the American public "knows" about the Court must, of necessity, be closely linked to what information they have received through television newscasts.

Clearly, nobody purports to claim that television's evening newscasts offer "model" citizens the broad informational base that they "need" to participate fully and effectively in a democratic polity. Recall the words of Doris Graber:

If judged in terms of the information needs of the ideal citizen in the ideal democracy, the end product . . . is inadequate. . . . [T]elevision . . . provides little more than a headline service for news . . . which mirrors the world like the curved mirrors at the county fair. Reality is reflected, but it seems badly out of shape and proportion. Most of us, however, only faintly resemble the ideal citizen, and most of us look to the media for entertainment. . . . By and large, American mass media serve the general public about as well as that public wants to be served in practice rather than in theory. (1989: 105)

The general situation that Graber describes is no better and, we think, considerably worse with regard to coverage of the Court. The portrait we have drawn suggests that there has been a precipitous decline in newscast attention to and coverage of the Court. As Fred Graham opined, "I think the network television coverage of the Supreme Court has atrophied to the point that it's not informing the public very much about what's going on." In a similar vein Carl Stern added, "I suppose there are still some urgent items off the top that people will tune in for, but they simply don't get enough knowledge of matters that are undramatic but which are important in a political society to civic participation."

We have argued throughout that the state of affairs we have portrayed in network newscasts has important consequences for the beliefs people hold about the Court and what it has done, as well as implications for the actions and behaviors people pursue based on what they have been told (and, indeed, not told) on the evening news. The situation is particularly acute for an institution such as the Court, which reaches the public almost exclusively through the limited news coverage that it receives. In effect, one could argue that the implications of the newscast coverage that the Court receives are considerably greater than they would be in a setting where an institution's message reached the public in alternative ways or in an institutional setting that was much less insulated, characteristics that define public linkages to Congress and the presidency.

We have offered evidence that the Court and its members "enjoy" their insularity, and, consequently, few initiatives have been pursued that would make the institution a more attractive venue for media attention. It appears that a majority of the justices are content with the scenario suggested in a conventional wisdom of long standing that the "myth" of the Court as an institution outside the realm of politics is best sustained by maintaining the Court's relative invisibility. As Gregory Casey outlined the argument years ago:

Myth sustains mystique, which shelters an institution from the public eye. . . . But if the mask of myth falls, people can see more clearly what is going on. If an institution's involvement in raw political decision making becomes visible, people may develop contempt for it. In contrast, invisibility and distance from the mass public sustain myth and thus legitimacy. . . . [The] common thesis is that the High Court's myth together with its essentially non-democratic ideology of judicial review flourish in the shade, but might wither in the bright glare of public attention. . . . [V]isibility would jeopardize the Court's mystique and cause a decline in its legitimacy. (1974: 387)

Whether this thesis is true, of course, is an empirical question. Even if it were answered in the affirmative, however, the question would still remain of whether the desire to maintain a mythic view of the Court ought to sustain its efforts at maintaining its relatively low public profile. Further, as an empirical matter, one might question whether there remains a "myth" about the Court's policy-making role to begin with. As Richard Davis notes:

One of the arguments for maintaining distance from the press is to preserve the mystique of the Court in the eyes of the public. The public, interest groups, and, to some extent, the press itself, however, may already be questioning the reality of the mystique. (1994: 148)

Perhaps even more to the point, there may be a good deal to be gained for the Court and its justices in eschewing the myth and letting the public in to see the Court and its work for exactly what it is. Rita Braver made the general point very well in the context of discussing the implications of cameras in the Supreme Court during the period when she covered the institution for CBS News:

To a certain extent to demystify anything is to undermine confidence in it, but I watch these arguments day after day and I find them inspiring. I think people's confidence in the Court would be, rather than undermined, . . . reinforced. They would see how serious these people are about their jobs, and how smart they are. When you hear constitutional principles talked about in language that you can understand, it's thrilling. I think it would be much better for the public. (Quoted in Davis, 1994: 151)

For the public to receive more and better information about the Supreme Court on television news, fundamental changes within the broadcast news industry and/or within the Court itself would appear to be the only avenues available for facilitating such an outcome. We are convinced that the impetus for change in the context of the commercial imperatives of the broadcast news industry will not emanate from television news as long as nothing changes about the nature of the Court as a news-making venue. We also recognize that this is not a state of affairs that is likely to cause many justices on the Court great concern. We feel, however, that it should. As Richard Davis has underscored:

The future of press relations does not hold great promise for maintaining the Court's traditions. If resisted, technological advances will increasingly isolate the Court from its most important base – the mass public. (1994: 159)

We do not mean to suggest, of course, that the Court should alter its docket to hear more "newsworthy" cases, or that it should strike out boldly to take new policy initiatives to attract media attention and public notice. We do not feel that justices should hold press conferences to "explain" their opinions, nor do we believe that the Court's Public Information Office should alter its role as a conduit for information to that of a "source" for journalists. Indeed, we do not even issue a call for the Court to immediately open its doors to "gavel-to-gavel" camera coverage of its public proceedings, oral arguments, and decision announcements. We recognize that the institution of the Court transforms its traditions slowly and that it must walk first before it tries to run, even in instituting relatively small changes considerably less radical and ill-advised than the notions addressed above.

We do believe, however, that it must adapt its traditions if it cares, as we think it should, about its relationship with the American public. Tim O'Brien has opined, "I think there ought to be an educative function in what the Court does, just as there is in what we do." Judge Gilbert Merritt, who chaired the Federal Judicial Conference's committee that examined the issue of cameras in federal courts, reminds us that "judges need to feel some obligation to communicate what they're doing" (quoted in Hodson, 1996).

And, indeed, we have recent evidence that one federal district court judge, James Graham, both felt the "obligation to communicate" and did something about it. Concerned about reactions in the black community to a decision he had rendered that dismantled an affirmative action program in Columbus, Ohio, Graham "mailed more than 60 copies of an 11 page summary of his decision along with a cover letter to black ministers, lawyers, and other leaders throughout the city." Graham's summary of his opinion was written "with the hope that it will help the average citizen to understand the court's decision," which ran 183 pages in length followed by a fifty-four page appendix. Explaining this unusual and, perhaps, unprecedented action in his cover letter, Graham wrote:

I think it is vitally important that the community understands why the court has found the plan unconstitutional, but I recognize that few, if any, will have the time, opportunity or inclination to read a decision of this length. (in Ruth, 1996)

While by no means suggesting that Supreme Court justices should routinely go to the lengths exhibited by Graham to communicate better with the public he serves, we do feel that there are steps that the Court and its justices could and should take that represent changes around the edges of the Court's relationship with the press generally and with television in particular. These changes could facilitate "better" and more inclusive news coverage of the institution.

For example, Supreme Court justices should, as several increasingly have, make themselves available to the press more routinely to illuminate the processes through which the Court decides cases. Nothing in such meetings should, or would, compromise the substantive deliberations in ongoing cases, nor, indeed, should justices discuss the substantive deliberations that occurred in those cases that they decided in the past. In addition, the public appearances of the justices should be open to press coverage.

Further, attention should be placed on possible alterations of the Court's decisional calendar with an eye toward spreading the announcement of decisions over a greater number of decision days and, as important, avoiding the issuance of multiple decisions on a given newsday. Little, we suspect, could or should be done to change the reality of most decisions coming down toward the end of the term. Thus, we are by no means suggesting that the justices should alter their decisional and opinion writing processes to reach decisions more quickly. Rather, we simply take note that, even at the end of the term, issuing decisions across a greater number of days and, perhaps, even extending the Court's term for a limited number of days to avoid massive decision days would facilitate news coverage, particularly on television, immeasurably. In the process, the Court will ensure that more of what it does reaches the public it serves.

We have saved for last a suggestion that is, we think, viewed as most radical by some and most inevitable by others. That is, of course, a call for opening the Court's doors to coverage by television cameras. At the outset this should be accomplished on a limited and experimental basis. There are many ways, of course, in which such a major change could be implemented. We feel that such an effort would be most likely to succeed if it followed in the wake of collective planning by the Court and the television news industry.

Indeed, it is important to underscore our more generalized belief that the responsibility for achieving more meaningful coverage of the Supreme Court lies jointly with the Court itself and the news media. Here, we echo the view articulated succinctly by Linda Greenhouse:

Despite our divergent interests – the press corp's interest in accessibility and information, the Court's in protecting the integrity of its decisional processes – I am naive enough and out of step enough with the prevailing journalistic culture, to think of these two institutions as, to some degree, partners in a mutual democratic enterprise to which both must acknowledge responsibility. The responsibility of the press is to commit the resources necessary to give the public the most accurate and contextual reporting possible about the Court, its work, its members, and its relationship with other branches of government. The Court's responsibility is to remove unnecessary obstacles to accomplishing that task. (1996a: 1561)

Following any one or, indeed, even all of our suggestions would not guarantee, necessarily, that the coverage television news gave the Court would be substantively "better" than what we have analyzed throughout this book. Clearly, however, the breadth of the coverage the Court received (and the "headline" information the public received) would increase considerably. Further, it is reasonable to assume, until proven otherwise, that a Court that was more receptive to media coverage generally, and television coverage in particular, would benefit from both greater breadth and depth of coverage as the institution attained added luster as a potential news source. In the "field of dreams" we have offered, if the Court builds it, television news will come. In the final analysis, it is the American public that will reap the greatest benefits from being introduced to an institution where, as Pete Williams observed, there are "people . . . wrestling with what the founding fathers had in mind when they formed this country":

To think that there are these people in America that struggle with what it is that we're supposed to be all about every day. That's their job, and I just think that's fascinating – that as we seem to spin further and further toward the twenty-first century and we don't know what the hell we are, well, here, there is this little . . . group of people who come in and say, "Wait a minute. Maybe George Washington and Thomas Jefferson meant this for us." . . . It shows that the Constitution is such a living document. That it really counts. And as we seem to get further and further away from these common touchstones in our lives, the Supreme Court really provides that. Now the trouble is, how do you call attention to that on television? I think that it can be done, and I think there's a real niche for it, but for some reason, the current attitude is that people don't want to see that. . . . I don't know. Maybe that underestimates what people are interested in.

Appendix
Schedule of Interviews

Fred Graham	March 9, 1996
Toni House	March 5, 1996
Tim O'Brien	September 27, 1995
Carl Stern	March 6, 1996
Jim Stewart	March 7, 1996
Pete Williams	March 5, 1996

Notes

1. TELEVISION NEWS: A CRITICAL LINK BETWEEN THE SUPREME COURT AND THE AMERICAN PUBLIC

1. McLeod, Kosicki, and McLeod (1994) present a very thorough review of the literature in this regard. For example, the research on agenda setting suggests that the media, by their choice of what to report, establish the salience of various political issues for American citizens (Funkhouser, 1973; Iyengar and Kinder, 1987; McCombs and Shaw, 1972). Additionally, some research suggests that the media can form and change public opinion in the realm of campaigns (for instance, Fazio and Williams, 1986; Granberg and Brown, 1989; Krosnick, 1988; Rice and Atkin, 1989). Priming, the idea that the media may encourage its users to think about certain topics, has also received scholarly attention (Berkowitz and Rogers, 1986; Iyengar and Kinder, 1987). Framing, or the process by which the media may package the news in such a way as to promote users to think about a topic in a particular way, has also been the subject of considerable research (Gamson and Lasch, 1983; Gamson, 1992; Tuchman, 1978). For evidence that the media may have the effect of actually limiting what viewers learn from the news, see Arterton (1984), Neuman (1976), Patterson (1980). For more recent evidence that the learning process of the media audience may be complicated by psychological factors, see Ferejohn and Kuklinski (1990), Gunter (1987), and Robinson and Levy (1986).
2. Some have even taken note that, "despite such limitations, network news finds plenty of time for frivolous subjects intended to entertain rather than inform. If the evening news were expanded to one hour, this would not guarantee more in-depth coverage. If anything the repetitious and evasive surface quality of television news would become more evident, and an hour more unsatisfying. . . . Time is not an iron-clad determinant of content" (Parenti, 1993: 56–57).

5. A TALE OF TWO TERMS:
THE 1989 AND 1994 COURT TERMS

1. The index to the archive was used to identify all stories referencing the Supreme
    Court during this term. While the October 1989 term dated from October 2, 1989,
    to June 27, 1990, our data set includes stories broadcast from August 23, 1989, to
    September 27, 1990, in our effort to cast a broad net to ensure that no stories re-
    lated to the Court's 1989 activities were excluded. Tapes of these stories were com-
    piled by the archive and then were viewed and coded, in their entirety, by both au-
    thors. Because we were so broad in our original selection, some stories in which
    the focus on the Court was peripheral were eliminated from further consideration
    in our analysis.
2. This total includes eight per curiam opinions, which are not signed by any one of
    the justices.
3. These three publications are reasonable choices for information about the relative
    prominence of cases heard each term by the Court and were used to identify the
    noteworthy cases of the 1994 Court term as well. While not necessarily exhaus-
    tive, this measure of "leading" or noteworthy cases is very inclusive as it includes
    all cases identified by at least one of these three publications, as already noted.
4. We collected these data by accessing the archive's World Wide Web site at http://
    tvnews.vanderbilt.edu/. News stories were selected by a very broad, comprehen-
    sive search that included key words such as *court, Supreme Court, U.S. Supreme
    Court,* and the names of the justices. As was the case for the 1989 term, our data
    set includes stories broadcast just prior to and after the 1994 term to include sto-
    ries and events related to the activities of the term. These dates are July 15, 1994,
    through August 12, 1995.
5. Four federal laws were overturned in 1994: one related to Congress's power to reg-
    ulate interstate commerce, two related to First Amendment protections, and one
    related to the separation of powers. According to Greenhouse, these represent "an
    unusually high number given that the Court had invalidated only 129 laws in its
    previous 205-year history" (Greenhouse, 1995: 4).
6. Of this total, four were per curiam decisions.
7. For both terms, the total number of stories analyzed were not discrete Court-
    related stories. Rather, when stories had multiple foci, such as instances when two
    or three decisions were reported in the same broadcast segment, each Court-
    related focus was recorded as a separate story. Additionally, both sets of stories
    consisted of those in which the Court and its work were the *central* focus as well
    as those in which the focus on the Court was more *peripheral.*
8. The number of signed opinions handed down by the Court has decreased steadily
    in the past decade. In the 1989 term, the Court wrote 129 such opinions, 14 fewer

than were delivered in 1986. In the 1994 term, the Court delivered 82 signed opinions, and during the 1995 term the Court signed only 75 opinions. (We are grateful to our colleague Larry Baum for sharing these data with us.)

9. *Hodgson v. Minnesota* is included in this list of thirty-two, but *Ohio v. Akron Center for Reproductive Health* is not. The reason for excluding *Akron* is that the networks more often than not treated the issue of parental consent for abortions through their coverage of *Hodgson*. The rulings were handed down on the same day and were reported in the same story in such a way that separating them into distinct stories was not possible. Furthermore, interviews that were part of the stories were with the interested parties in *Hodgson*. To avoid confusion and undue complexity, we treat *Akron*'s coverage as part of *Hodgson*, referring in most instances to *Hodgson* only.

10. *Sandin v. Conner*, which limited civil rights claims by prisoners against prison officials, and *Arizona v. Evans*, a search-and-seizure case involving computerized warrants, were not covered by any one of the three networks.

11. Also reported in Tables 5.3 and 5.4 are stories about these cases that were broadcast between the three major stages of the decision-making process. These tables, however, do not include the total number of stories broadcast on each case. Because a few stories reported in each term included only general information on multiple cases, by way of introducing the Court's docket for the term, it was difficult to identify some of the cases and impossible to distinguish them as discrete stories. As a consequence, these stories were not included in the tables.

12. We should note that the Court may have granted certiorari to some of the cases in both terms prior to the starting date of our data sets. As a consequence, our analysis may not include stories that were broadcast about some cert decisions.

13. For the 1989 data set, given the availability of actual videotapes, both the entire length of each story in addition to the length of the specifically Court-related components of each story were coded. In most cases, however, the two measures were equivalent, and we chose to utilize the more meaningful Court-related length. For the 1994 data set, though, we were limited in measuring length because the archive's indices do not allow for a precise distinction between the story length and the Court-related length. Consequently, we have used in our analysis of the 1994 data the story length, which is an overestimated measure of length in the seventeen (15.3%) stories that included components that were not specifically Court-related.

14. Comparison between the 1989 and 1994 terms on the placement dimension is not perfect because at the time of our data collection the commercial-break information was not readily accessible for 1994–95. Nevertheless, we were able to divide the broadcasts into ten-minute increments, roughly estimating the commercial breaks in a typical half-hour broadcast, and we were also able to identify

the leading stories of the broadcast. Both help us to make some comparisons between the terms.

15. Of the thirty-one stories that mentioned Brennan, eight were in the context of
his resignation and twenty-two were docket-related. In contrast, thirty-one of
the thirty-three stories that mentioned Souter were about his nomination and
confirmation, and only one was docket-related.

16. Recall, though, that our data for the 1994 term came from the annotated index
of stories, which may not be totally inclusive of references to the justices.

17. Seven of the twelve stories that mentioned Breyer were in the context of his appointment and five were docket-related. All of the stories reported about Rehnquist were docket-related.

6. "THE SUPREME COURT DECIDED TODAY . . ." –
OR DID IT?

1. Actually, two stories reported on the Court's decision to deny an application for
a stay but, for our purposes, given the manner in which the stories were presented
(that is, as if they were merits rulings), they have been included in the category
of certiorari denials. Justice Kennedy, in fact, in his dissent from the decision to
deny the stay, suggested that the application was analogous to a certiorari petition: "The lower court's actions require us to treat the stay application as a petition for certiorari" (109 L.Ed 2d 493). Subsequently, after the case worked its
way up through the Georgia court system, it was denied certiorari (without dissent) by the Supreme Court. (See 502 U.S. 818.)

2. Actually, the story about the case of disputed water rights in Wyoming was also
quite thorough in its presentation of substantive information about the case. This
story was anomalous in the data set, however. Focused on a rather narrowly
framed case, it was one of the longest stories and one of only two news/feature
stories on certiorari. Broadcast on a Saturday night, we suspect that it provided
filler for a light newsday.

3. The authors are indebted to Stephen Wasby for this succinct phrasing of a solu-
tion to the problem examined here.

7. WHICH DECISIONS ARE REPORTED?
IT'S THE ISSUE, STUPID!

1. Due to missing data on the case vote variable, as will be explained in the following pages, the number of cases included in our analysis is actually 125.

References

Abraham, Henry J. 1993. *The Judicial Process*, 6e. New York: Oxford University Press.

Arterton, F. C. 1984. *Media Politics: The News Strategies of Presidential Campaigns.* Lexington, Mass.: D. C. Heath.

Behuniak-Long, Susan. 1991. "Friendly Fire: Amici Curiae and *Webster v. Reproductive Health Services.*" *Judicature* 74: 261–270.

Berelson, Bernard R., Paul F. Lazarsfeld, and William N. McPhee. 1954. *Voting: A Study of Opinion Formation in a Presidential Campaign.* Chicago: University of Chicago Press.

Berkman, Ronald and Laura W. Kitch. 1986. *Politics in the Media Age.* New York: McGraw-Hill.

Berkowitz, L. and K. H. Rogers. 1986. "A Priming Effect Analysis of Media Influences." In J. Bryant and D. Zillmann (Eds.), *Perspectives on Media Effects.* Hillsdale, N.J.: Lawrence Erlbaum.

Berkson, Larry C. 1978. *The Supreme Court and Its Publics.* Lexington, Mass.: Lexington Books, D. C. Heath.

Blackside, Inc. 1989. "The Keys to the Kingdom (1974–81)." Boston: PBS Videos.

Caldeira, Gregory A. 1986. "Neither the Purse nor the Sword: Dynamics of Public Confidence in the Supreme Court." *American Political Science Review* 80: 1209–1226.

———. 1991. "Courts and Public Opinion." In John B. Gates and Charles A. Johnson (Eds.), *The American Courts: A Critical Assessment.* Washington, D.C.: Congressional Quarterly.

Caldeira, Gregory A. and John R. Wright. 1988. "Organized Interests and Agenda Setting in the U.S. Supreme Court." *American Political Science Review* 82: 1109–1128.

Canon, Bradley. 1995. "The Supreme Court Didn't Decide Today: Television News' Reporting of Certiorari Denials." Presented at the Annual Meeting of the Midwest Political Science Association. Chicago.

Casey, Gregory. 1974. "The Supreme Court and Myth: An Empirical Investigation." *Law and Society Review* 8: 385–419.

Coyle, Marcia. 1990. " '89–'90 Term Concludes with a Bang." *National Law Journal,* August 13: S2 ff.

———. 1995. "A Working Majority." *National Law Journal,* July 31: C1.

Craig, Barbara Hinkson and David M. O'Brien. 1993. *Abortion and American Politics.* Chatham, N.J.: Chatham House.

C-SPAN. March 14, 1996. "Cameras in the Courtroom." Washington, D.C.

Davis, Richard. 1994. *Decisions and Images: The Supreme Court and the Press.* Englewood Cliffs, N.J.: Prentice Hall.

Delli Carpini, Michael X. and Scott Keeter. 1996. *What Americans Know about Politics and Why It Matters.* New Haven, Conn.: Yale University Press.

Devol, Kenneth S. (Ed.). 1982. *Mass Media and the Supreme Court: The Legacy of the Warren Years,* 3e. New York: Hastings House.

Dolbeare, Kenneth. 1967. "The Public Views of the Supreme Court." In Herbert Jacob (Ed.), *Law, Politics, and the Federal Courts.* Boston: Little, Brown.

Dreyfuss, Joel and Charles Lawrence III. 1979. *The Bakke Case: The Politics of Inequality.* New York: Harcourt, Brace Jovanovich.

Epstein, Edward J. 1973. *News from Nowhere: Television and the News.* New York: Random House.

Ericson, David. 1977. "Newspaper Coverage of the Supreme Court: A Case Study." *Journalism Quarterly* 54: 604–607.

Fallows, James. 1996. *Breaking the News: How the Media Undermine American Democracy.* New York: Pantheon Books.

Fazio, R. H. and C. J. Williams. 1986. "Attitude Accessibility as a Moderator of the Attitude-Perception and Attitude-Behavior Relations: An Investigation of the 1984 Presidential Election." *Journal of Personality and Social Psychology* 51: 505–514.

Ferejohn, J. A. and J. H. Kuklinski. 1990. *Information and Democratic Processes.* Urbana: University of Illinois Press.

Funkhouser, G. R. 1973. "The Issues of the Sixties: An Exploratory Study in the Dynamics of Public Opinion." *Public Opinion Quarterly* 37: 62–75.

Gamson, W. A. 1992. *Talking Politics.* Cambridge: Cambridge University Press.

Gamson, W. A. and K. E. Lasch. 1983. "The Political Culture of Social Welfare Policy." In S. Spiro and E. Yuchtman-Yaar (Eds.), *Evaluating the Welfare State: Social and Politial Perspectives.* New York: Academic Press.

Gans, Herbert J. 1979. *Deciding What's News: A Study of CBS Evening News, NBC Nightly News,* Newsweek, *and* Time. New York: Pantheon Books.

Gates, Melissa and Jan P. Vermeer. 1992. "Reporting Supreme Court Decisions: Conflict, Dissents, and Other Cues." Presented at the Annual Meeting of the Western Political Science Association. San Francisco.

Ginsburg, Ruth Bader. 1995. "Communicating and Commenting on the Court's Work." *Georgetown Law Journal* 83: 2119–2129.

Goldman, Sheldon and Thomas P. Jahnige. 1985. *The Federal Courts as a Political System*, 3e. New York: Harper and Row.

Graber, Doris. 1989. *Mass Media and American Politics*, 3e. Washington, D.C.: Congressional Quarterly Press.

_____. 1997. *Mass Media and American Politics*, 5e. Washington, D.C.: Congressional Quarterly Press.

Graham, Fred. 1990. *Happy Talk: Confessions of a TV Newsman*. New York: W. W. Norton.

Granberg, D. and T. A. Brown. 1989. "On Affect and Cognition in Politics." *Social Psychology Quarterly* 52: 171–182.

Greco–Larson, Stephanie. 1989. "Supreme Court Coverage and Consequences." Presented at the Annual Meeting of the Midwest Political Science Association. Chicago.

Greco–Larson, Stephanie and Bryan Tramont. 1993. "The Supreme Court and Television: Predicting Case Coverage." Presented at the Annual Meeting of the Midwest Political Science Association. Chicago.

Greenhouse, Linda. 1990. "A Divided Supreme Court Ends the Term with a Bang." *New York Times*, July 1: E3.

_____. 1995. "Farewell to the Old Order in the Court: The Right Goes Activist and the Center Is Void." *New York Times*, July 2: Section 4:1.

_____. 1996a. "Telling the Court's Story: Justice and Journalism at the Supreme Court." *Yale Law Journal* 105: 1537–1561.

_____. 1996b. "Court Says It Will Not Hear Appeal on Affirmative Action." *New York Times*, July 1: A1.

Grey, David L. 1968. *The Supreme Court and the News Media*. Evanston, Ill.: Northwestern University Press.

Gunter, B. 1987. *Poor Reception: Misunderstanding and Forgetting Broadcast News*. Hillsdale, N.J.: Lawrence Erlbaum.

Harvard Law Review. 1990. "The Supreme Court 1989 Term: Leading Cases." 104: 129–372.

Harvard Law Review. 1995. "The Supreme Court 1995 Term: Leading Cases." 109: 13–340.

Hiebert, Ray E. (Ed.). 1966. *The Press in Washington*. New York: Dodd, Mead.

Hodson, Thomas, moderator. March 9, 1996. "Courts and the News Media." Chicago: American Judicature Society. Roundtable panel discussion broadcast on C–SPAN.

Iyengar, Shanto and Donald R. Kinder. 1987. *News That Matters*. Chicago: University of Chicago Press.

Katsh, Ethan. 1980. "Law in the Lens: An Interview with Tim O'Brien." *American Legal Studies Forum* 5: 31–46.

_____. 1983. "The Supreme Court Beat: How Television Covers the United States Supreme Court." *Judicature* 67: 6–12.

Krosnick, J. A. 1988. "The Role of Attitude Importance in Social Evaluation: A Study of Policy Preference, Presidential Candidate Evaluations, and Voting Behavior." *Journal of Personality and Social Psychology* 55: 196–210.

Larson, Stephanie. 1985. "How the *New York Times* Covered Discrimination Cases." *Journalism Quarterly* 62: 894–896.

Lewis, Anthony. 1959. "Problems of a Washington Correspondent." *Connecticut Bar Journal* 33: 363–371.

Linzer, Peter. 1979. "The Meaning of Certiorari Denials." *Columbia Law Review* 79: 1227–1302.

Lippmann, Walter. 1922. *Public Opinion.* New York: Macmillan.

Marshall, Thomas R. 1989. *Public Opinion and the Supreme Court.* Boston: Unwin Hyman.

McCombs, Maxwell. 1994. "News Influence on Our Pictures of the World." In Jennings Bryant and Dolf Zillmann (Eds.), *Media Effects: Advances in Theory and Research.* Hillsdale, N.J.: Lawrence Erlbaum.

McCombs, M. E. and D. L. Shaw. 1972. "The Agenda-Setting Function of the Mass Media." *Public Opinion Quarterly* 36: 176–187.

McLeod, J. M, G. M. Kosicki, and D. M. McLeod. 1994. "The Expanding Boundaries of Political Communication Effects." In Jennings Bryant and Dolf Zillmann (Eds.), *Media Effects: Advances in Theory and Research.* Hillsdale, N.J.: Lawrence Erlbaum.

Morin, Richard. 1989. "Wapner v. Rehnquist: No Contest." *Washington Post,* June 23: A21.

_____. 1995. "Unconventional Wisdom: A Nation of Stooges." *Washington Post,* October 8: C5.

Moyers, Bill and Richard Cohen, producers. 1989. "The Public Mind: Image and Reality in America." WNET/WETA PBS Video.

Neubauer, David. 1991. *Judicial Process: Law, Courts and Politics in the United States.* Pacific Grove, Calif.: Brooks Cole.

Neuman, W. R. 1976. "Patterns of Recall among Television News Viewers." *Public Opinion Quarterly* 40: 115–123.

Newland, Chester A. 1964. "Press Coverage of the United States Supreme Court." *Western Political Quarterly* 17: 15–36.

Newsweek. July 10, 1978. "The Landmark Bakke Ruling." 19–31.

O'Brien, David M. 1990. *Storm Center: The Supreme Court and American Politics,* 2e. New York: W.W. Norton.

O'Brien, Tim. 1990. "Best Kept Secrets of the Judiciary." *Judicature* 73: 341–343.

_____ . 1991. Personal correspondence to Slotnick.

O'Callaghan, Jerome and James O. Dukes. 1992. "Media Coverage of the Supreme Court's Caseload." *Journalism Quarterly* 69: 195–203.

Paletz, David E. and Robert M. Entman. 1981. *Media Power Politics.* New York: Free Press.

Parenti, Michael. 1993. *Inventing Reality: The Politics of News Media.* 2e. New York: St. Martin's Press.

Patterson, T. E. 1980. *The Mass Media Election: How Americans Choose Their President.* New York: Praeger.

Press, Charles and Kenneth VerBurg. 1988. *American Politicians and Journalists.* Glenview, Ill.: Scott Foresman.

Rice, R. E. and C. K. Atkin (Eds.). 1989. *Public Communication Campaigns,* 2e. Beverly Hills, Calif.: Sage.

Robinson, John P. and Mark R. Levy. 1986. *The Main Source: Learning from Television News.* Beverly Hills, Calif.: Sage.

Robinson, Michael J. and Margaret A. Sheehan. 1983. *Over the Wire and on TV: CBS and UPI in Campaign '80.* New York: Russell Sage Foundation.

Ruth, Robert. 1996. "Judge Tries Mailings to Explain His Ruling." *Columbus Dispatch* August 28: B1.

Schudson, Michael. 1983. *The News Media and the Democratic Process.* New York: Aspen Institute for Humanistic Studies.

_____ . 1995. *The Power of the News.* Cambridge, Mass.: Harvard University Press.

Shaw, David. 1981. "Media Coverage of the Courts: Improving but Still Not Adequate." *Judicature* 65: 18–24.

Sherman, Rorie. 1988. "Media and the Law." *National Law Journal,* June 6: 32–36.

Sindler, Alan P. 1978. Bakke, DeFunis, *and Minority Admissions: The Quest for Opportunity.* New York: Longman.

Slotnick, Elliot E. 1990. "Television News and the Supreme Court: The Case of Allan Bakke." Presented at the Annual Meeting of the American Political Science Association. San Francisco.

_____ . 1991a. "Television News and the Supreme Court: 'Game Day' Coverage of the Bakke Case." Presented at the Annual Meeting of the Midwest Political Science Association. Chicago.

_____ . 1991b. "Media Coverage of Supreme Court Decision Making: Problems and Prospects." *Judicature* 75: 128–142.

_____ . moderator. September 4, 1993. "The Media and the Supreme Court." Washington, D.C.: American Political Science Association. Roundtable panel discussion broadcast on C-SPAN.

Slotnick, Elliot E. and Jennifer A. Segal. 1992. "Television News and the Supreme

Court." Presented at the Annual Meeting of the American Political Science Association. Chicago.

———. 1994. "'The Supreme Court Decided Today . . . ,' or Did It?" *Judicature* 78: 89–95.

Slotnick, Elliot E., Jennifer A. Segal, and Lisa M. Campoli. 1994. "Television News and the Supreme Court: Correlates of Decisional Coverage." Presented at the Annual Meeting of the American Political Science Association. New York.

Stern, Carl. 1993. Personal correspondence to Slotnick.

Tarpley, J. Douglas.1984. "American Newsmagazine Coverage of the Supreme Court, 1978–1981." *Journalism Quarterly* 61: 801–804.

Tuchman, G. 1978. *Making News.* New York: Free Press.

Wasby, Stephen L. 1988. *The Supreme Court in the Federal Judicial System,* 3e. Chicago: Nelson Hall.

———. 1990. Personal correspondence to Slotnick.

Index

ABC News: and *Bakke* case, 98, 100–1, 103,
108, 110–11, 119–21, 123, 125–7, 140–3,
145, 146; and certiorari denials, 202, 203,
206–7; Court coverage by, 53, 59–60, 76,
79, 166, 168, 170–4, 178–9, 184; misinformation by, 206–7; reporters' training at,
24; and *Webster* case, 99, 102, 114–15, 117,
129–33, 135–9, 147–9. *See also* O'Brien,
Tim
abortion clinics, 197
abortion rights, 53, 104, 178, 200–1; counseling, 198, 200; interpretation of decisions
on, 21; interest groups and, 114–16,
127–33; issues surrounding, 93–7; news
coverage of, 100, 107, 134–9, 147–51, 154.
*See also Roe v. Wade; Webster v. Reproduc-
tive Health Services*
*Abortion Rights Mobilization, Inc., v. U.S.
Catholic Conference,* 201
Abraham, Henry, 196
Adarand Constructors, Inc. v. Pena, 47, 162,
170, 173, 174, 179
Adler, Stephen, 24
affirmative action cases, 53, 66, 82, 162,
191–3; and Court, 154, 155; coverage of,
107–12, 141–6; speculation about, 119–27.
See also quotas; *Regents of the University of
California v. Bakke*
agenda setting, 44, 247
Alabama v. White, 171, 226
American Airlines v. Wolens, 174
American Bar Association, 80
American Civil Liberties Union (ACLU), 185
*American Federation of Government Employ-
ees, AFL-CIO, et al. v. Skinner,* 201
American Jewish Committee, 113, 121
amicus briefs, 186; in *Bakke* case, 110–13,

121; and decisional coverage, 218–19,
220–3, 224–5, 228; in *Webster* case, 95–6.
See also interest groups
Andrews, Wyatt, 148
Ann Arbor News, 11
Arizona v. Evans, 249
Associated Press, 44
Association of American Law Schools
(AALS), 51
Association of American Medical Colleges,
122
Austin v. Michigan Chamber of Commerce, 171

Babbitt v. Sweet Home, 174, 175, 181
Babcock, By and Through Babcock v. Tyler,
201, 206
"Baby Richard" case, 191
Bakke, Allan, 89, 98; reporting on, 106,
107–10, 140, 141, 144, 154, 155, 234; sup-
port for, 112–13, 120
*Baltimore City Department of Social Services
v. Bouknight,* 172, 206
Baltimore Sun, 24, 44
Barrett, Paul, 42
Behuniak-Long, Susan, 95
Bell, Griffin, 120, 121
Bell v. Thornburgh, 201
Ben-Shalom v. P. W. Stone, 201
Berkson, Larry, 8, 20
Bernard v. Gulf Oil Corporation, 201
Bernstein, Carl, 38
Black, Hugo, 83
Blackmun, Harry, 37, 83, 93, 116; and *Bakke*
case, 142, 145, 146; retirement of, 168, 179;
and *Webster* case, 134, 136, 149, 150–1
*Board of Education of the Westside Community
Schools v. Mergens,* 171, 226

257